EASY
DOES
IT

EASY DOES IT

Alcoholism Treatment Outcomes, Hazelden and the Minnesota Model

J. Clark Laundergan

First published March, 1982.

ISBN: 0-89486-119-0

Printed in the United States of America.

TO
Sister Mary Leo Kammeier, C.S.J.
Friend, Colleague
Late Director of Hazelden
Evaluation and Research Department

About the author:

J. Clark Laundergan is Associate Professor of Sociology at the University of Minnesota, Duluth. Since 1974 he has served as an evaluation and research consultant to the Hazelden Foundation. He has published monographs and journal articles on alcoholism and treatment, and presented papers at national alcoholism conferences. As a member of the Board of Directors of the Duluth Center for Alcohol and Drug Problems, he is presently serving as Chairperson for the Outpatient Program Planning Committee. At Hazelden, he is involved in ongoing projects with the Evaluation and Research Department and serves as an instructor for Continuing Education Department workshops.

Contents

List of
Tables and Figures

X

Acknowledgments

A project such as this requires considerable effort on the part of many people other than the author. The book is dedicated to the late Sister Mary Leo Kammeier who, as Director of the Hazelden Evaluation and Research Department, helped to stimulate my interest in researching alcoholism recovery processes and facilitated my desire to pursue the present study. If it had not been for her untimely death, Sister Mary Leo would have been a co-author. Although that collaboration was not possible, she and her staff should be credited with the careful data gathering on which the analysis is based.

Staff members who were especially helpful are Peggy Barnett, Loretta Anderson, Ron Johnson, and Kevin Johnson. Kevin Johnson's contribution as computer programmer and data base manager was of special importance both in the enthusiasm and skill with which he approached his work and in his careful implementation of data analysis techniques. Michael Patton, past Director of the Minnesota Center for Social Research, helped to develop the research design and data analysis strategy. Dow Lambert, recently with the University of Washington Alcoholism Studies Center, reviewed the resulting research design and data analysis plan. Jerry Spicer continued the support of the project and made useful suggestions after being appointed manager of Hazelden's Evaluation and Research Department.

Apart from the data analysis, Daniel Anderson, President and Director of Hazelden, generously helped identify the Hazelden conceptualization of alcoholism presented in the second chapter and reviewed the entire manuscript. A. Neil Pearson also reviewed the entire manuscript as did Rachel Caldwell who made valuable editorial recommendations and constructed the index. Tim Pegors's editorial suggestions and other help contributed to the readability of the final manuscript. Selected chapters were read by Robert Franz and typing was done in a timely and efficient manner by Marian Braff.

Considerable time away from home and seclusion while at home were required to complete the project. This was possible because of the consideration of my colleagues and students at the University of Minnesota, Duluth and the encouragement and understanding of my wife, Jean, and sons, Jeff and Jeremy.

Financial support for the project came from two research grants: one from the National Council of Alcoholism and the other from the University of Minnesota, Alcoholism and Other Drug Abuse Programming Office. Time, an important resource in completing a project of this scope, was granted by the University of Minnesota Sabbatical Program and through the work load assignment within the Sociology-Anthropology Department, University of Minnesota, Duluth. Hazelden retained me as a consultant during the 1977 sabbatical year and since that time and also supported project costs not covered by external support.

Not to be forgotten are the people treated at Hazelden for chemical dependency who completed the mail questionnaire follow-up surveys. By participating in the treatment follow-up study, they shared of themselves to benefit the treatment program at Hazelden and to further the understanding of chemical dependency treatment and recovery. The questionnaires were intended both to solicit information and to help construct an inventory of the recovery process. This work is, therefore, reciprocal in the sense that it is part of the chemical dependency treatment and recovery process of sharing and examining experiences as a way of helping others and being helped. It is, then, the people who have come to recognize their chemical dependency and to accept sharing their personal struggle as a means to recovery, who have made this work possible.

Preface

As one travels rural byways and metropolitan highways of Minnesota it is not uncommon to encounter the bumper sticker proclaiming, "Easy Does It." This Alcoholics Anonymous motto also graces the winding road leading to the Hazelden Foundation rehabilitation center on South Center Lake, northeast of Minneapolis-St. Paul. In a sense, the "Easy Does It" symbolizes chemical dependency treatment as it is carried out in the Minnesota Model. It was, in part, for this symbolism that the motto was selected as the title for the present work, but it was also chosen because of the relationship between the meaning that it conveys and the research findings that will be reported.

The motto "Easy Does It" appears at the end of the "Big Book" chapter entitled, "The Family Afterward." This chapter deals with numerous problems and concerns that are likely to affect an alcoholic's recovery. The alcoholic and the alcoholic's family often have overly optimistic expectations concerning the speed and magnitude of recovery. Recovery from active alcoholism does not mean that social relationships will automatically become smooth or that all bad habits will be discarded. What it does mean, from a Hazelden treatment perspective, is that the alcoholic has admitted powerlessness over alcohol, recognized the unmanageability of life revolving around alcohol and acknowledged the existence of a Higher Power as a source of strength and direction. To quote from the "Big Book," "Whether the family goes on a spiritual basis or not, the alcoholic member has to if he would recover."* The central focus of the recovering person is the personal growth and guidance that can be realized in an active and meaningful relationship with a Higher Power. This is best expressed in Step 11, "Sought through prayer and meditation to improve our conscious contact with God *as we understood Him,* praying only for knowledge of His will for us and the power to carry that out."

The research findings reported in this book empirically support the wisdom of Step 11 and the importance of spirituality as a major part of recovery. This study further suggests that recovery consists of interrelated processes found within the physical, psychological, social and spiritual realms of existence that may not always be, and frequently are not, in phase with one another. It is understandable that the recovering person would wish for a rapid and orderly progress toward physical and mental health and more satisfying interpersonal and spiritual relationships. Such a wish appears to be both unrealistic and the potential source of frustration and anxiety that may serve as an impediment to recovery. Instead, an attitude of acceptance and patience as expressed in the three mottos, "First Things First," "Live and Let Live," and "Easy Does It" stand as reminders of the surrender that was necessary before

---

Alcoholics Anonymous: The story of how thousands of men and women have recovered from alcoholism. rev. ed., New York: Alcoholics Anonymous World Services, Inc. 1955, p. 135.

recovery could begin and that continues to be a necessary part of ongoing recovery.

"Easy Does It" signifies the surrender of recovery, with its active spiritual dimension, in opposition to the attempted control and personal isolation of active alcoholism. For this reason, it also summarizes the central research findings that emerge from this study of 1652 treated alcoholics who were followed up by mail questionnaires at four, eight and twelve months after treatment. These alcoholics were treated at Hazelden, which may be considered a model of the chemical dependency treatment modality characteristic of Minnesota. The conclusion reached in this study is that the Minnesota Model of treatment is effective in dealing with alcoholism and, accordingly, that "Easy Does It" is an appropriate motto that conveys the essence of a philosophy of recovery, the commonality of treatment in Minnesota and the empirical findings from this study of recovering alcoholics.

EASY
DOES
IT

Chapter One

Introduction to the Minnesota Model

During the past three decades, great advances have been made in understanding alcoholism as a condition responsive to treatment. This emerging understanding is by no means universal. In some states and regions, alcoholics are considered untreatable and troublesome by both the medical and social service professions. In other states and regions, effective treatment models are being developed and refined, with the result that they have gained national and international recognition.

Minnesota is viewed by many as a leader in the treatment of alcoholism. The facilities for such treatment in Minnesota are numerous—38 residential treatment programs (both public and private), 27 outpatient programs, 35 halfway house programs, 35 regionally located detoxification centers, 183 information and referral centers, and myriad AA chapters. Minnesota's alcoholism treatment programs have approximately 3800 inpatient beds and 1000 outpatient slots.[1] Minnesota has more primary treatment centers for chemical dependency than any other state, a per capita capacity for inpatient treatment four times the national average, and a per capita expenditure on chemical dependency care nearly 50% higher than the national average. With more information and referral services provided by employers, courts, public and private agencies than any other state, and with state laws requiring broad health insurance coverage for chemical dependency care, Minnesota has a well-organized capacity for intervention with individuals experiencing chemical dependency problems.[2]

Most alcoholism services in Minnesota are based on what may be called the *Minnesota Model of Chemical Dependence Intervention and Treatment.* This treatment model began to develop in the early 1950's and since that time has been revised, refined in practice, and is still evolving. The model represents considerable diversity while maintaining common premises and practices. Hazelden's variation of the Minnesota Model of Chemical Dependency Intervention and Treatment, hereafter called the Minnesota Model, will be discussed in greater detail in Chapter Two.*

The Minnesota Model had its origin in the Alcoholics Anonymous program of recovering alcoholics helping other alcoholics to initiate recovery through the Twelve Steps of AA. Two small Minnesota treatment programs, Pioneer House (started in 1948) and Hazelden (started in 1949), used the AA approach without professional staff and had apparent success.[3] At the same time, professionals of Willmar State Hospital were aware of the overall lack of success they and other professionals had experienced in trying to treat alcoholics. Their failure was characterized by patient noncooperation and a high frequency of posttreatment return to drinking. They began looking for an alternative treatment program.

The alternative program that became seminal to the Minnesota Model was a blend of professional behavioral science and AA principles. It began at Willmar State Hospital in the early 1950's under the direction of Drs. Nelson Bradley and Daniel Anderson. Their program involved unlocking the treatment wards and using as counselors recovering alcoholics with five years or more of sobriety and at least a high school education. They also used lectures and group and individual therapy integrated with a working knowledge of Alcoholics Anonymous principles.

The results of these changes were encouraging. Unlocking the wards drastically reduced the number of patients who left the alcohol section of the hospital without staff permission. Apparently, the patients had seen a challenge in escape, but when they knew that they could leave, they chose to stay. This may be seen as an early example of the importance of freedom of choice in the treatment of alcoholics. Using recovering alcoholics as therapists was successful because these therapists were working on their own recovery, were familiar with AA and had their own past alcoholism in common with the patients. Lectures were valuable in providing patients with information about alcoholism. Group and individual therapy focused on personal growth and discovery. The AA emphasis involved both outside AA members visiting Willmar to work with patients and counseling staff promoting the AA program. Steps Four and Five of AA began to take on a special significance in the Will-

---

*An in-depth discussion of the Minnesota Model by one of its pioneers, Dr. Daniel J. Anderson, can also be found in the booklet *Perspectives on Treatment* published by Hazelden Educational Services.

mar program, a significance which was to remain as the Minnesota Model evolved.[4]

A mimeographed "Handbook on the Treatment of Alcoholism" made available at Willmar in 1951 emphasized three treatment goals: 1) restoration of the alcoholic to good physical condition as soon as possible, 2) provision for as much individual psychiatric treatment as possible, and 3) presentation of the AA program. In 1952 Willmar began a clergy training program specifically to give spiritual support and hear patients' AA Fifth Steps. By 1956, Willmar established Alcoholic Follow-up Clinics in Willmar and Minneapolis under Daniel Anderson's direction. These Follow-up Clinics combined aftercare and outpatient services and demonstrated the willingness of alcoholics to use outpatient resources.

In the Minnesota Model today, attention to improved physical functioning is still stressed, but psychiatric treatment has shifted to a small group therapy emphasis since few alcoholics require intensive psychiatric treatment. Exposure to AA during the treatment experience remains paramount in the Minnesota Model, with clergy playing an important role in guiding and hearing the Fifth Step. Aftercare is generally considered important, although there are variations in the aftercare services promoted by different rehabilitation programs within the Minnesota Model. Training for both clergy and counselors has become increasingly important, with 13 training programs presently available in the state.

The Minnesota Model has emerged as a comprehensive model of rehabilitation supported by key underlying assumptions: 1) alcoholism can be described and identified, 2) alcoholism is an involuntary disablement, and 3) alcoholism is responsive to treatment. Alcoholism is described as a pathological relationship between a person and the mood-modifying properties of alcohol. Further, it is a multiphasic condition affecting the person physically, psychologically, socially and spiritually. The deterioration that occurs in these areas in the lives of alcoholics has a consistency, although the resulting patterns are seldom recognized by the alcoholic. Accordingly, denial is one of the symptoms of alcoholism, along with personality manifestations such as grandiosity, defiant individuality, anxiety and resentment.

The question of personal responsibility for the alcoholic's present condition is related to the idea of involuntary disablement, according to the Minnesota Model. The alcoholic did not choose to become alcoholic; instead, a host of contributing factors moved the person into alcoholism. Still, personal responsibility has an important role in the recovery process, although it is unlikely that without the benefit of treatment an alcoholic person would assume responsibility for change.

Treatment is any systematic form of intervention aimed at modification. For the Minnesota Model, treatment is based on an experiential philosophy of rehabilitation: the learning necessary to recovery comes primarily through experience. An essential part of Minnesota Model treatment is direct intervention in the alcoholic's life. Direct intervention creates an awareness of the experience of being an alcoholic and provides an opportunity to consider alternative behaviors. Since denial is a central characteristic in alcoholism, the Minnesota Model supports getting the practicing alcoholic into treatment through constructive coercion if necessary, by using either involuntary commitment or "voluntary" admission resulting from an arranged crisis confrontation. The alcoholic is a motivated person, motivated to feel better, and drinking is used as a means of trying to feel better. Once the denial system is dismantled, the motivation to feel better can be used constructively in the rehabilitation process.

The Minnesota Model of treatment is a comprehensive and systematic program of rehabilitation. Its central tenet is that scientific and spiritual understanding can merge to provide a powerful catalyst for healing. Thus, the recovery process is seen as change occuring through a series of stages. This process is aided by systematic procedures blending physical and behavioral science findings with basic spiritual-theological principles. The program of treatment takes place within a healing community designed to provide an intensive experience geared to produce rapid changes in the participants. Positive changes promoted during treatment are to be sustained following treatment through a personal care plan designed to meet the individual needs of program participants.

As it has evolved, the Minnesota Model has taken the form of a multidisciplinary approach utilizing medical personnel, psychologists, clergy, lay counselors and, more recently, recreation specialists, aftercare planners and an assortment of resource persons called upon as needed. Therapy has become more multifaceted, including group therapy and reading about alcoholism, individual counseling and regulated confrontation, nutrition and other areas of individual responsibility reinforcement, lectures and informal patient interaction; all of these reinforcing the patient's developing grasp of the Twelve Steps of AA.

Although the original treatment concern was alcoholism, it became increasingly apparent that many alcoholics also had drug dependencies, and that the psychological and behavioral manifestations of drug dependencies were similar to those recognized for alcoholism. Thus, the Minnesota Model broadened to include abuse of mood-altering chemicals other than alcohol. Techniques that were effective in intervening with and treating the alcoholic were found to work with the person whose drug of choice was other than alcohol.[5] Furthermore, persons having dependence on alcohol, alcohol and drugs, and drugs other than alcohol could be treated in the same therapeutic group without diminishing the effectiveness of the therapy. When users of different drugs communicated the psychological and behavioral manifestations of their dependence, a shared recognition emerged that all were harmfully dependent on mood-altering chemicals.

Within Minnesota, most professionals and nondegreed professionals, instead of talking about "alcoholism" or "drug dependence other than alcoholism" refer to themselves as chemical dependency specialists and talk about alcoholism and other drug dependencies as "chemical dependency." The state organization of chemical dependency workers is known as the Minnesota Chemical Dependency Association and provides yet another forum in which the Minnesota Model is elaborated and communicated.

One of the important components of the growth of the Minnesota Model was that nondegreed* counselors and clergy were prepared for their counseling and spiritual support roles by non-college-based training programs consisting of formal instruction and on-the-job training. After their training period, clergy and counselor trainees could find employment elsewhere in the state and the nation. The training component of the Minnesota Model thus provided manpower for the growing alcoholism treatment enterprise, while effectively diffusing the evolving techniques and philosophy of alcoholism intervention and treatment developed through the Minnesota Model. Today, treatment personnel trained in the Minnesota Model approach to chemical dependency treatment are found in many states.**

The Minnesota Model is both dynamic and diverse. Most of the treatment innovations are pragmatically tested and their effectiveness clinically communicated. The procedures of adopting, diffusing and discarding treatment techniques is not formal, and most chemical dependency workers functioning within the Model are permitted to try new approaches. As a result, the Minnesota Model is many different techniques subject to modification but having in common the use of recovering or affected persons as principal therapists and the AA philosophy, as set out in the Twelve Steps, as an essential adjunct to the treatment process.

In such a diffuse approach, formal communication about techniques is difficult. Still, clinical communication of techniques is an important part of the dynamic nature of the Minnesota Model, although there are some obvious shortcomings in relying on clinical impressions to evaluate the effectiveness of therapeutic approaches. The most apparent of these shortcomings is the short time frame for which the judgment is made. If a patient appears to respond well to a therapeutic approach, a logical question is, "How long will the desired response be maintained?" Also a strictly clinical judgment is based on the perception of the therapist and does not usually allow for the patient's ap-

---

*Nondegreed refers to persons without college level preparation in counseling.
**As an example, Hazelden training alumni as of summer 1979 were working in 19 states other than Minnesota and in 6 foreign countries.

praisal of the therapy. These shortcomings in the clinical evaluation of what works and what does not work in chemical dependency treatment do not suggest that clinical impressions and their dissemination are not important. Rather, they point to the need for systematic empirical outcome evaluation as another way of judging the effectiveness of treatment. More will be said about this as it is of central interest to this book.

The approach referred to as the Minnesota Model, with its origin at Willmar State Hospital, was adopted and modified at Hazelden, a chemical dependency treatment center located forty miles northeast of Minneapolis/St. Paul on South Center Lake near Center City, Minnesota. Hazelden, recognized nationally and internationally for chemical dependency treatment, began as a guesthouse for alcoholic businessmen and clergy in 1949. Actually, the first patients to receive treatment were mainly poverty-level chronic male alcoholics from the Twin Cities whose treatment costs were paid by a grant from the Hill Foundation of St. Paul. Treatment in 1949 was modest by present standards, with a staff of three in contrast to a present staff of approximately 400. The average daily patient population of seven men constrasts with a present daily patient population of 147 men and women. Development of the Hazelden treatment facility and program was aided by: 1) a realignment of financial arrangements in 1952, 2) the acquisition and development, in 1954, of Fellowship Club, a Twin Cities-based halfway house, 3) procurement of the rights to publish *Twenty-Four Hours a Day*[6] in 1954, 4) the establishment of a women's treatment center near White Bear Lake, Minnesota in 1956, 5) employment in 1961 of Daniel Anderson, formerly of the Willmar State Hospital staff, as Director, 6) the construction of a building complex made ready between 1965 and 1977 and location of treatment for women at the South Center Lake site in 1966, 7) development of a clergy and counselor training program in 1966, 8) the growth of the Literature Department to one of the largest distributors of alcoholism and chemical dependency literature in the world during the 1960's and 1970's and 9) the establishment of an Evaluation and Research Department in 1971. Apart from the physical and program growth, Hazelden was instrumental in further refining some elements of the Minnesota Model, as well as disseminating those refinements through the training programs and the Literature Department's publications.[7, 8]

Hazelden's growth also led to the establishment of a patient follow-up survey procedure for determining treatment outcomes. The first phase of Hazelden's patient follow-up began in 1969 under a grant from the Northwest Area Foundation. Assessment of 1970-71 patient follow-up data showed a therapeutic and informational and evaluational benefit from the use of questionnaires sent out at regular intervals following a patient's treatment.

The therapeutic benefit of patient follow-up questionnaires has been commented on by many former Hazelden patients. Their comments indicate that the questionnaire provides a useful inventory for the respondent and encourages periodic self-assessment. Daniel Anderson, President and Director of Hazelden, expresses patient and staff sentiments about the therapeutic effect of the follow-up procedure:

> Much of the activity involved in data collecting turned out to be extremely helpful therapeutically, especially for those persons still trying to clarify their own personal coping skills. This therapeutic bias probably runs through all of the data, and we feel it belongs there; patient outcome studies cannot be done in a sterile neutral vacuum. Rather, patients do need and want to know that people care about them and are concerned about their recovery—their joys and sorrows, strengths and weaknesses.[9]

Keeping in touch with patients after they leave the residential treatment program and asking questions that will help them in their own recovery progress is therapeutically useful, and such attention, by all indications, does not seriously limit either the validity or reliability of the resulting follow-up data (see Appendix A by Michael Patton).

Another justification for using a patient follow-up procedure, apart from the therapeutic, informational and evaluation reasons, is the politics of accountability in an era of inflation and public skepticism about social services. Public agencies, private insurance carriers and consumers are increasingly demanding to know the effectiveness of the services they are paying for. Alfonso Paredes, a recognized alcoholism treatment authority, states that:

> In order to define priorities and predict costs, we need reliable information on the performance of alcoholism programs, including outcome data. In the past, providers of rehabilitative services have assumed that the therapeutic manipulations or rehabilitation procedures incorporated into their programs would benefit their patients. This expectation might not be fulfilled in practice. Without ongoing outcome evaluations, we cannot reliably ascertain if we are helping induce favorable changes, if we are doing harm, or we are just contributing to support greater numbers of care-givers and sheltering more people from the responsibilities of productive daily living.[10]

The politics of accountability simply necessitate that outcome evaluation become a standard procedure in the delivery of alcoholism services. Without treatment outcome data it is impossible to justify the public, corporate or individual investment in alcoholism treatment by means other than generalized arguments for human and social concern.

Related to the politics of accountability are the informational and evaluational payoffs of outcome data. Hazelden's experience has been that installing patient outcome and related information gathering procedures improves the overall collection and accessibility of patient data and prompts significant staff attitude changes regarding the usefulness of patient information in the treatment process.[11] The informational and evaluational procedures make possible still further program refinements which, in turn, provide further informational advances. The patient follow-up requirement improves the quality and accessibility of information, upgrades existing record-keeping procedures and increases both the acceptance and enthusiasm for further information gathering and processing procedures.

An example serves to illustrate how improvements in information quality and availability prompted further refinements. The Medical Records Department and the Evaluation and Research Department at Hazelden both recognized the need for patient information which would be quickly retrievable. The departments cooperated in identifying information that would be valuable for evaluation and management purposes. The sociodemographic and treatment variables used in the following analysis and the computer procedures were developed during 1975. The patient sociodemographic information retrieval system was established as a functioning tool in 1976.

Considerable savings in labor and improved accuracy of patient information resulted. With patient information accessible by computer, it became possible to respond to requests from management for patient information, to supply rehabilitation staff with patient summaries and to answer unique inquiries from the staff promptly and accurately. Hazelden patient data are now summarized in monthly reports and are used as a quality assurance monitoring device.[12] This computer-based patient information system may be seen as a by-product of the follow-up procedures which necessitated both improved quality and accessibility of patient information.

With patient sociodemographic, treatment, and follow-up information readily available to management and rehabilitation staff, it became possible to make more informed program decisions. Having patient sociodemographic and treatment data summarized both monthly and annually made it possible to be aware of changing patient characteristics and to consider program decisions more rationally. When it was noted, for instance, that the age of the patient population had been dropping and more patients had never been married, it was possible to reflect on the implications of these changes for the treatment program. In this manner, follow-up and related informational resources provide a useful input into the treatment decision-making process.

This study is a more detailed analysis of the Hazelden patient data than has been carried out to date. Orientation for the analysis is offered in Chapters Two and Three. Chapter Two will explain the conceptualization of alcoholism that prevails at Hazelden and will describe the Hazelden treatment process. Past outcome studies of treated alcoholics reported in the alcoholism literature will be reviewed in Chapter Four with special attention given to the "alternative to abstinence" studies including the Rand Report by Armor and his associates.

In later chapters the analysis of the Hazelden treatment outcome data gathered between 1973 and 1975 will be presented. This analysis will consider posttreatment alcohol use, posttreatment participation in Alcoholics Anonymous and posttreatment social/psychological functioning. These three interrelated variables will be considered in sequence and then will be examined in combination in order to determine the interrelationships between them and a host of independent variables in identifying successful treatment outcomes.

Within this broad analysis, timely research questions will be explored: 1) What are appropriate alcohol treatment outcome measures? 2) Can treated alcoholics drink following treatment without remission? 3) What are the characteristics of AA participators? 4) How is improved social/psychological functioning related to abstinence, AA participation and other sociodemographic, treatment and posttreatment variables? It is not anticipated that these and other related questions will be conclusively resolved. But, it is hoped that a further empirical examination will add to the research presently available and will thereby bring closer their eventual answers.

Reference Notes Chapter 1

[1]*State of Minnesota directory chemical dependency programs.* St. Paul, MN. Chemical Dependency Programs Division, Department of Public Welfare, 1977.

[2]B. Shellum, Sobriety, Minnesota's newest industry. *Minneapolis Tribune* (summary supplement) May 20-28, 1979.

[3]E. A. Shepard, (ed.) Reports on government sponsored programs. *Quart. J. of Studies on Alc.* 1950 *11,* 351-359.

[4]F. Richeson, *Courage to change: Beginnings and influence of Alcoholics Anonymous in Minnesota,* Minneapolis, MN. M&M Printing, 1978.

[5]D. J. Anderson, S. M. L. Kammeier, and H. Holmes, *Applied research: Impact on decision making.* Center City, MN. Hazelden Foundation, 1978, p. 6.

[6]*Twenty-four hours a day.* Center City, MN. Hazelden Foundation, 1955.

[7]C. Crewe, A short history of Hazelden. In V. Groupe (ed.) *Alcoholism rehabilitation: Methods and experiences of private rehabilitation centers.* New Brunswick, N.J.: Rutgers Center of Alcohol Studies, 1978, pp. 51-55.

[8]F. Richeson, op. cit., pp. 186-197.

[9]S. M. L. Kammeier and J. C. Laundergan, *The outcome of treatment: Patients admitted to Hazelden in 1975.* Center City, MN: Hazelden Foundation, 1977, p. iii.

[10]A. Paredes, The history of the concept of alcoholism. In R. E. Tarter and A. A. Sugarman (eds.) *Alcoholism: Interdisciplinary approaches to an enduring problem.* Reading, MA: Addison-Wesley Publishing Co., 1976, p. 46.

[11]D. J. Anderson, S. M. L. Kammeier, and H. Holmes, op. cit.

[12]J. C. Laundergan and K. Johnson, Hazelden's research data terminals can get it for you quickly. *Hazelden Research Notes,* Hazelden Foundation, 1977 (No. 1).

Chapter Two

Conceptualization of Alcoholism and Process of Treatment: Hazelden

Introduction

The intent of this chapter is not to present a refined model of alcoholism. The conceptualization of alcoholism found here is the working understanding that is generally accepted by practitioners at Hazelden. Practitioners are often not concerned with theory and are only secondarily familiar with empirical research. Much of the view of alcoholism at Hazelden has its base in practical clinical experience, in-service education and popular readings that may summarize formal theory and research.

The prevailing understanding of alcoholism at Hazelden appears to have been influenced by its President, Dan Anderson. Dr. Anderson is a clinical psychologist who has been associated with the Minnesota model of chemical dependence and treatment since its early development at Willmar State Hospital. He participates in a number of national conferences, workshops, and alcoholism schools each year and keeps abreast of the behavioral science literature relating to addiction and treatment. Many of the ideas that he encounters are synthesized and presented to Hazelden staff, either indirectly in lunchroom conversation, or through formal in-service workshops and the literature that Anderson authors, co-authors and heavily influences.

In part, the conceptualization of alcoholism that will be presented here was identified in Anderson's writings, both published[1] and unpublished, and through taped interviews with him. During interviews, Anderson mentioned readings from papers, journal articles and books. These became additional sources of elaborating his conceptualization of alcoholism.

One of the books Anderson discussed was *Emerging Concepts of Alcohol Dependence* by the well-known proponents of controlled drinking, E. Mansell Pattison, Mark Sobell and Linda Sobell. This work represents a point of view which is, at first glance, contrary to the Hazelden position and understanding. Pattison and the Sobells begin their work by presenting a critical analysis of what they identify as the "traditional model"* of alcoholism. Following this presentation they raise an issue of importance: "It is possible and even likely that many persons will tend to misinterpret our purpose in attempting to summarize traditional concepts of alcoholism. In particular, it may be argued that in doing so we have fabricated a straw man for the purpose of setting it aflame."[2] Indeed, the reader is likely to get that impression. Whether the traditional model of alcoholism as presented by Pattison and the Sobells accurately reflects the established and more traditional view of alcoholism remains a question, but it is clear that their representation of this model does not conform to what was being identified as the Hazelden conceptualization of alcoholism.

Later in their work, Pattison and the Sobells present what they call an emergent model** of alcoholism in the form of seven propositions which parallel the six propositions made for the traditional model of alcoholism; the seventh proposition having to do with treatment implications. It is not surprising to note that the conceptualization of alcoholism identified at Hazelden does not fully concur with the emergent model of alcoholism.

It did seem helpful, however, to use the seven propositions of the emergent model of alcoholism as both a format and a starting point for describing the Hazelden conceptualization of alcoholism. Using this format permits a contrast with both the traditional and the emergent model of alcoholism. The seven propositions clearly identify major elements that must be addressed in a conceptualization of alcoholism, outlining relevant categories of concern that need to be considered in identifying the alcoholism conceptualization current at Hazelden.

---

*The "traditional model" was synthesized from three primary sources: 1) AA literature; 2) E. M. Jellinek's, *The Disease Concept of Alcoholism,* and 3) *Marty Mann's New Primer on Alcoholism* (both editions) and other writings based on AA positions and Jellinek's work.

**The "emergent model" was based on empirical studies that challenged and elaborated some of the concepts included in the "traditional" model. Both the inclusion and interpretation of the studies that serve as a basis for the "emergent model" suggest the author's point of view and corresponding selection of supporting evidence.[3]

After seven propositions and supporting statements thought to be representative of Hazelden's conceptualization of alcoholism had been developed, copies were sent to Hazelden treatment staff for their reaction. Staff were asked to respond by way of the categories "agree," "somewhat agree" and "disagree" with sufficient space provided for comments and reaction. The results of this treatment staff survey will be presented as a part of this chapter.

The second part of the chapter focuses both on alcoholism treatment goals and on the process of treatment. Goals of treatment have relevance for treatment outcome, and the treatment process describes the actual intervention experience that is intended to promote changes in the lives of Hazelden patients. Looking at treatment goals and their relationship with outcome goals, and considering the process of treatment, it is possible to formulate a context in which to consider the follow-up data. Treatment process data were gathered in three ways: as a participant-observer in the treatment process, through interviews and conversations with staff and persons participating in treatment and through documentation of the treatment process available in the Rehabilitation Department.

Conceptualization of Alcoholism

Alcoholism as a single entity

Although understanding of alcoholism is in its infancy, the Hazelden treatment perspective asserts that alcoholism can be identified behaviorally. The crucial identifying behaviors involve a relatively consistent pattern of excessive and/or inappropriate use of alcohol with directly associated negative or harmful consequences. However, excessive use of alcohol and negative consequences are sometimes difficult to consensually define because drinking norms are vague and variable judgments about harmful consequences associated with drinking are socially mediated.[4,5]

Nevertheless, the Hazelden position is that alcoholism has behavioral characteristics which supercede the diverse norms and variable definitions of deviance and problems. Preoccupation with alcohol use is one of these behavioral characteristics. When a person is preoccupied with alcohol use, social relationships and activities become secondary to drinking, which serves increasingly to structure the drinker's existence. Preoccupation with drinking is closely associated with protecting the supply of alcohol. As such, a person makes certain not to become obligated to participate in nondrinking social situations. Instead, stockpiling or otherwise assuring ready access to alcohol becomes paramount.

A ready supply of alcohol is certainly important when its use is more medicinal than social. When drinking alcohol is used to make a person functional by steadying the hand or affecting the psychological state of the user, it may be said to be a self-prescribed and administered medicine. It is not surprising that such use is often solitary and rapid, since medicine is seldom taken as a group activity. The user is seeking the effect of the alcohol rather than the group conviviality. Preoccupation with alcohol, protecting the supply of alcohol, use of alcohol as medicine, solitary use and rapid intake of alcohol for effect are five interrelated behaviors that are useful in the identification of alcoholism.

Other characteristics of alcoholism are more physiologically based than the five characteristics just mentioned. Adaptive cell metabolism, associated with increased tolerance to alcohol, has a physiological basis, but displays itself behaviorally in the greater quantity of alcohol consumed. Similarly, blackouts have a physiological basis but have behavioral and social/psychological consequences too. The role of physiology as a catalyst in unplanned drinking episodes* will be discussed later, but whatever combination of cues prompt unplanned overuse of alcohol, it is clear that the drunken episode and its aftermath create behavioral sequences that may identify alcoholism. Increased tolerance to alcohol, blackouts or memory holes created by alcohol use, and episodes of unplanned excessive drinking combine with the previous five characteristics to constitute eight characteristics of alcoholism. Evidence of four or more of the characteristics is considered sufficient by Heilman for positive alcoholism diagnosis.[7]

The eight characteristics may not appear in all alcoholic persons, a fact which may be said to suggest a variable condition rather than a single entity. What strongly supports the conceptualization of alcoholism as a single entity, however, is the presence of harmful consequences linked to the excessive abuse of alcohol. The bottom line in the definition of alcoholism is that the person's drinking is resulting in harmful consequences for the drinker and others close to the drinker. Often the harmful consequences take a multifaceted form with physical, psychological, social and spiritual involvement creating what may be called adaptive impoverishment. More will be said about adaptive impoverishment in the following discussion, but it is sufficient for the present to identify harmful consequences resulting from repetitive patterns of alcohol use as central to the identification of alcoholism as an entity.

Another way of saying this is that alcoholism may be identified by stereotyped, repetitive, maladaptive behavior which is generally associated with excessive and inappropriate use of alcohol. The stereotyped behaviors are associated with the eight characteristics identified by Heilman. Preoccupation with alcohol and control of its use will serve to illustrate a stereotyped behavior. The usual pattern occurs when there is less than a full awareness by the

---

*Mark Keller's definition of an alcoholic is "One who is unable consistently to choose whether he shall drink or not, and who, if he drinks, is unable consistently to choose whether he shall stop or not."[6]

drinker that drinking has become destructive. Others have probably pointed out problems and that there is too much drinking taking place. As a defense, the drinker may develop a morbid preoccupation with control and spend considerable mental energy either thinking about the promised limit of two drinks or waiting for a self-imposed drinking time. Added to the frustration of agonizing decisions about the quantity and starting time of drinking, there may be the added frustration of an inability to consistently regulate alcohol use according to these criteria. The preoccupation with drinking and its control, the periodic failures resulting from unintended overuse, and the rationalizations for those failures constitute a stereotyped behavior. When this stereotyped behavior is repeated and accompanied by other repeated stereotyped behaviors, social/psychological maladaptation occurs.

Social/psychological maladaptation both results from and contributes to a defensive life-style, self-justification, fixated and inflexible behavior, and self-isolation which in turn serves to stimulate the urge to repeat the intoxification experience. In this fashion alcohol use becomes an autonomous objective preempting other life goals and evolving as a central life focus. Adaptive impoverishment is a corollary of making alcohol use a central life focus. A person is not likely to function well in the numerous social roles related to family, work and voluntary association membership when alcohol use is life's primary concern.

The identification of alcoholism as a behavioral entity or unitary phenomena may be said, in part, to support the disease concept of alcoholism. The disease concept of alcoholism has been both repeatedly defended and challenged.[8] Arguments in the alcoholism literature against classifying excessive and inappropriate use of alcohol as a disease have to do with: 1) medical model definitions that are thereby assumed, 2) lack of personal responsibility for change that may be implied,* 3) stigma attached to the illness "alcoholism," and 4) a "self-fulfilling prophesy" phenomenon as a reinforcer of maladaptive behavior. Further arguments against considering alcoholism as a disease are its uncertain etiology, its varied symptomology and possibilities of spontaneous remission.[9] Benefits of classifying alcoholism a disease are associated with the public support and treatment acceptance that have resulted from the legitimation alcoholism has gained by having the status of a disease.

It should not be concluded, however, that the disease concept is assumed

---

*One of the assumptions of the medical model that needs to be commented on here is the relationship between the ill person, or patient, and the physician. There are social roles that have developed in this patient-physician relationship that may be detrimental to alcoholism recovery. Some providers of alcoholism services prefer to use the "client" designation in an attempt to discard the passive sick role connotation of the patient label. In the present discussion persons receiving treatment for alcoholism will be referred to as *patients* without intending to ascribe either a passive sick role or a dominant and manipulative therapeutic role.

to be either correct or incorrect in the Hazelden conceptualization of alcoholism, but rather that it is a convenient and necessary metaphor.* The "alcoholism as a disease" metaphor refers to a complex behavioral disability usually having chronic medical, social and psychological components which result in multiple negative consequences. But just as the moral ethical model of alcoholism was too limited and led to intervention involving primarily the criminal justice system or church, so too is the disease concept too limited for the full understanding of alcoholism: a complex, multiphasic, existential condition of dis-ease.

The medical-behavioral conditions are a broad range of stereotyped, repetitive, maladaptive behaviors over which the individual has some presumably voluntary control. Such behavior disabilities include conditions such as smoking-emphysema, eating-obesity, medication taking-drug addiction. The category of behavior disabilities presents the greatest difficulty for causal conceptualization within the traditional illness model. Little is known about the dynamics of behavioral disabilities but it appears that a complex interaction of multiple *predisposing* factors, multiple *precipitating* "triggers" and *perpetuating* conditions are involved. At this time the multiple "trigger" notion is in need of both theoretical and empirical elaboration. However, even with its limitations it seems well suited to the consideration of behavioral disabilities.[12]

The predisposing factors cover a broad range of physical, psychological and social-cultural ingredients that may combine in a number of ways. Thus, there is no unitary cause, but instead a complex of variable linkages. While the predisposing factors combine to create the potential for behavioral disabilities, the immediate antecedent behaviors and events (precipitating triggers) are far more evident in the description of problem behavior. Social environment may contribute to a behavioral disability in the form of peer pressure or interpersonal conflict. Conflict and pressure may combine with the person's emotional state so as to heighten anxiety or impulsivity patterns and stimulate cognitive components including perfectionism and negative self-assessment. These in turn interact with physiological conditions such as chronic physical pain or vitamin dietary reactions resulting in the manifestations of some form of stereotyped, repetitive, maladaptive behavior. Each "trigger" may be seen as a weak causal factor, but when certain combinations of weak causal factors are linked, the result may be a category of behavior disability such as "alcoholism."

---

*Metaphor, a figure of speech literally denoting by word or phrase one kind of object or idea in place of another to suggest a likeness or analogy between them.[10] In describing alcoholism's classification as a disease in a metaphorical way, it is suggested that alcoholism has some of the properties of disease. Its use is not in the "illness as metaphor" context discussed by Susan Sontag,[11] where she states that it is best not to attribute the metaphorical inferences to actual illness.

Perpetuating conditions may be found in the social-situational and the emotional-cognitive milieu, and in the physiological status of a person to reinforce the emergence and development of a behavioral disability. These perpetuating conditions interact with an assorted combination of predisposing factors and precipitating "triggers" so that it is not possible to conceptualize a single etiology for behavioral disabilities. Instead, the unitary phenomenon of each behavioral disability is found in the stereotyped-repetitive-maladaptive behavior rather than the etiology. Someone with an eating and obesity problem may have a history of a mother concerned about feeding her child "too well" as an act of love, reinforced by food definitions of an ethnic subculture, coupled with the later life experiences that eating reduces anxiety and the stereotype that fat people are jolly. All this, combined with a hereditary predisposition toward plumpness could result in an eating and obesity problem. Another person may have come to the same problem by way of different combinations of predisposing, precipitating and perpetuating ingredients. Obesity is a single entity, its etiology is not in the kinds of food and types of consumption, but in its manifestations: overeating with resulting overweight and other maladaptive consequences.

Such a multi-path and multi-factor view of etiology for behavior disabilities is not especially helpful except to suggest that for alcoholism and other behavior disabilities a single causative agent is unlikely. The position taken at Hazelden, unlike Tarter and Schneider who conclude that alcoholism may not be a unitary disorder because the etiology is varied, is that the behavior topography in alcoholic persons has enough commonality, despite the variables of the condition, for it to be seen as a unitary disorder having varied etiologies.[13]

For strategic purposes, it is considered better to look at the behavior associated with alcoholism as a separate and distinct condition, deserving a clear intervention approach. Perhaps in the future other viable perspectives or conceptualizations may develop that suggest other ways of intervening and treating alcoholism. For instance, Pattison and others suggest that the behaviors associated with alcoholism are symptoms of other conditions and disturbances. This may be, but in the Hazelden view, the condition of alcoholism at the point of intervention has sufficient power and autonomy that it needs to be approached as a primary condition and the principal focus of treatment.

Although it is contended that alcoholic people exhibit similar stereotyped, repetitive, maladaptive behavior, closer inspection may indicate that alcoholism could be separated into distinct categories and within these categories types of alcoholic behaviors identified. Since Jellinek suggested a possible typology of alcoholics over twenty years ago, there has been little advancement in refining his contribution or developing other useful subclassifications.[14] Given the current state of knowledge about types of alcoholism from a treatment conceptualization, it seems reasonable to continue to view alcoholism as an entity. The Hazelden conceptualization of alcoholism on this point is as follows:

> *There is a single entity which can be defined as alcoholism.* Although alcohol dependence subsumes a variety of symptoms and behaviors, there is enough commonality in the array of symptoms and behaviors to consider alcoholism as a unitary phenomenon. There have been subclassifications of alcoholism developed, but for the purpose of providing treatment none of the subclassifications have provided a therapeutic advantage. The symptoms common to alcoholism have been corroborated over time and are such that alcoholism may be identified in the person using alcohol in a stereotyped, repetitive, maladaptive fashion.

Prealcoholics, alcoholics and nonalcoholics

In the Hazelden treatment experience, it has not been possible to identify sociopsychological characteristics that would suggest a prealcoholic profile. Part of the treatment experience requires patients to "tell their story." Early use of alcohol and other drugs and some of the sociopsychological conditions of this early use, as well as the later appearance of problems associated with drinking and/or drug use, are verbally shared and critically examined during the therapeutic exercise of telling one's story and receiving feedback. Unit staff within one of the seven treatment units at Hazelden hear approximately two hundred thirty patients tell their story each year. Although some suggestive prealcoholic patterns have been noted by these counselors and by researchers, no clear prealcoholic identifiers have emerged.[15, 16, 17, 18]

These observations concur with other research which indicates that some personalities of alcoholics prior to alcoholism are relatively aggressive, impulsive and antisocial, but that not all persons with such personality configurations become alcoholic.[19] The risk of alcoholism is higher in families having an alcoholic member, although the interplay of sociocultural and genetic factors associated with this risk is presently uncertain.[20, 21, 22] And, although treatment staff observations do not include physiological factors other than alcoholism symptoms, it appears safe to conclude from the relevant alcoholism literature that there are no biochemical, endocrinological or metabolic indicators for identifying prealcoholics.[23, 24, 25]

Hazelden treatment maintains that once alcoholic behaviors have become manifest, it is possible to separate alcoholics from nonalcoholics by their ability to use alcohol with and without experiencing repeated harmful consequences. For the vast majority of alcoholics, alcohol cannot be used without a high risk of returning to medical, sociopsychological and spiritual problems. There may be some persons who display behavior used to diagnose alcoholism who could return to the use of alcohol with a reduction or cessation of problems; however, at the present level of knowledge there is no satisfactory way that such persons may be identified. Because of the risk involved, for the vast majority of alcoholics, it is considered prudent to support the abstinence goal for all patients. In part the abstinence position is supported by the ethical consideration that far less harm can come to the patient who has been prescribed abstinence from alcohol than in the modified or reduced drinking prescription. If there is a mistake in the intervention strategy, Hazelden prefers to err on the side of caution and safety for the patient.

The Hazelden conceptualization of the prealcoholic, alcoholic, nonalcoholic question is stated as follows:

> There are no identifiable differences between the individual who will become an alcoholic and the individual who will not become an alcoholic (assuming that the individuals use alcohol). However, once alcoholism develops, the alcoholic is distinguished from the nonalcoholic by an inability to use alcohol without a high probability of experiencing harmful consequences. Although individuals may have differing susceptibility to both the use of alcohol and the development of alcohol problems as a result of genetic, physiological, psychological and sociocultural factors, no technology exists which permits identification of the prealcoholic. Accurate assessment of alcohol problems is best achieved through operational descriptions of the pattern of alcohol use and the consequences of such use for an individual, which could range from no adverse effects to severe or even fatal consequences.

Biological predispositions to alcoholism

As there are no known methods for identifying prealcoholics through biochemical, metabolic or endocrinological measurement, so researchers have not isolated basic biological processes that predispose persons to become alcoholic. Neurochemical imbalance, dietary deficiency and glandular disorder have all been suggested as causal factors in alcoholism but none of these appears to have gained much research support.[26]

It is recognized that continued and heavy use of alcohol has neurochemical, glandular and dietary implications for the user. Sleep disturbance, principally in the form of insomnia, is one of the well-documented neurochemical effects of heavy drinking.[27, 28] Research on alcohol-endocrine relationships is conflicting with no definite patterns established for alcoholics. However, clinical impressions suggest endocrine imbalance in alcoholics may be related to nutritional deficiencies.[29] Dietary problems among alcoholics are well-recognized and the effects of malnutrition and low vitamin intake are the subject of ongoing research.

Either a biological-, a psychological- or a combination-based craving for alcohol and loss of control have been offered as explanations of why alcoholics abuse alcohol. Biological craving alone has received popular support even though the empirical evidence is largely to the contrary. There is, however, support for the psychological situational-based craving in the work of Ludwig and his associates.[30] Their work indicates that a combination of socio-psycho-physiological cues interact to bring about what has been called the craving and loss of control response in alcoholic persons.

The Hazelden understanding of this response pattern links the etiology of alcoholism to certain combinations of triggers. The triggers in various combinations may be seen as a constellation of cues that become indelibly learned over time. The intake of alcohol alone is not sufficient to bring about a heavy drinking response. Situational and socio-psychological factors need also to be in place to result in uncontrolled use of alcohol.

According to this conceptualization of craving and loss of control in alcoholism, an alcoholic person may use alcohol in moderation on some occasions, but when the relevant cues are activated the preoccupation with obtaining alcohol for its direct pharmaceutical effect becomes dominant. The Hazelden conceptualization, unlike that of the behaviorists who support conditioning therapy with controlled drinking outcome, views the learned response to the relevant cues as a heavily overlearned adaptive strategy that is not amenable to permanent modification. Because drinking itself is an identifiable and essential ingredient in the constellation of relevant cues leading to heavy drinking with associated dysfunctional physiological, psychological and social consequences, total abstinence from alcohol is a reasonable and effective way of directly intervening in the alcoholic behavior. In summary, the Hazelden conceptualization of alcoholism relative to biological process is as follows:

> *There is little evidence to date for a basic biological process that predisposes an individual toward dysfunctional use of alcohol. However, once the pattern of alcoholism is established the use of alcohol by an individual has a high probability of triggering dysfunctional physiological, psychological and social responses.* There is no generally accepted physiological predeterminer of alcoholism that may be identified in an individual. There is evidence that physical dependence is established after the consumption of large amounts of alcohol. This condition may activate psychophysiological response patterns which in turn serve as stimuli to engage in further drinking.

Progressive development of alcoholism

Becoming alcoholic is a process, but it may not be a straight line progression in terms of continually more and more excessive drinking and associated maladaptation. It is the process of *learning how not to learn*. Behavior becomes fixated at some level of development thereby affecting all aspects of a person's life.

Several objectively observable indicators may suggest that a person is behaving in an impoverished fashion. The physiology of the alcoholic may evidence some dysfunction, but with the exception of blackouts coupled with the social misunderstandings and psychological defensiveness they can produce, physiological dysfunction is usually of least concern from the treatment perspective—most alcoholics do not have bad livers. The Hazelden treatment perspective is primarily concerned with the social/psychological functioning of the person.

Behavior that shows adaptive impoverishment is characterized by both interpersonal and intrapersonal conflicts, frustration, low tolerance for stress and high anxiety. These characteristics seem to emerge as a result of using alcohol as a primary adaptive technique, a technique relatively ineffective for short term problem solving. For example, if a person who does not work out interpersonal conflicts very well discovers that alcohol seems to make relationships with others less stressful, drinking will possibly become the temporary remedy for this and other perceived shortcomings. This person finds what appears to be a solution to troublesome interpersonal relationships by using alcohol. However, regular and heavy use of alcohol leads to a curtailment of the learning process which affects the person's entire web of social relationships. Drinking alcohol then, becomes the temporary solution to a problem of adaptation. But over time, unnoticed by the person utilizing alcohol as the answer, there is a disruption of the facility of ongoing long-term successful adaptation. Thus, the process of meaningful socialization is interrupted by the use of alcohol and *the person learns how not to learn.*

Curtailment of the learning process occurs in ways that we are just beginning to be aware of and have not yet adequately examined empirically. Some things do seem clear, however. The dynamic of disrupted socialization produced by heavy alcohol use is related to the twin pathologies of rejection and enabling. Feedback from others is filtered through the alcohol-impaired reality but, the two main forms of feedback are rejection for "disgusting, drunken, irresponsible behavior" interwoven with subtle adjustments that enable the drinking and consequent behavior to continue. The enabling feedback message is "I don't like what you are doing - I will make adjustments that will permit me to coexist with you." Frequently this feedback message is translated by the alcoholic as, "My behavior is alright because (as a result of the enabling actions of others) I am adapting successfully; others have hangups."

Selden Bacon discusses these processes in his article entitled "The Process of Addiction: Social Aspects."[31] Disrupted socialization, or the process of learning how not to learn, is implied in Bacon's discussion of dissocialization and the "pampering" function of alcohol. In dissocialization a person becomes less socially active, disengaging from social roles. Dissocialization and disrupted socialization appear to happen in combination and are facilitated by the pampering function of alcohol; (a concept borrowed from Jellinek and further elaborated by Bacon).

> The pampering function of alcohol . . . changes the process of sensitivity of cues, of recognizing the environment of accepting input from outside the brain, it changes the process within the brain of integrating new input with older learning, changes the mode and quality of bodily and motor responses which follow upon sensation, integration and the sending of messages to other bodily systems.[32]

Psychological and social functioning are altered in major ways, referred to here as disrupted socialization and dissocialization, because of the pampering function of the alcohol.

To be sure, patients come into treatment with many social roles apparently intact: married and living in a family, holding a job and working forty hours each week, and holding memberships in voluntary associations. Upon closer inspection, however, it becomes evident that meaningful social relationships are missing or are badly deteriorated for many of these people. But the alcoholic, because of the "pampering" function of alcohol, is only vaguely aware of the deteriorated sociopsychological environment.

Creating an awareness of the deteriorated sociopsychological environment may require some dogmatic persuasion and overstatement to penetrate the denial system. One tool which helps is the Jellinek Chart of alcoholism progression. Jellinek's presentation includes footnotes indicating that not all symptoms need to occur in every alcoholic, and that the sequence of their occurrence does not have to be the same as depicted in the chart. Treatment staff are generally aware of the variability of developmental sequences in alcoholism, but are interested in promoting awareness and motivation in patients. Patient identification with Jellinek's presentation of symptoms and progression can be an effective tool to this end. Most patients, because they are able to identify with some of the symptoms identified on the Jellinek Chart, may initially give more credence to a linear progression of alcoholism than might be warranted. In later recovery, the Jellinek progression is often reinterpreted by patients so that a less rigid progression is inferred. However, the fear of exhibiting symptoms of alcoholism that have not yet been experienced, should drinking be resumed, remains a real threat for most alcoholics.

Considering the interaction of the disrupted socialization (curtailment of the learning process) dissocialization (becoming less socially active) and the pampering effect of alcohol, it is highly probable that continued alcohol use will result in the occurrence of some of the symptoms listed in the Jellinek Chart. But alcohol abstinence, coupled with a program of personal growth and support, is equally as likely to interrupt a developmental sequence of these maladaptive behaviors. The Hazelden rehabilitation program is intended as an intervention to acquaint alcoholics with a therapeutically viable alternative to their patterns of physical, social and psychological problems.

Hazelden's conceptualization of alcoholism progression is summarized as follows:

> *The developmental sequence of adverse consequences associated with alcoholism appears to be highly variable.* The variation ranges from an almost immediate and rapid progression to a slow progressive development. At times the alcohol problem may remain static or appear to become less severe. Despite the variation, most alcoholics find that physiological, psychological and social problems produced by alcohol abuse continue to increase unless reversed through a therapeutic program that includes abstinence from alcohol.

Alcoholism and life problems

Related to dissocialization and sociopsychological behavior fixation is the stagnation of spiritual life. Spiritual life apparently plays a very significant role in a person's ability to deal with everyday problems. The behavioral sciences have not yet adequately explored the function of spiritual elements in sociopsychological adaptation. Spiritual elements, in the context of AA, refer to a person's relationship to a Higher Power. Another aspect of the spiritual element is related to what might be called "existential anxiety." Human beings have to face many different and demanding situations and most people experience considerable anxiety in facing up to life.

It may be that alcoholics are rebelling against the limitations of being human. They may be people who, because of the rewarding effect of chemical use for them, have had a glimpse of what it is like to be transposed out of the limitations of being human. Such a glimpse becomes a force difficult to deal with. Something seems to happen in chemical dependency in that a person is increasingly living a lie by denying or minimizing the ingredients of sociopsychological reality. The alcoholic person gets into a condition, one symptom of which is constantly making excuses for what is happening—trying to justify the inexorable complications of alcoholic behavior. As a result of the strain of trying to excuse this behavior and balance it with reality, the alcoholic's character (ethical value system, sense of honesty, responsibility, concern for others) begins to deteriorate. To cope with a character defective self, alcoholics undergo personality and self-concept changes. In general, alcoholics have identity conflicts because they are not well integrated psychopaths. For most chemically dependent people, being chemically dependent promotes situations that force them to violate their own consciences. If they were truly successful psychopaths, they wouldn't have conflicts resulting from the violation of ethical standards. In order to make that violation of conscience acceptable, it is necessary to say "to hell with everybody," an attitude which results in increasing egocentricity. As egocentricity increases, there is either a further sociopsychological withdrawal or regression, including a spiritual withdrawal, into what might be called defiant individuality.

Alcoholics feel omnipotent when they are drinking. When they are not drinking they are anxious about the world around them, wanting to control it and not being able to deal with the high level of frustration of not controlling. When they drink, although their lives may be falling apart, they think that they have control. The result, of course, is further social and psychological conflict. Many psychiatrists describe alcoholics and drug addicts as people who feel inadequate, inferior and anxious. AA people who have learned to be sober say that grandiosity is the dominant characteristic of alcoholics. Grandiosity is the outward manifestation of not accepting the limitations of being human; inadequacy, inferiority and anxiety result when human limitations are made evident.

All people have grandiose ideas and impulses, as well as feelings of inadequacy and inferiority, but most people keep these ideas and feelings regulated. Outwardly, alcoholics appear to be normal, but alcohol lets them regress for a while into the grandiosity of narcissism. At the same time that the alcoholic is experiencing grandiosity, unanticipated mood swings begin to occur where feelings of inadequacy, inferiority and anxiety become dominant. What follows is an emotional roller coaster ride through the high of grandiosity and the low of ego deflation. Psychiatrists tend to focus on the inadequacy, inferiority and anxiety, believing that alcoholics need support and that to help them, caution must be exercised so that tasks are not made too great. AA chooses to focus on grandiosity, concluding that the alcoholic needs to be deflated. In a treatment environment such as Hazelden there is both acceptance and deflation.

The emotional roller coaster ride contributes, along with disrupted socialization, dissocialization and the pampering effect of alcohol, to further social and psychological difficulties. With this complex of factors, interpersonal relationships for both the alcoholic and others in association with the alcoholic are guided by suspicion, resentment and anger. What may have been close emotional relationships become difficult if not impossible to maintain, with the result that the alcoholic feels abandoned and may seek to fill the void either by participation in extralegal behavior or the oblivion of alcohol which may lead to legal, economic and further sociopsychological problems. Alcoholics seeking help speak of their growing desperation as the problems in their lives multiply.

In the Hazelden conceptualization of alcoholism, the core difficulty or primary condition needing treatment is the dependence on alcohol, with the multiple and complex disruptions that dependence creates in social and psychological adaptation. This is not to say that other problems in the alcoholic's life are not real or are unimportant, but comes from the conviction, based on considerable clinical experience, that other problems which either predate or were prompted by alcohol abuse, cannot be adequately addressed unless drinking is stopped. For instance, if a patient has sexual guilt traceable to an early exposure to incest it is important to acknowledge this as a problem area which will need attention following the intensive treatment focusing on alcoholism. Similarly, if a patient has a recent history of theft and related criminal behavior, it may be that alcohol was instrumental in facilitating these illegal acts, but the alcohol behavior needs to be addressed so that rehabilitation for criminal behavior may be productively undertaken. Problems other than alcoholism need to be acknowledged as a part of alcoholism treatment and in some instances further diagnosis and initial intervention is appropriate. But from the Hazelden perspective it is most productive to work on one principal problem area at a time, and it is the alcoholism that is most immediate and manifestly disturbing. For the practicing alcoholic, then, the most productive intervention strategy is to provide direct treatment for alcoholism before dealing with other related problems in living. Other problems identified during alcoholism treatment need to be incorporated into posttreatment aftercare planning and referral.

The Hazelden conceptualization of the relation of alcoholism and other life problems may be summarized as follows:

Alcohol problems are typically related with other life problems. The relationship between alcoholism and other life problems is a complex web of interacting multiple linkages where it is difficult to distinguish between cause and effect relationships. We do know that strategically, if we treat alcoholism as a primary problem that needs treatment in its own right, a remarkable number of life problems are resolved once the alcoholism recovery process is under way. In other instances, other life problems are put into sharper focus so that sober, a person may identify these life problems and begin to deal with them successfully with appropriate help.

Alcoholism and the goal of abstinence

As stated previously, the Hazelden conceptualization of alcoholism advocates abstinence and views alcoholism as a chronic condition subject to recovery, but resistant to cure. Both clinical and research evidence support the position that abstinence is an appropriate and logical goal as a partial means of recovery from alcoholism. Abstinence alone will not suffice to resolve the sociopsychological functioning problems experienced by alcoholics, but it appears to be an important, if not necessary, means to that end.

Studies reporting the incidence of posttreatment normal drinking recognize the importance of abstinence. Davies' 1962 report of 7 men out of 93 treated alcoholics who engaged in posttreatment normal drinking for periods of 7 to 11 years concludes with the recommendation that ". . . all patients should be advised to aim at total abstinence."[33] Although strongly recommending consideration of alternative treatment outcome goals, Pattison and the Sobells acknowledge that ". . . abstinence is a legitimate and feasible outcome goal" and further that "More practically, it is likely that for some individuals with alcohol problems, abstinence would be both an easier and more appropriate treatment goal, with less danger to their ongoing stability."[34] Abstinence is certainly the safer treatment outcome goal considering that the techniques for identifying alcoholics who would be successful with controlled drinking have not been developed as reliable assessment tools.

Treatment outcome research indicates that about five to nine percent of treated alcoholics report drinking without problems at the time of follow-up.[35] These findings, however, have shortcomings concerning: 1) definition of controlled or normal drinking, 2) duration of time during which drinking without problems was carried out, 3) accuracy of alcoholism diagnosis, 4) follow-up interval, return rate, size and characteristics of the population, and 5) reliability and validity of the information. As will be pointed out in the next chapter, there are many limitations on the generalizability of treatment outcome studies. Still, it is plausible that some small percentage of treated alcoholics may successfully drink in moderation without related problems, but the caveat is that there is no way of identifying who will be among this small percentage. From a probability standpoint, the odds against being able to resume moderate drinking without problems are so great that even a careless gambler would be unwilling to wager on the outcome.

Considerably more research will certainly be done on the abstinence versus controlled drinking question, but for the present, from a treatment strategy perspective, the Hazelden conceptualization favoring abstinence seems justified. This position is stated as follows:

> *The empirical evidence suggests that alcohol problems are chronic and are not responsive to therapy advocating nonabstinence.* Practically, abstinence is the most effective immediate treatment goal for the overwhelming majority of individuals identified as alcoholic. Psychological and physiological dependence on alcohol are not separate phenomena but are linked together in complex and, as yet, not understood ways. The consumption of small amounts of alcohol by a person does not necessarily initiate a physical need that in turn causes further drinking, but the psychophysiological risk of using small amounts of alcohol is high relative to the probability of returning to alcoholic drinking and problems.

Alcoholism treatment implications

The advantage of using an alcoholism problem focus with alcoholic and chemically dependent people may be best illustrated from the perspective of the "patient in treatment experience." Three Hazelden patients were taking a midday walk and engaging in active conversation. Speaking of the treatment experience one patient said, "The main purpose, as I see it, is to make you look at things you don't want to look at and to put you into contact with others whose problems are similar to yours." Another spoke up supporting the forced awareness about oneself as having great benefit and then referred to a statement from the group session that morning that although each of the participants had a unique set of problems, there were numerous similarities among the problems of all the patients. He said, "We become so preoccupied with our own problems that we don't realize that the other guy has problems too. When you hear about someone else's problems you don't feel so alone." The third patient agreed with his companions and added, "What I got out of that is, I wouldn't want to trade my problems for someone else's, but by talking about my problems I can now think about ways of working on them."

It is unlikely that these three patients drank the same alcoholic beverage in the same quantities at the same intervals. The drinking patterns were probably as different as their life problems and their characters as varied as their physical statures. Their common bond was that they abused chemicals, had problems in their lives as a direct result of this abuse, and were learning to look at their chemical abuse problems as one of their major life problems. The recognition that their problem situations were similar in many respects to those of other patients grew out of their ability to identify with other alcoholics.

Even where the drug of choice is different, patients seem able to find a unifying bond in their feelings and experiences resulting from chemical dependency and associated life problems. Youth are seen to form strong mutual bonds with older patients whose life circumstances and chemical use patterns are quite different from their own. Binge drinkers and daily drinkers become aware of ways in which alcohol has affected their lives, noting that the differences in their styles of drinking is of little consequence.

Still, each Hazelden patient's individual circumstances and characteristics are recognized as important in the treatment experience. Chemical use history, social background, life problems and personality assessment all contribute to the formulation of an individual treatment plan for each patient. Patients are assigned different change objectives and different means of working toward these objectives. What provides the commonality is that everyone is working on change objectives, learning about themselves through sharing their assets and weaknesses in a group setting and recognizing the detrimental effect that chemical abuse has had for them. Patient differences that warrant special attention are referred to special resources, but differences that do not affect treatment process are not seen as important.

Hazelden's position in support of a single treatment modality, meaning a chemical dependency problem focus, for alcoholics and other chemically dependent people is expressed in the statement that follows:

> *Treating alcoholics and other chemically dependent people by way of a single treatment modality, while also recognizing the individual differences of people, is an effective treatment approach.* For the purposes of treatment, individuals with alcoholism and other chemical dependencies have more in common than they have to differentiate them. Practically, differences that do not make any difference are not differences. It does not seem warranted at our present level of therapeutic knowledge to develop separate programs for different categories of persons with other chemical dependencies. Within a single treatment approach it is possible to acknowledge and deal with individual differences thereby treating both the common condition of alcoholism-chemical dependency and the problems unique to individual patients.

Agreement with and comparison of the seven statements

Members of the Hazelden staff were asked to react to the seven foregoing statements about the conceptualization of alcoholism current at Hazelden. The statements were presented in a mailing which included a cover letter explaining the purpose of the survey, some background questions for the respondent and the seven statements. The staff was asked to indicate "agree," "somewhat agree" or "disagree" and to make comments to supplement their reaction to any of the statements. A total of 36 (45%) of the 80 Hazelden staff surveyed responded to the questionnaire. As shown in Table 2-1 the response rate was above 60% for counselors, clergy and clergy trainees and psychologists. Staff in these three classifications have considerable patient contact whereas the consultants and administrators, with a lower return rate (34.8%), have a varied but generally lower patient contact. Trainees had the lowest return rate (20%) as well as a high level of patient contact. The lower return rate for trainees may be accounted for by their temporary status at Hazelden (training lasts for one year for the majority of trainees) and the heavy expectations placed on their time as they participate in a demanding work/study situation.

Of the 36 respondents, 17 were female with an average age of 43, and 19 were male with an average age of 46. Education for both male and female staff respondents averaged 17 years or slightly beyond college graduation. Although some of the respondents had no formal education beyond high school, most had some college or held undergraduate or graduate college degrees.

The female staff respondents had worked in the alcoholism field for an average of 3.7 years, 71% were recovering alcoholics and 82% were active in AA or another self-help group. Males had a longer average working experience in alcoholism at 6.8 years but fewer were recovering alcoholics (53%) and fewer were active in AA or other self-help groups (74%).

Agreement levels were consistently high as shown in Table 2-2. Highest agreement (97%) was with the idea that "alcohol problems are typically related to other life problems" and lowest agreement (75%) was with the idea that "there is little evidence to date for a basic biological process that predisposes an individual toward dysfunctional use of alcohol." Those respondents indicating that they "somewhat agree" or "disagree" with the statement on biological predisposition were not of any single background category except that they were overrepresented in the consultant-administrator category. Highest disagreement was with the idea that "there is a single entity which can be defined as alcoholism." Those disagreeing with this idea represent a cross section of Hazelden staff, with being a recovering alcoholic the only background factor that was common to all except one.

It may be concluded that the seven statements do represent a conceptualization of alcoholism that is generally accepted at Hazelden. In what ways, then, does this conceptualization of alcoholism differ from the "traditional" and "emergent" conceptualizations of alcoholism put forth by Pattison and the Sobells?[36] Table 2-3 presents the "Traditional," "Hazelden" and "Emergent" conceptualizations of alcoholism for the purpose of comparison, Although the "traditional" statements are more abbreviated than the Hazelden and "emergent" statements, a comparison of the Hazelden conceptualization of alcoholism with the other two views should be possible.

Table 2-1 Hazelden Staff Return Rate by Job Classification for Questionnaire on Alcoholism Conceptualization and Treatment Goals

Job Classification	Total in Job Classification	Questionnaires Returned	Percent Returned
Counselors	16	10	62.5
Clergy & Clergy Trainees	13	9	69.2
Consultants & Administrators	23	8	34.8
Psychologists	8	5	62.5
Trainees	20	4	20.0
TOTAL	80	36	45.0

Table 2-2 Hazelden Staff Responses to Seven Statements Representing Hazelden's Conceptualization of Alcoholism

	Agree		Somewhat Agree		Disagree		No Information		Total	
	f	%	f	%	f	%	f	%	f	%
1. Single Entity	29	80.5	2	5.6	5	13.9	0	—	36	100.0
2. Prealcoholic Predictors	30	83.3	4	11.1	2	5.6	0	—	36	99.9
3. Biological Predisposition	27	75.0	6	16.6	3	8.3	0	—	36	99.9
4. Developmental Sequence	33	91.6	1	2.7	2	5.5	0	—	36	99.9
5. Life Problems	35	97.2	1	2.7	0	—	0	—	36	99.9
6. Chronic Condition	30	83.3	4	11.1	2	5.6	0	—	36	100.0
7. Single Treatment	31	86.1	5	13.9	0	—	0	—	36	100.0

To begin with, the Hazelden statement recognizing a single entity called alcoholism is in basic agreement with the "traditional" idea, but acknowledges various symptoms and behaviors within alcoholism. The "emergent" statement recognizes the variations in symptoms and behavior, but sees them as more important or useful from a treatment perspective than does the Hazelden view. Given diversity, the Hazelden conceptualization contends that alcohol use with associated health, personal and social problems constitutes enough commonality to be viewed as a single entity.

According to both the Hazelden and "emergent" conceptualizations, there is no way of identifying prealcoholics as different from nonprealcoholics. However, the Hazelden position agrees with the "traditional" view that there is an identifiable difference between alcoholics and nonalcoholics. It is possible to define alcoholism by symptoms and behaviors and within that definition to diagnose some persons as alcoholic, whereas others could not be so classified.

More research such as that of Goodwin, needs to be focused on the presence of a biological predisposition to alcoholism.[37] Once alcoholism is evident, a psychophysiological response may be activated which, in turn, serves to stimulate drinking. The "traditional" conceptualization has viewed the drinking response mechanism as largely physiological, but research indicates that it may be more of a multiple cue reaction. Essentially, however, the "traditional," "emergent" and Hazelden conceptualization appear to differ very little at this point, with all three accepting physical dependence on alcohol and psychophysical stimulation which may prompt further drinking.

There is agreement between the Hazelden and the "emergent" conceptualizations of alcoholism as to the variable rate of progression. However, the Hazelden conceptualization holds that a therapeutic intervention is necessary for recovery and that abstinence is essential to effective intervention. The "emergent" conceptualization accepts "spontaneous remission" and holds that changes other than abstinence can result in an alteration of drinking problems. Hazelden's position favoring therapeutic intervention and abstinence is in accord with the "traditional" conceptualization of alcoholism because both accept the likelihood of "loss of control," a psychophysiological response pattern which may serve to stimulate further drinking. It appears that the "emergent" conceptualization accepts the presence of a psychophysiological response pattern, as indicated in statement C3, but implies either a self-correcting action or reversal of the pattern by changes other than stopping drinking altogether.

Statement D follows from the preceding statement in all three conceptualizations. Loss of control appears to be associated with an inevitable movement through the phases and symptoms of the Jellinek Chart in the "traditional" conceptualization. Hazelden's conceptualization accepts a variable progression, but considers that as life problems multiply, it is the abuse of alcohol and associated maladaptive behaviors that need to be addressed as the primary problem in the intervention. Other life problems are all seen as being of equal importance to alcohol abuse in the "emergent" conceptualization, with treatment addressing all problems simultaneously and treatment outcome not judged by whether drinking has stopped. In contrast, abstinence may be seen as a necessary end for the "traditional" conceptualization both as a means to improving sociopsychological functioning as well as an outcome objective for the Hazelden conceptualization.

Is it possible that some individuals displaying alcoholic behaviors may begin to drink again without abuse or associated life problems? For the "traditional" conceptualization the answer in an emphatic NO. The Hazelden conceptualization accepts the idea that a small percentage of alcoholics may return to drinking without alcohol abuse or life problems, but the probability of this happening is very slight. On a normal probability curve the alcoholic who can change a drinking pattern to moderate consumption with no associated problems may be seen as three standard deviations from the mean, i.e., extremely rare. Abusive drinking may be a symptom of other problems according to the "emergent" conceptualization, but it should not be considered the principal problem although, for some, abstinence might be a helpful remedy. In contrast, the Hazelden conceptualization supports abstinence as an effective, practical and prudent alcoholism treatment strategy that will promote overall improved functioning.

The concluding statement for the Hazelden and "emergent" conceptualizations contrasts a chemical dependency problem focus with pluralistic problem focus. If alcoholism is seen as the primary condition, treatment needs to focus on alcoholism: Hazelden's treatment approach is consistent with this alcoholism conceptualization. On the other hand, if a variety of problems are conceived of as equally important, as is true for the "emergent" conceptualization, then a diversity of treatments each with special approaches and capabilities would provide the most responsive treatment programming. The Hazelden conceptualization does not preclude individual differences, but does see alcoholism as the common denominator. In the "emergent" conceptualization with its objective of effecting minimal changes in remedying life problems, alcohol abuse, the principle commonality, loses emphasis.

It is not the purpose of the preceding comparisons to reject either the "traditional" conceptualization or the "emergent" conceptualization. The "traditional" conceptualization, to the extent that it was accurately portrayed by Pattison and the Sobells, has been useful in the development of alcoholism treatment and still provides a therapeutic construct that may be helpful. The "emergent" conceptualization is an obvious attempt to explore alternatives, but it is still questionable whether the positions taken can be translated into effective large-scale therapies. Hazelden conceptualization differs from either approach in that it reflects some of the newer empirically based understandings used to support the "emergent" conceptualization, while drawing different conclusions from some of the findings, and at the same time it maintains some continuity with the "traditional" conceptualization. In a sense, the Hazelden conceptualization may be seen as a pragmatic, "middle of the road" position. What is more important is that it is a position that appears to work as will be shown in later chapters. Before proceeding with outcome findings, treatment goals and treatment process need to be discussed.

Treatment Goals and Means

Contrast with other modalities

Three objectives are seen as being at the core of recovery in the Hazelden model: 1) growth of transcendental, spiritual awareness, 2) recognition of choice and personal responsibility, 3) acceptance of peer relationships. The Hazelden challenge to patients is to grow spiritually, to make choices and to relate openly to others. In order for this challenge to be effected, there needs to be a systematic development of spontaneity, free will and dignity. The following is abstracted from a statement of the Hazelden primary rehabilitation program philosophy:

> The primary rehabilitation program is based on the belief that the chemically dependent person has the capacity to abstain from mood-altering chemicals and the capacity to actualize his human potential: to demonstrate personal freedom and responsibility, to exercise self-determination

and personal choice, to realize personal growth and change, to form meaningful and workable relationships with the world outside himself. These factors are vital to recovery from chemical dependency.

The mission of the primary rehabilitation program is to help the chemically dependent person achieve two long-term goals:

1. Abstinence from mood-altering chemicals, and

2. An improved life-style.

Of necessity, the final realization of these long-term goals is a lifelong pursuit, and the primary rehabilitation program is viewed as only the beginning of what must be a continuing effort to maintain a life-style that is conducive to remaining free from mood-altering chemicals. However, movement toward these goals can be demonstrated in the here and now, during the person's stay in the rehabilitation program. Achievement of the following four short-term goals is a satisfactory indication of progress toward long-term goal attainment.

1. To help the chemically dependent person recognize the illness and its implications.

2. To help the chemically dependent person admit that he/she needs help . . ., that the illness cannot be cured, and to concentrate on learning to live with it in a constructive manner.

3. To help the chemically dependent person identify specifically what he/she needs to change in order to live with the illness in a constructive manner.

4. To help the chemically dependent person translate that understanding into action; that is, to actively assist the patient in the changes necessary to increase his/her level of functioning and to develop a new life-style.

To accomplish these purposes, Hazelden uses a variety of means, some of which are similar to those used in other chemical dependency treatment models and others which are adaptations of therapeutic means utilized in the mental health field.

Hazelden follows the medical model in the detoxification and withdrawal process, but only in its methodology and not in its mechanistic assumptions. Chemical dependency, in Hazelden's view, is more than a medical problem or a disease. The medical model regards alcoholism as a progressive disease, possibly hereditary, which is the symptom of a psychological disturbance.[38] Treatment within the medical model utilizes tranquilizers, often administered for several weeks or months, and deterrent medications (Antabuse) with either hospitalization or periodic physician visits focusing on medical symptoms.[39] The initiating and manipulative role of the physician is central to the medical model. At Hazelden, although medical symptoms are attended to and medications are used in the detoxification phase of treatment, the greater

Table 2-3 Three Contrasting Conceptualizations of Alcoholism

Traditional Conceptualization of Alcoholism*	Hazelden Conceptualization of Alcoholism	Emergent Conceptualization of Alcoholism*
A¹ THERE IS A UNITARY PHENOMENON WHICH CAN BE IDENTIFIED AS ALCOHOLISM.	A² THERE IS A SINGLE ENTITY WHICH CAN BE DEFINED AS ALCOHOLISM. Although alcohol dependence subsumes a variety of symptoms and behaviors, there is enough commonality in the array of symptoms and behaviors to consider alcoholism as a unitary phenomenon. There have been subclassifications of alcoholism developed but for the purpose of providing treatment none of the subclassifications have provided a therapeutic advantage. The symptoms common to alcoholism have been corroborated so that alcoholism may be identified by the person using alcohol in a stereotyped, repetitive, maladaptive fashion.	A³ THERE IS NO SINGLE ENTITY WHICH CAN BE DEFINED AS ALCOHOLISM. Alcoholism is not a thing but a collection of various symptoms and behaviors that collectively comprise different types of syndromes. There appears to be a broad array of life situations—dependent upon psychological disposition, past learning, sociocultural influences, and physiological states—that lead to inappropriate use of alcohol, which in turn leads to deleterious physical, psychological, and social consequences for the individual. These consequences are manifested in different patterns. Alcohol dependence is a health problem that may involve various organ systems of the body and affect one's personal and social well-being.
B¹ ALCOHOLICS AND PREALCOHOLICS ARE ESSENTIALLY DIFFERENT FROM NONALCOHOLICS	B² THERE ARE NO IDENTIFIABLE DIFFERENCES BETWEEN THE INDIVIDUAL WHO WILL BECOME AN ALCOHOLIC AND THE INDIVIDUAL WHO WILL NOT BECOME AN ALCOHOLIC (ASSUMING THAT THE INDIVIDUALS USE ALCOHOL). HOWEVER ONCE ALCOHOLISM DEVELOPS THE ALCOHOLIC IS DISTINGUISHED FROM THE NONALCOHOLIC BY AN INABILITY TO USE ALCOHOL WITHOUT A HIGH PROBABILITY OF EXPERIENCING HARMFUL CONSEQUENCES. Although individuals may have differing susceptibility to both the use of alcohol and the development of alcohol problems as a result of genetic, physiological, psychological and sociological factors, no technology exists which permits identification of the prealcoholic. Accurate assessment of alcohol problems is best achieved through operational descriptions of the pattern of alcohol use and the consequences of such use for an individual, which could range from no adverse effects to severe or even fatal consequences.	B³ THERE IS NO CLEAR DICHOTOMY BETWEEN EITHER ALCOHOLICS AND NONALCOHOLICS, OR BETWEEN PREALCOHOLICS AND NONPREALCOHOLICS even though individuals may have differing susceptibility to both the use of alcohol and the development of alcohol problems as a result of genetic, physiological, psychological, and sociocultural factors. Accurate assessment of alcohol problems is best achieved through operational descriptions of the pattern of alcohol use and the consequences of such use for an individual, which could range from no adverse effects to severe or even fatal consequences.
C¹ ALCOHOLICS SOMETIMES EXPERIENCE AN IRRESISTIBLE PHYSICAL CRAVING FOR ALCOHOL OR A STRONG PSYCHOLOGICAL COMPULSION TO DRINK	C² THERE IS LITTLE EVIDENCE TO DATE FOR A BASIC BIOLOGICAL PROCESS THAT PREDISPOSES AN INDIVIDUAL TOWARD DYSFUNCTIONAL USE OF ALCOHOL. HOWEVER, ONCE THE PATTERN OF ALCOHOLISM IS ESTABLISHED	C³ THERE IS NO EVIDENCE TO DATE FOR A BASIC BIOLOGICAL PROCESS THAT PREDISPOSES AN INDIVIDUAL TOWARD DYSFUNCTIONAL USE OF ALCOHOL. That is, there is no mysterious "cell hunger" or metabolic "need."

Table 2-3 Three Contrasting Conceptualizations of Alcoholism - Continued

Traditional Conceptualization of Alcoholism*	Hazelden Conceptualization of Alcoholism	Emergent Conceptualization of Alcoholism*
	THE USE OF ALCOHOL BY AN INDIVIDUAL HAS A HIGH PROBABILITY OF TRIGGERING DYSFUNCTIONAL PHYSIOLOGICAL, PSYCHOLOGICAL AND SOCIAL RESPONSES. There is no generally accepted physiological predeterminer of alcoholism that may be identified in an individual. There is evidence that physical dependence is established after the consumption of large amounts of alcohol. This condition may activate psychophysiological response patterns which in turn serve as stimuli to engage in further drinking.	However, there is evidence that physical dependence is established after the consumption of large amounts of alcohol. This condition may activate psychophysiological response patterns, which in turn serve as stimuli to engage in further drinking.
D¹ ALCOHOLICS GRADUALLY DEVELOP A PROCESS CALLED "LOSS OF CONTROL" OVER DRINKING, AND POSSIBLY EVEN AN INABILITY TO STOP DRINKING	D² THE DEVELOPMENTAL SEQUENCE OF ADVERSE CONSEQUENCES ASSOCIATED WITH ALCOHOLISM APPEARS TO BE HIGHLY VARIABLE. The variation ranges from an almost immediate and rapid progression to a slow progressive development. At times the alcohol problem may remain static or appear to become less severe. Despite the variation, most alcoholics find that physiological, psychological and social problems produced by alcohol abuse continue to increase unless reversed through the therapeutic program that includes abstinence from alcohol.	D³ THE DEVELOPMENTAL SEQUENCE OF ADVERSE CONSEQUENCES APPEARS TO BE HIGHLY VARIABLE, ranging from an almost immediate and rapid progression to a slow progressive development. The alcohol problem may also remain static or even become less severe. Further, with or without treatment, various types of alcohol problems may moderate or simply desist. Such remission bears no necessary relationship to abstinence, for it may accompany a change in patterns of drinking and the consequences thereof.
E¹ ALCOHOLISM IS A PROGRESSIVE DISEASE WHICH FOLLOWS AN INEXORABLE DEVELOPMENT THROUGH A DISTINCT SERIES OF PHASES	E² ALCOHOL PROBLEMS ARE TYPICALLY RELATED WITH OTHER LIFE PROBLEMS. The relationship between alcoholism and other life problems is a complex web of interacting multiple linkages where it is difficult to distinguish between cause and effect relationships. We do know that strategically, if we treat alcoholism as a primary problem that needs treatment in its own right, a remarkable number of life problems are resolved once the alcoholism recovery process is underway. In other instances, other life problems are put into sharper focus so that sober, a person may identify these life problems and begin to deal with them successfully with appropriate help.	E³ ALCOHOL PROBLEMS ARE TYPICALLY INTERRELATED WITH OTHER LIFE PROBLEMS. Therefore, treatment plans and goals should be determined on an individual basis, with specific assessment of dysfunction in each major area of life function. This is necessary to evaluate treatment effectiveness and to assess unintended or detrimental side effects. Abstinence should not be the only criterion used for assessing the effectiveness of treatment.

35

Table 2-3 Three Contrasting Conceptualizations of Alcoholism - Continued

Traditional Conceptualization of Alcoholism*	Hazelden Conceptualization of Alcoholism	Emergent Conceptualization of Alcoholism*
F¹ ALCOHOLISM IS A PERMANENT AND IRREVERSIBLE CONDITION	F² THE EMPIRICAL EVIDENCE SUGGESTS THAT ALCOHOL PROBLEMS ARE CHRONIC AND ARE NOT RESPONSIVE TO THERAPY ADVOCATING NONABSTINENCE. Practically, abstinence is the most effective immediate treatment goal for the overwhelming majority of individuals identified as alcoholic. Psychological dependence and physical dependence on alcohol are not separate phenomena but are linked together in complex, and as of yet, not understood ways. The consumption of small amounts of alcohol by a person does not necessarily initiate a physical need that in turn causes further drinking but the psychophysiological risk of using small amounts of alcohol is high relative to the probability of returning to alcoholic drinking and problems.	F³ THE EMPIRICAL EVIDENCE SUGGESTS THAT ALCOHOL PROBLEMS ARE REVERSIBLE. It would appear that the more severe and long-term patterns of alcohol dependence are more resistant to change than less entrenched patterns. The potential for reversibility may lie along a continuum so that theoretically, except for irreversible cellular damage, it might be possible to reverse any drinking pattern. More practically, it is likely that for some individuals with alcohol problems, abstinence would be both an easier and a more appropriate treatment goal, with less danger to their ongoing stability. For others, it may be more judicious and appropriate to change their patterns of alcohol use rather than to insist on abstinence. Further, clinical research on drinking goals is needed to clarify the most efficacious and appropriate long-term clinical options.
	G² TREATING ALCOHOLICS AND OTHER CHEMICALLY DEPENDENT PEOPLE BY WAY OF A SINGLE TREATMENT MODALITY, WHILE ALSO RECOGNIZING THE INDIVIDUAL DIFFERENCES OF PEOPLE, IS AN EFFECTIVE TREATMENT APPROACH. For the purposes of treatment, individuals with alcoholism and other chemical dependencies have more in common than they have to differentiate them. Practically, differences that do not make any difference are not differences. It does not seem warranted at our present level of therapeutic knowledge to develop separate programs for different categories of alcoholics or different categories of persons with other chemical dependencies. Within a single treatment approach it is possible to acknowledge and deal with individual differences thereby treating both the common condition of alcoholism-chemical dependency and the problems unique to individual patients.	G³ IT MAY BE CLINICALLY USEFUL TO DEVELOP TYPOLOGIES OF SUBPOPULATIONS FOR ADMINISTRATIVE PROGRAM DEVELOPMENT since people with alcohol problems characteristically differ from one another in many respects, yet may share common treatment problems. Efficient treatment, from the recipient's viewpoint, is that strategy which includes the minimal necessary changes in life function to obtain amelioration of alcohol-related life problems.

*From E. M. Pattison, M. Sobel and L. Sobell, *Emerging Concepts of Alcoholism*, Springer, New York, 1977. The order of presentation has been changed portion of the rehabilitation program following detoxification is drug free and coordinated by therapists other than physicians or other medical health practitioners.

Treatment at Hazelden uses some of the interpretations common to the psychoanalytic model. The psychoanalytic model accepts the concept of an alcoholic personality which is seen as passive-dependent, emotionally immature and experiencing difficulty relating meaningfully to others. This alcoholic personality configuration is classified largely as a character disorder, although a small portion (20-30 percent) of the alcoholic population may be categorized as either psychotic or neurotic.[40] Psychoanalytic treatment involves creating an awareness of the satisfaction of relating meaningfully to other persons and thus breaking the ego defense system of denial found to be well entrenched in most alcoholics.

In the psychoanalytic treatment model, the professional therapist's personality is a principal instrument in therapy. In contrast, Hazelden's treatment model utilizes both intensive and long-term group therapy. Personalities of the paraprofessional counselors and peer group members are important within the rehabilitation process, but they use a more transitory, confrontive and caring style than a directive, passive manner. The patient is encouraged to take an active role with the nondegreed professional counselors and members of the peer group in developing meaningful relationship experiences and clarifying feelings and definitions of reality. Breaking the denial system is a principal objective of treatment, but unlike the psychoanalytic model with its past and causal orientation, the Hazelden model with its strong AA influence does not focus on cause and is concerned with the past only as a means of orienting attention to the present and future.

The Hazelden model has little in common with the classic behavioral modification model of alcoholism treatment apart from an agreement that some behavior can be modified. Classic behavior modification may use either aversive conditioning techniques, positive reinforcement or systematic desensitization.[41] All these techniques are predicated on a manipulative strategy where the therapist conditions the subject to respond in an "acceptable" fashion. Hazelden's treatment model considers freedom and choice crucial to recovery. Accordingly, the patient is not manipulated or conditioned, but is instead presented with cognitive information through peer interaction, group therapy, readings and lectures. This information is helpful in understanding behavior, feelings and physical symptoms characteristic of chemical dependency. The didactic presentation of this information is intended to provide a basis for intellectual awareness about chemical dependency but is not seen as sufficient for recovery. Instead, intellectual awareness about chemical dependency is viewed as contributing to the insight necessary for rehabilitation to take place. This approach follows the treatment known as cognitive behavior modification with the goal of teaching behavioral self-control through cognitive restructuring and training.

The social model of treatment and the Hazelden model of treatment are most closely aligned. Within the social model, abuse of alcohol and other chemicals is considered to be an overlearned mechanism of coping with problems of living. At Hazelden, because social factors are seen as having a major part in contributing to chemical dependency, social techniques are important in the process of rehabilitation. Treatment utilizing a peer group and paraprofessionals (who are often recovering alcoholics) constitutes a social milieu of therapeutic community in which resocialization occurs guided by the principles of Alcoholics Anonymous.

Because the Hazelden treatment model is multifaceted, professionals and nondegreed professionals from a range of disciplines and applied specialities are required for an effective treatment team. It is most accurate, therefore, to consider the Hazelden treatment model part of the multidisciplinary approach to chemical dependency treatment. The multidisciplinary treatment prescribed by the Hazelden model uses physicians and nurses in the detoxification and withdrawal care, psychologists, psychiatrists in individual problem assessment, nondegreed professional counselors and clergy in the experience of resocialization, dietitians to help rekindle an interest in proper nutrition, recreation and relaxation specialists to introduce alternative coping skills, and experienced chemical dependency workers to provide information in lectures, identify supplementary books and pamphlets for reading, and coordinate needs and community resources for aftercare planning. These multidisciplinary resources constitute a team that promotes the previously mentioned objectives of the Hazelden model: 1) transcendental growth, 2) free will, choice and personal responsibility awareness, and 3) interpersonal relationship skill development.

Goals and process

One treatment goal seeks to encourage an outward orientation for patients. Transcendental awareness refers to the development of meaningful relationships with people and the total social and physical environment external to man.* The Hazelden model holds that the past and present affect human behavior but that man can transcend these seeming constraints by developing new external relationships. Individuals face a choice between relating transcendentally to other people and the universe or relating inwardly. Chemically dependent people have either made the inward choice or gravitated to it as a

---

*Revell Howe discusses this in the context of two opposing life principles: The exclusionist principle and the inclusionist principle. His position is that, "inclusion (openness to new people, new values, new ideas, and change of all kind) is the only way in which one can achieve wholeness."[42]

result of their use of alcohol or other drugs. The chemically dependent person pursues the inward course with the conviction that being affected by others at a deep level may have only negative consequences. Others are viewed as objects to be related to with minimal emotional involvement. Accordingly, almost all stimulation and motivation is internally based, and other people are seen as uncaring and alien. The result is a growing aloneness which, in turn, promotes the use of chemicals and the use of chemicals, in turn, promotes aloneness.

Entering into treatment, the patient is introduced to a radically new style of living. This new view emphasizes a way of relating that may make a person feel whole and productive. Transcendental awareness is similar to, although somewhat more expansive than, the Alcoholics Anonymous idea of spiritual awareness. The revolutionary idea is that man has the ability to identify transcendentally. Although the dynamics of identifying transcendentally are not fully understood scientifically, patients are made aware that there is a creativity and vitality in relating transcendentally that has the capability of making one whole and productive. The result is that the chemically dependent person can dramatically alter past forms of behavior because a new definition of reality has been adopted which rejects the limited aloneness perception that guided past behavior. Life as a transcendentally aware individual has the potential to become full of new and fulfilling relationships which provide meaning and direction for living.

Free will, choice and personal responsibility operate in the Hazelden model's contention that a person does not have to remain chemically dependent and that recovery is largely self-effected, although the rehabilitation program serves as a catalyst for change. Recovery from active alcoholism and other chemical dependencies cannot be accomplished by other people doing things to and for the patient. Only through the chemically dependent person's thoughts and actions can recovery come about. Hazelden's treatment approach is designed to challenge the pathological props that are both the symptoms and behavioral traps of chemical dependency by making persons aware of what their lives have become as well as providing a glimpse of alternative life-styles.

Chemically dependent persons need to be made aware that much of the social and personal pathology that dominates their lives is attributable to the effects of being dependent on chemicals. If much of their maladaptation is seen as the direct result of alcohol and/or drug abuse then the obvious conclusion, supported strongly by Hazelden, is that life would be much better without the use of chemicals.

Confrontation, as used at Hazelden, is a supportive but probing encounter and an effective tool in helping patients gain insights into themselves and their life condition. To be effective, this confrontation requires patients to play an active rather than a passive role. Patients must engage in serious self-examination intended to help the patients become primary teachers about themselves. Compliance with the expectations of others will not contribute productively to the self-discovery process, although partial and temporary compliance may lead to new patterns of self-examination. Self-honesty and working at developing insight are promoted by the First Step of AA coupled with the recognition that positive changes can be effected in areas of life over which a person has some control.

Part of developing a sense of free will, choice and personal responsibility is a redefinition of control in relation to self and the social/physical environment. The redefinition of control is communicated in the frequently repeated Serenity Prayer* and the implications of this redefinition are dealt with in a variety of activities which make up the rehabilitation process. Free will and personal responsibility are put into perspective with the recognition that man is not omnipotent. There are areas of life over which a person has control and other areas of life that are outside a person's control. As stated in the Serenity Prayer, the critical factor is being able to determine the difference between the control and noncontrol areas of life.

Developing interpersonal relationship skills requires transcendental growth and an awareness of free will, choice and personal responsibility. In turn, meaningful relationships positively reinforce transcendental growth and the awareness of free will, choice and personal responsibility. Some chemically dependent persons are so withdrawn that they relate to others only in a perfunctory manner. Other chemically dependent people are outwardly gregarious, but other people are seen as objects rather than human beings. Counselors and other patients engage each chemically dependent person in an effort to draw them out of themselves. The counselor is like an older sibling sharing experience with a younger sibling or a "midwife" of values and ideas in this process.

The therapy guided by the character defect assessment of the staff psychologist and by the counselor within the peer group is part of what has been labeled "reality therapy" or "existential therapy." Peer group members who have been in treatment for several weeks develop the ability to begin to relate to others in the group meaningfully and become adept at identifying superficial and manipulative-destructive relationship patterns. Group norms require meaningful participation, and the approval or disapproval of the peers constitutes a powerful sanctioning (reward and punishment) system that is highly constructive for the interpersonal relationship skill development goal.

The Hazelden physical plant is unique in that it was designed as a functional and architecturally attractive low-rise complex. There are seven self-con-

---

*God grant me the serenity to accept the things I cannot change, courage to change the things I can, and wisdom to know the difference.

tained treatment units which are spatially distinct, but are linked by connecting concourses to the dining hall, lecture hall and office area. Courtyards, flower beds, trees and the shoreline of South Center Lake are visible through the numerous windows that complement the designed openness of the interior physical space. The decor of brick and glass with modern furnishings and paintings adorning the walls is intended to provide an environment that will stimulate the patients' personal awareness and change.

After being admitted, patients are assigned a room in the intensive care (detoxification) unit. Patients here have no contact with those on the primary treatment units. Meals are brought to the patients and in other ways the intensive care unit is hospital-like including nursing personnel on duty twenty-four hours a day. These staff are concerned with the necessary physical workups, such as the general physical examination, blood tests, blood pressure, urine analysis, medication and monitoring of detoxification. Most patients remain in the intensive care unit for twenty-four hours, although some remain longer if necessary.

The following summary of treatment events traces the patient through the rehabilitation process which lasts an average of 30 days, with the length of stay variable depending on patients' needs. A more detailed discussion of the Hazelden rehabilitation process is available in Groupe's *Alcoholism Rehabilitation: Methods and Experiences of Private Rehabilitation Centers.*[43]

*Summary of Treatment Events**

DAY ONE   Admission and assignment to the intensive care unit/physical testing/all chemicals taken from the patient.

DAY TWO   Transfer to the Primary Treatment Residence/short tour of the physical complex/explanation of the daily routine and unit expectations

Unit Expectations
a. Patients are expected to interact only with others in their treatment unit.
b. Patients are expected to participate in meals, lectures and other unit activities.
c. Patients are expected to perform a 15-20 minute therapeutic duty such as washing floors.
d. Patients are expected to sign in and out when they leave the unit during free time.

Assignment of the basic readings: The AA "Big Book" and *The Twelve Steps and Twelve Traditions.*

---

*The days on which these events occur are variable with different tasks lasting different lengths of time depending on the patient.

DAY THREE   Assessment Interview-the patient chemical use history is taken to be used in the later problem identification interview/patient begins to meet staff and fellow patients/a senior peer who has been selected by the patients serves as a nominal leader of the 20 to 22 patients on the unit/the daily routine is followed every day but Sunday.

Daily Routine

7:00 a.m.	Personal time*
7:45	Meditation (optional)
8:00	Breakfast
8:45	Therapeutic duty
9:15	Lecture
10:00	Split group ("Hot Seat" Tues., Wed., Fri.)
11:00	Personal time
12:00 p.m.	Lunch
12:45	Personal time
1:30	Lecture
2:15	Group sessions
3:30	Community meeting
4:00	Personal time
6:00	Dinner
7:00	Lecture
8:00	Patient group objectives
approx. 11:00	Bed

*Personal time is used for reading, or conversing about group or lecture, or for exercising and is often done as small groups of patients from the unit.

DAY FOUR   Diagnostic Interview; the Jellinek chart is discussed with the patient and symptoms associated with patient problems and behavior are explored/patient tells own story to the full group and is given written feedback from peers.

DAY FIVE   "Hot Seat," a structured confrontation where peers evaluate a patient and patient evaluates self/problem identification interview—counselor discusses previous interview findings with patient and begins to formulate patient change objectives/psychological testing—personality and intellectual functioning tests are given with results communicated by the staff psychologist both to the patient and to the treatment staff/clergy interview—discussion with the patient concerning use of chemicals, family problems, and personal problems.

DAY SIX   Staff review—medical data, interview findings, family questionnaire and psychological test results are discussed by unit staff and a rehabilitation plan is developed/Phase one: a) acceptance of powerlessness over chemicals, and b) acceptance of unmanageability of one's life will proceed according to the rehabilitation plan.

DAY SEVEN   Change objectives (e.g., overcome hopelessness) and specific tasks related to Phase One are assigned to patient (assemble three peers and discuss ways in which alcohol use has interfered with a close interpersonal relationship).

DAYS 8-11   Completion of Phase One/AA Step One.

DAY 12   Begin Phase Two: a) recognize need for change, b) recognize ability to change, c) recognize that the continuum of care process is a vehicle for change.

DAYS 13-17   Completion of Phase Two/AA Step Two.

DAYS 18-23   Begin Phase Three: a) make a decision to change, b) modification of the need to control/AA Step Three and the beginning of Step Four.

DAYS 24-27   Continue to refine AA Step Four using the *Hazelden Guide to the Fourth Step Inventory* and frequent counselor, clergy and peer assistance.

DAYS 28-29   Prepare for and take the AA Fifth Step which is usually taken with the unit clergy/meetings with counselor and aftercare staff/arrangement for AA contact in the patient's home community.

DAY 30   Presentation of medallion in the unit during the afternoon group meeting/discharge procedure includes reinforcement of change and continuum of care processes.

A full appreciation of the treatment experience cannot be gained by reading over the summary of treatment events. The dynamics of treatment are instead found in the interpersonal dynamics, the personal discovery and the spiritual presence that permeates the demanding schedule of the rehabilitation program. Different patients gain from different aspects of the program. For example, when a lecture deals with drinking and driving, those who had received DWI arrests identify closely and others relate to the topic in a less personal way. Also, individual treatment programs focus different patients in different directions, such as reading a particular pamphlet or chapter from a book or going daily to relaxation therapy, but these different directions are still a part of the mainstream of treatment. Treatment is a pluralistic process with differences identified and appreciated, but with a commonality based on the impact of chemical dependency on the patients' lives.

Summary

In this chapter the Hazelden conceptualization of alcoholism has been systematically presented using the format employed by Pattison and the Sobells in their discussion of what they term the "traditional" and "emergent" conceptualizations of alcoholism. Although the Hazelden conceptualization shares elements with the other two views of alcoholism, it stands as a separate pragmatic model that is based in the clinical experience of a treatment facility and draws both from the principles and practices of the Alcoholics Anonymous fellowship and from the empirical research into alcoholism treatment and recovery processes. The high level of agreement with these working definitions of alcoholism among Hazelden staff was verified in a staff survey. Although no evidence was gathered outside of the Hazelden staff, the majority of professionals and paraprofessionals working in the alcoholism treatment field in Minnesota would probably have a high agreement with these working definitions. It is therefore suggested that what has been called the Hazelden conceptualization of alcoholism may safely be referred to as the Minnesota Model conceptualization of alcoholism.

The emphasis of Hazelden goals corresponds to the conceptualization of alcoholism: 1) abstinence from mood-altering chemicals, and 2) an improved life-style. Treatment is seen as a catalyst to trigger the changes necessary in the achievement of these goals. The changes necessary for recovery require cognitive, relational, and behavioral redirection. Learning of the effects of alcohol abuse, recognizing the need to relate outside oneself both interpersonally and spiritually, accepting the possibility of change through taking personal responsibility for behavior and working to implement a new chemically-free life-style commensurate with the chronic condition of alcoholism are what the Hazelden rehabilitation program is designed to promote.

The described processes of treatment should be seen as an intensive intervention. How effective and long-lasting is this intervention in bringing about abstinence and an improved life-style? This question will be addressed in the later chapters which consider the patient follow-up survey findings. Before considering those findings, however, the research procedures used in the alcoholism follow-up studies and a review of other alcoholism treatment outcome studies will be presented.

Reference Notes Chapter 2

[1]*Hazelden caring community guidebooks: Identification, Implementation, the Crises, the New awareness, Emergency care, Dealing with denial, the New understanding, Winning by losing/the decision, Personal inventory and planned re-entry, Challenges to the new way of life.* Center City, MN: Hazelden Foundation, 1975.

[2]E. M. Pattison, M. B. Sobell, and L. C. Sobell, *Emerging concepts of alcoholism.* New York: Springer, 1977, pp. 9-28.

[3]Ibid, pp. 189-211.

[4]National council on alcoholism committee. Criteria for the diagnosis of alcoholism. *Amer. J. Psychiat.,* 1972, *129,* 127-135.

[5]C. Ringer, H. Kufner, K. Antons, and Feuerlein, The NCA criteria for the diagnosis of alcoholism. *J. of Studies on Alc.,* 1977, *38,* 1259-1273.

[6]M. Keller and M. McCormick, *A dictionary of words about alcohol.* New Brunswick, NJ: Rutgers Center of Alcohol Studies, 1968, p. 12.

[7]R. O. Heilman, *Early recognition of alcoholism and other drug dependence.* Center City, MN: Hazelden Foundation, 1980.

[8]J. H. Mendelson, Biochemical mechanisms of alcohol addiction. In B. Kissin and H. Begleiter (eds.) *The biology of alcoholism: Biochemistry* (Vol. 1). New York: Plenum Press, 1971.

[9]M. Keller, The disease concept of alcoholism revisited. *J. of Studies on Alc.,* 1976, *37,* 1694-1777.

[10]*Webster's third new international dictionary of the English language,* unabridged. Springfield, MA: G. and C. Merriam Co., 1967, p. 1420.

[11]S. Sontag. *Illness as metaphor.* New York: Farrar, Straus and Giroux, 1978.

[12]P. M. Miller and M. A. Mastria, *Alternatives to alcohol abuse: A social learning model.* Champaign, IL: Research Press, 1977.

[13]R. E. Tarter and D. V. Schneider, Models and theories of alcoholism. In R. E. Tarter and A. A. Sugarman (eds.) *Alcoholism: Interdisciplinary approaches to an enduring problem.* Reading, MA: Addison-Wesley, 1976, p. 101.

[14]E. M. Jellinek, *The disease concept of alcoholism.* New Haven, CT: College and University Press, 1960.

[15]J. Curlee, *Alcoholism and the empty nest.* Center City, MN: Hazelden Foundation, 1969.

[16]S. M. L. Kammeier, H. Hoffman, and R. G. Loper, Personality characteristics of alcoholics as college freshmen and at the time of treatment. *Quart J. of Studies on Alc.,* 1973, *34,* 390-399.

[17]R. G. Loper, S. M. L. Kammeier, and H. Hoffman, MMPI characteristics of college freshmen males who later became alcoholics. *J. of Abnor. Psy.,* 1973, *82,* 159-162.

[18]H. Hoffman, R. Loper and S. M. L. Kammeier, Identifying future alcoholics with MMPI alcoholism scales. *Quart. J. of Studies on Alc.,* 1974, *35,* 490-498.

[19]A. F. Williams, The alcoholic personality. In B. Kissin and H. Begleiter (eds.) *The biology of alcoholism: Social aspects of alcoholism* (Vol. 4). New York: Plenum Press, 1976, pp. 243-247.

[20]R. J. Cadort, Genetic determinants of alcoholism. In R. E. Tarter and A. A. Sugarman (eds.) *Alcoholism: Interdisciplinary approaches to an enduring problem.* Reading, MA: Addison-Wesley, 1976, pp. 225-256.

[21]D. Goodwin, *Is alcoholism hereditary?* New York: Oxford University Press, 1976.

[22]R. J. Lucero and K. F. Jensen, Alcoholism and teetotalism in blood relatives of abstaining alcoholics. *Quart J. of Studies on Alc.,* 1971, *32,* 183-185.

[23]P. E. Stokes. Alcohol-endocrine interrelationships. In B. Kissin and H. Begleiter, *The biology of alcoholism: Biochemistry* (Vol. 1). New York: Plenum Press, 1971, pp. 397-436.

[24]J. H. Mendelson, Biochemical mechanisms of alcohol addiction. In B. Kissin and H. Begleiter, (eds.) *The biology of alcoholism: Biochemistry* (Vol. 1). New York: Plenum Press, 1971.

[25]Tarter and Schneider, op. cit., 86.

[26]Ibid., p. 84.

[27]M. M. Gross and J. M. Hastey, Sleep disturbances in alcoholism. In R. E. Tarter and A. A. Sugarman (eds.) *Alcoholism: Interdisciplinary approaches to an enduring problem.* Reading, MA: Addison-Wesley, 1976, pp. 309-358.

[28]H. L. Williams and A. Salamy, Alcohol and sleep. In B. Kissin and H. Begleiter (eds.) *The biology of alcoholism: Physiology and behavior* (Vol. 2). New York: Plenum Press, 1972.

[29]Stokes, op. cit.

[30]A. M. Ludwig, A. M. Winkler, and L. H. Stark, The first drink: Psychobiological aspects of craving. In E. M. Pattison, M. B. Sobell and L. C. Sobell, *Emerging concepts of alcohol dependence.* New York: Springer, 1977, pp. 71-95.

[31]S. D. Bacon, The process of addiction to alcohol: Social aspects. *Quart. J. of Studies on Alc.,* 1973, *34,* 1-27.

[32]Bacon, op. cit., 11.

[33]D. L. Davies, Normal drinking in recovered alcohol addicts. *Quart. J. of Studies on Alc.,* 1962, *23,* 94-104.

[34]Pattison, Sobell and Sobell, op. cit., pp. 190-201.

[35]F. Baekeland, L. Lundwall, and B. Kissin, Methods for the treatment of chronic alcoholism: A critical appraisal. In J. Gibbins, Y. Israel, H. Kalant, R. E. Popham, W. Schmidt, and R. G. Smart (eds.), *Research advances in alcohol and drug problems* (Vol. 2). New York: John Wiley & Sons, 1975, pp. 247-327.

[36]Pattison, Sobell and Sobell, op. cit.

[37]Goodwin, op. cit.

[38]Tarter and Schneider, op. cit., p. 82

[39]B. Kissin, Theory and practice in the treatment of alcoholism. In B. Kissin and H. Begleiter (eds.), *The biology of alcoholism: Treatment and rehabilitation of the chronic alcoholic* (Vol. 5). New York: Plenum Press, 1977, pp. 32-34.

[40]Ibid, pp. 11-17.

[41]Ibid, pp. 34-35.

[42]R. L. Howe. *Survival plus.* New York: The Seabury Press, 1971.

[43]D. J. Anderson and J. P. Burns, Hazelden Foundation: Part of the caring community. In V. Groupe (ed.), *Alcoholism rehabilitation: Methods and experiences of private rehabilitation centers.* New Brunswick, NJ: Rutgers Center on Alcohol Studies, 1978, pp. 39-50.

[44]Pattison, Sobell and Sobell, op. cit.

Chapter Three

Research Design and Methodology

Study Background

The research design and methodology used in the present study had its origins in an evaluation and research project begun in 1969. At that time a grant from the Northwest Area Foundation allowed Hazelden to investigate the impact of treatment on Hazelden patients. Resulting findings were to be used as an empirical base in decision making about services provided at Hazelden.[1] The primary thrust of this effort was a mail questionnaire follow-up of patients treated between May of 1970 and mid-November of 1971. The nearly two thousand patients discharged from Hazelden treatment during this period were sent similar mail questionnaires at 6, 12, and 18 months after treatment discharge. Questionnaires relating to patient posttreatment functioning were also sent to "significant others": persons designated by the patients as being aware of their lives (spouses, patients, AA sponsors) and able to assess the patients' posttreatment functioning.

The 24-month questionnaire was more detailed than the briefer 6-, 12-, and 18-month questionnaires. It sought information on patients' posttreatment chemical use, AA involvement, maturation and growth, life problems and treatment satisfaction. This 24-month questionnaire was returned by over 50% of all patients discharged during the project period and became the prototype for questionnaires used in the present study.

In addition to developing and testing the format for the mail questionnaire follow-up in the 1970-71 project, procedures were established for gathering sociodemographic (age, sex, etc.) and diagnostic information necessary for patient treatment planning and for evaluation research. Initially, large quantities of detailed sociodemographic information were collected. Such a mass of information was difficult to assess, but selected sociodemographic and treatment variables were computerized and made accessible in both interactive and batch modes so as to maximize their usefulness. Thus, the sociodemographic treatment variables used in the present research are the result of the procedures used in working with the 1970-71 patient information.

The 1970-71 procedures and project data were considered during the period from November 1971 through June 1973 during which time no follow-up data were gathered and preparation was made for a second project phase. In July of 1973, patients were asked to participate in a mail questionnaire. These detailed questionnaires were sent out 4, 8, and 12 months after discharge from treatment, and selected sociodemographic information was simultaneously abstracted from patient record information. As in the 1970-71 follow-up, every patient who remained in treatment for five days or more and agreed to participate in the project was included in the study.

The intention of the data collection in 1973 was descriptive rather than analytical. No hypotheses were formulated and the research questions were implicit rather than explicit. It was thought that more data were needed to establish a base-line on the posttreatment population before a predictive study could be undertaken. The implicit objective of the descriptive survey was to examine treatment outcome for the purpose of assessing overall treatment effectiveness. The objective was then one of global evaluation, although the design was comprehensive enough to allow for detailed analysis as well as description.

It may be appropriate to categorize the present study as a mix of retrospective and prospective research. The research is prospective in the sense that it started with a chosen cohort population on which measurement was made at the time of treatment and at three intervals after treatment. An experimental design was rejected at the outset because of ethical concerns and methodological complexities which may, for some, disqualify the research as prospective. A more important limitation of the original research design, and one that would more likely designate it as retrospective relative to the current purpose, was the lack of either specific research questions or hypotheses at the inception of the study, coupled with the lack of specifications for analytical procedures or specific operationalizations* of variables.

---

*An operational definition describes a set of procedures used to measure an abstract concept, i.e., AA participation as measured by the frequency of AA meeting attendance at present: more than once a week, about once a week, about two or three times a month, about once a month, less than once a month, I do not attend.

The present study was initiated in 1977 after working with the 1970-71 data and engaging in some preliminary inspection of the 1974 data. Because the data collection format and procedures were the same for the last 6 months of 1973 and the calendar years 1974 and 1975, the data collected during that 30-month period was used to initially define the study population. Three thousand six hundred thirty-eight patients were discharged from Hazelden during this study period. Sociodemographic information abstracted for these patients was incorporated with the follow-up data gathered at 4, 8, and 12 months after treatment discharge and constitutes the data base for the study.

All three of the follow-up questionnaires asked five questions each about posttreatment alcohol and drug use. Nineteen questions addressed posttreatment maturation and growth changes at each follow-up, and eight questions sought information on AA involvement. Other questions related to common health complaints; behaviors in reaction to anger, anxiety and depression; resources turned to and reasons for any alcohol and/or other chemical use after treatment; present employment situation and assessment of treatment. Not all of the "other" questions were asked on all three of the follow-up questionnaires (see questionnaires in Appendix B).

In a general sense, the present study was designed to examine some of the current questions in the chemical dependency treatment evaluation and outcome literature which will be reviewed in the next chapter. Because the Hazelden 1973-75 data gathering was not established to analytically consider most of these questions, it became necessary to construct the new research design retrospectively within the constraints of the existing data base. Principal constraints of the data base had to do with the form and content of the sociodemographic and questionnaire follow-up information. The research design task then became one of determining ways to operationalize the measurement that had been done and identify indicators that could be used in an *ex post facto* research design to yield information relevant to the topics of posttreatment chemical use, AA participation, sociopsychological functioning and outcome prediction. Before elaborating the research design used to investigate these topics, the issues of sampling bias, validity and reliability of the 1973-75 Hazelden data base will be explored.

Sampling Bias

The thorough review of methodological issues in the alcoholism treatment outcome literature by Baekeland et al. will be used as a checklist for the identification of possible sampling biases within the 1973-75 data base.[2] In this manner it should be possible to establish both strengths and weaknesses of the data base used in the present study.

Potential diagnostic bias

Who is excluded from treatment, and what sampling biases are inherent in that exclusion? In this regard, diagnosis of alcoholism and other drug dependency is an important sampling bias concern. As previously stated, alcoholism may be identified behaviorally as excessive and inappropriate use of alcohol with associated negative consequences. Baekeland et al. point out that "Although varying definitions of alcoholism are a real obstacle to comparing the results of prevalence studies, which may deal with rather different populations, they probably do not pose much of a problem in facilities that specialize in the treatment of alcoholism."[3] At Hazelden, somewhat less than 1% of the patients admitted annually are determined not to be chemically dependent. The determination of chemical dependency is accomplished through a series of measurement and testing procedures including medical assessment, patient interviews at two different time periods, a detailed questionnaire completed by the patient while in treatment, and a questionnaire completed by a family member (concerned other) about the patient. These inputs are summarized, along with insights revealed by the patient during the treatment process, in a final diagnostic impression included in a narrative report prepared by the patient's counselor.

Because strong denial by the patient is quite prevalent, there is a potential "Catch 22" in the diagnosis of alcoholism and other chemical dependencies. If persons do not admit to being dependent they are denying, which identifies them as being dependent; at the same time, persons admitting dependency are dependent by admission. Although some aspects of the "Catch 22" situation may indeed exist, it is reasoned that multiple measurement and multiple corroboration will provide information adequate to formulate a reasonable diagnostic judgment by those competent to work with alcoholics and other chemically dependent people. Following these procedures results in less than 1% of the patients admitted to Hazelden being ultimately found not chemically dependent. This is evidence that although a person's presence as a patient in a chemical dependency treatment center is not *prima facie* evidence of chemical dependency; the selection and referral of persons into such a treatment milieu carries with it a strong probability for chemical dependency diagnosis.

Potential demographic bias

A private chemical dependency treatment facility such as Hazelden is more accessible to some patients than to others. As will be seen in a later review of patient sociodemographic data, Hazelden patients are disproportionately of middle or upper-middle socioeconomic backgrounds and over half are from outside Minnesota. The patients may be characterized as white, middle-aged and, for the most part, employed and married. According to Ogborne's review of patient characteristics as outcome predictors and other similar summaries of favorable outcome indicators, the Hazelden patient population is likely to have good prognosis overall.[4, 5] This spotlights an issue that is of concern in generalizing about treatment effectiveness. Baekeland et al. pose the patient vs. treatment outcome indicator question by asking, "Which is the tail and which is the dog?"[6] Are patient characteristics more important than treatment characteristics in predicting outcome? To the extent that Hazelden patients are of high socioeconomic status (SES) and socially intact, they are likely to experience favorable treatment outcome. Still, it is possible to examine this influence empirically by comparing different background characteristics of patients in relation to outcome. In a brief study of patients committed to treatment by the court, most of whom were lower SES than the noncommitted patients at Hazelden, no significant treatment outcome differences were found between the two groups in drinking, AA attendance and sociopsychological functioning.[7] These findings suggest that treatment is more important to outcome than are the characteristics of patients for the study population. But there is also some evidence that middle-aged patients have more favorable treatment outcome than either youthful or elderly patients.[8]

Potential "no-show" bias

An issue related to treatment selectivity is patient rejection of treatment and the possible sampling biases that may be produced as a result. There are two apparent forms of treatment rejection: the person who inquires about treatment and makes arrangements to enter but never shows up, and the patient who is admitted into treatment and drops out prematurely. Some research has attempted to use the treatment "no shows" as a control group by comparing alcohol use and social functioning of treated persons with "no shows." This procedure seems impractical given the contaminating factors that may be in effect and the difficulties in initiating and maintaining contact with the "no shows." Annually, about 11.5% of the persons who make arrangements to enter inpatient treatment at Hazelden do not show up on their appointed admission date. Given the size of Hazelden's average annual population (1550), the small number of "no shows" would probably not have a significant sampling bias effect.

Potential dropout bias

Treatment rejection, in the form of dropping out of treatment, is a more complex issue and one that will be examined in greater detail relative to sociodemographic characteristics and posttreatment alcohol use. Within the context of sampling bias, patients who drop out after six days and patients who drop out after twenty-eight days have had very different levels of exposure to the rehabilitation process. Because early treatment dropouts have a low commitment to the program, it is very difficult to follow them successfully after they leave. For this reason, persons in treatment for fewer than five days have been routinely omitted from Hazelden follow-up, creating what may be criticized as an intentional sampling bias. Patients who did not complete treatment but stayed five days or longer are included in the follow-up, and their questionnaire return rate is found to be related to the length of stay as shown in Table 3-1. Dropouts whose length of stay approaches the average treatment stay of thirty days are likely to have left because of external pressures such as home or job demands, as well as for reasons related to dissatisfaction with or lack of progress in their treatment. Because of the heterogeneity and number of treatment dropouts (nearly 20 percent), both their inclusion and exclusion in the analysis of follow-up data relative to treatment outcome presents a sampling bias that needs to be acknowledged in generalizing the findings.

Potential death bias

What about the patients who subsequently die? At twelve months after treatment about 2.5% of the Hazelden patients are dead. How should these patients be accounted for in order not to create a sampling bias? Baekeland et al. state, "It appears that at least half of the patients who die at follow-up should be considered treatment failures."[9] Given the present level of knowledge it seems pessimistic yet prudent to follow this recommendation and

Table 3-1 Treatment Dropouts Length of Stay by Whether or Not They Returned the 12-Month Follow-up Questionnaire

	Returned		Not Returned		Total	
	f	%	f	%	f	%
5-9 days	26	3.9	103	15.3	129	19.2
10-14 days	31	4.6	90	13.4	121	18.0
15-19 days	37	5.5	58	8.6	95	14.1
20-24 days	29	4.3	44	6.5	73	10.9
25-29 days	38	5.7	60	8.9	98	14.4
30-34 days	33	4.9	37	5.5	70	10.4
35-39 days	15	2.2	29	4.3	44	6.5
40 or more days	19	2.8	23	3.4	42	6.3
Total	228	33.9	444	66.1	672	100.0

Somer's D (Asymmetric) = $-.107$ with follow-up questionnaire return response dependent

$X2 = 25.68$, DF $- 7$, $p < .001$

judge half of the patients who die during the follow-up period as unsuccessful treatment outcomes.

Other patients cannot be found or do not respond to the questionnaires. The recommendation of Baekeland et al. is that these patients should be considered treatment failures. This recommendation must be rejected as too harsh. It would seem far more realistic to use a compromise and estimate that seventy-five percent of all patients lost to follow-up because of death, disappearance, or refusal to cooperate, should be classified as unsuccessful treatment outcomes.* Using this standard procedure should result in judging about 7% of the total annual patients as treatment failures. Another 2 to 4% of the patients return to Hazelden for further treatment during the follow-up period, and it seems reasonable to judge all of these patients as treatment failures even though the awareness that they needed more help may be interpreted as a level of treatment success. In total, between 9 and 11% of all patients treated in a year should be judged as treatment failures and are so considered.

A more detailed account of the sociodemographic characteristics for the Hazelden patient population will be presented later in this chapter. Questions related to other possibilities of sampling bias may be considered by the reader in light of these data. It is probably safe to say that the Hazelden patient population is most similar to patients found in other private treatment centers and in some established hospital-based programs, possibly excluding state and veterans' hospitals. An effort will therefore be made to qualify generalizations made from the findings (so that a criticism of sampling bias will not be directed at concluding and summary remarks).

Validity and Reliability Concerns

Probably of greater importance than sampling bias are the issues of reliability and validity of the data. These topics are dealt with in Appendix A by Michael Patton. What will be done here is to address some questions related to the validity and reliability of the Hazelden data that are outside of the purview of Patton's chapter.

Validity involves the issue of accuracy, and reliability relates to the consistency of response. Patton reports that in the Hazelden follow-up questionnaire, both validity and reliability are high. Measurement, the actual content and structure of the questions asked on the questionnaire, also has an implication for validity and reliability. A case in point is the format of the alcohol and drug usage questions asked on the Hazelden questionnaires. The first of the five posttreatment alcohol use questions asks, "Which of the following best

---

*This recommendation is based on an interpretation of the abstinence rate of telephone respondents in contrast with mail respondents. Approximately one-third of the telephone respondents were abstinent. Telephone respondents are thought to be similar to non-respondents in their unwillingness to return the mail questionnaire.

categorizes your drinking at present?" Six choices of response are given: Abstinent, Light or moderate drinking, Inappropriate drinking restricted mainly to social events and weekends, Inappropriate drinking on more than one occasion most weeks but not restricted to social events or weekends, Inappropriate drinking occurring almost everyday or weekend, and Periodic binge drinking. This question is phrased to elicit ". . . drinking at present," whereas response on this question has consistently resulted in overreporting of abstinence if compared to the other four posttreatment drinking questions. Because the questionnaire includes a series of questions assessing different aspects of posttreatment drinking, it is possible to identify the "bad" question that seems to result in information inconsistent with a more dominant response pattern. In this way a check on the reliability of the instrument itself is maintained.

Some posttreatment follow-up surveys have used quantity-frequency drinking measures as a way of gauging posttreatment alcohol use.[10] Although quantity-frequency measures appear to identify exact levels of consumption that may in turn be converted into an average daily amount of ethanol consumed, it is not possible to know the levels of behavioral or physiological impairment for all persons *relative* to their levels of ethanol intake. For this reason, in the Hazelden questionnaires, an alternative approach was used to construct the posttreatment use items. A frequency question asked how many times alcohol was used since treatment, a quantity question asked how much was consumed (more or less) relative to before treatment, another asked, "How long ago did you last take a drink?" and the final question sought information on the duration of the longest period of nonuse. All these questions require the respondent to give a comparative response relating their present alcohol use to the period immediately preceding treatment.

Do these questions yield the most valid and reliable information possible on posttreatment drinking? It is not possible to answer this question with any level of certainty. Some readers might question the measurement sensitivity of these questions because of their comparative phrasing, but what better ways exist for asking respondents to report their posttreatment alcohol use? With no reason to question the performance of the questions, and with the assurance of validity and reliability reported in the Patton chapter, the alcohol and drug use questions can be considered acceptable as valid and reliable measurements.

The measurement of validity and reliability for most of the other questions in the Hazelden 1973-75 follow-up questionnaires will be accepted too, because of the lack of usable standardized instruments that would accomplish the study objectives. More will be said about the performance of these questions in the discussion of measurement operationalization and construction of indicators. It is sufficient to say here that it was possible to develop a series of outcome measures from the questionnaires that consider other aspects of a patient's posttreatment behavior than just alcohol and drug use.

Another related issue has to do with the follow-up interval. At what point following treatment should the patient be contacted, and should the questions deal with how the patient is presently doing or should they deal with what has been happening over the period of time since treatment? The follow-up interval debate in alcoholism literature has resulted in a tentative agreement, "Provisionally, a one-year follow-up seems reasonably safe."[11] More will be said about movement in and out of drinking in the next chapter.

With aftercare and other extensions of treatment, caution needs to be exercised so that the error of follow-up while a person is still receiving treatment, as was the case with the follow-up done for the NIAAA Treatment Centers,[12, 13] can be avoided. In the 1973-75 Hazelden treatment follow-up data, gathered at three intervals (4, 8, and 12 months) during the year following discharge from treatment, persons who had been referred to either extended care, aftercare, or a half-way house program are accounted for when such post-treatment therapy is known. Certainly, a more comprehensive inventory of posttreatment support and therapy would have been helpful in controlling for posttreatment influence on primary treatment outcome.

The present questionnaire was designed to gauge both how the patient was doing after treatment and how the patient was doing at the point of response. The operationalization of questions will address these two dimensions and the manner of incorporating several questions into single measures. Generally the measurement favors how and what a person has been doing since leaving treatment. In part, then, the relative improvement since treatment is reflected both in the research design and in the operationalization of concepts.

Study population and study design

The study population included all Hazelden patients discharged between June 1, 1973 and December 31, 1975 who: 1) had completed treatment by successfully meeting the program objectives and been discharged with a medallion*, 2) were classified as having problems with either alcohol or alcohol and drugs (excluding only drugs) at the time of treatment as reported by respondents on the 4-month questionnaire, and 3) had returned the 4-month questionnaire and responded to the questionnaires at 8 and 12 months. These inclusion categories imply particular exclusions as well. Also excluded from the study were patients who either returned to treatment at Hazelden or entered extended care treatment at Hazelden.

---

*Regularly discharged patients are presented with a medallion in a full group meeting in their treatment unit usually about twenty-four hours before leaving Hazelden.

Table 3-2 shows the overall questionnaire response information at the three follow-up periods for all patients discharged during the study period (N = 3638). Table 3-3 shows the questionnaire response for the study population resulting from imposing the selection criteria referred to above (N = 1652). The table pertaining to the study population shows that there was further attrition in the study population over the 8- and 12-month follow-up periods. The study population of 1652 at the four month follow-up and the reduced number of cases for the other two follow-up periods represent the cases on which the analysis presented in the following chapters was based (with the exception of that portion of the analysis about alcohol and drug use found in Chapter Five). The 568 cases excluded from the larger population (2220) at the 4-month follow-up interval were those who were treatment dropouts and those having problems with drugs only at the time of treatment.

Questionnaire return rates are of importance and should be commented on here. Fifty-six percent of the 3638 cases returned questionnaires or responded to telephone interviews at 12 months following treatment discharge, as reported in the subtotal row of Table 3-2. The 56% return rate may be considered as a gross return rate because it did not take into account either the cases where the permission to follow-up was denied or the questionnaires that were not sent because the patient was in treatment less than five days or was excluded because of clerical error. Still, this gross return rate is a pessimistic one.

Table 3-2 Questionnaire Responses For 3638 Patients Discharged Between June 1973 and December 1975

	4 months		8 months		12 months	
	f	%	f	%	f	%
Returned	2200	60.5	1862	51.2	1639	45.1
Telephone	20	.5	101	2.8	401	11.0
Subtotal	2220	61.0	1963	54.0	2040	56.1
Not Returned	865	23.8	980	26.9	809	22.2
Cannot Locate	124	3.4	166	4.6	183	5.0
Permission Denied	173	4.8	229	6.3	268	7.4
Form Not Sent	139	3.8	138	3.8	134	3.7
Returned to Hazelden	69	1.9	96	2.6	122	3.3
Deceased	48	1.3	66	1.8	82	2.3
Total	3638	100.0	3638	100.0	3638	100.0

Table 3-3 Questionnaire Responses for the Study Population of 1652 Patients

	4 months		8 months		12 months	
	f	%	f	%	f	%
Returned	1640	99.3	1311	79.4	1171	70.9
Telephone	12	.7	47	2.8	163	9.9
Subtotal	1652*	100.0	1358	82.2	1334	80.8
Not Returned			245	14.8	240	14.5
Cannot Locate			14	.8	18	1.1
Permission Denied			16	1.0	21	1.3
Returned to Hazelden			13	.8	24	1.4
Deceased			6	.4	15	.9
Total	1652	100.0	1652	100.0	1652	100.0

*568 respondents were excluded according to the selection criteria used to identify the study population.

The adjusted return rate excluded cases that were intentionally not sent questionnaires and were therefore not given an opportunity to respond. In addition to the cases where permission was denied (268 cases at 12 months) and where questionnaires were not sent (134 cases at 12 months), patients who returned to Hazelden during the study period (122 cases at 12 months) and those deceased (82 cases at 12 months) were not participants in the study. Excluding these 606 cases reduced the total population to 3032 and resulted in an adjusted return rate of 67.3%. As pointed out earlier, the return rate for treatment completers was higher than that for patients who dropped out of treatment. The higher rate of return for patients completing treatment was reflected in the 80.8% gross return rate and the adjusted return rate of 83.8% for the study population.

Men comprised 75% of the study population (1652) and women 25%. This was essentially the same male/female ratio as was found for all treatment completers (2670), although there was a higher proportion of females in the total patient population (3638). The mean age of the study population was 42.5 years, for the patients completing treatment 41.3 years, and for the total population 41 years. More of the patients in the study population were married (61.3%) than were either the patients completing treatment (57.2%) or the total patient population (54.5%). There were no meaningful differences between patients whose home residence was outside of Minnesota for the study population (59.3%), treatment completers (58.1%), and the total population (57.9%). Only 15% of the study population had not completed high school, while 36.4 percent were college graduates; 17.9% of patients completing treatment had less than high school and 32.4% were college graduates. Of the total patient population, 19.5% had less than high school and 30.3% had completed college.

What are the implications of these sociodemographic characteristics? Proportionately more women than men drop out of treatment; younger patients drop out of treatment more frequently than do middle-aged and older patients. Youth are also more commonly found among the "drug only" patients, resulting in their proportional underrepresentation in the study population compared to the total population at Hazelden. In part, the underrepresentation of youth in the study population may explain the differences in marital status as well as other differences between the study population, the treatment completers and the total population. Youth also had a low questionnaire return rate as well as a lower treatment completion rate when contrasted with patients 25 years and older and were drawn more heavily from the geographic area of the metropolitan Twin Cities and surrounding counties which, again, served to explain sociodemographic differences, including the educational attainment differences among the three populations. The study population may be characterized as predominantly middle-aged (with an underrepresentation of youth and a slight underrepresentation of women), well educated and including few (2%) racial minorities.

Research Questions

These study population data were used to examine eight research questions:

1) *What are the alcohol and drug use outcomes of Hazelden?*
2) *How much change is there in posttreatment alcohol and drug use outcomes over time?*
3) *What variables are important in predicting posttreatment abstinence?*
4) *What evidence is there from the Hazelden data to refute or support the claim that treated alcoholics can resume drinking without negative consequences?*
5) *What effect does posttreatment AA participation have on alcohol use outcomes?*
6) *What are the characteristics of AA affiliates in contrast with nonaffiliates?*
7) *What variables are important in predicting posttreatment AA participation?*

8) *What sociodemographic, treatment and posttreatment variables explain social/psychological functioning improvement during the year following treatment?*

The study design for each of these eight research questions is probably best approached by way of the key variables associated with the research questions and the ways in which they are operationalized.

Operationalizations

Operationalization of the information about posttreatment alcohol and drug use into accurate and responsive indicators of posttreatment alcohol-drug use was seen as a critical task in that it had major implications for the research results. Both frequency and quantity questions categorized use relative to what it was before treatment, rather than measuring the number of drinking episodes in a given period of time and fluid intake during an average drinking episode. Various combinations of the frequency and quantity questions were made with the "time since last drink" and "longest period dry" questions. In examining these combinations it was determined that it was best to use the quantity questions in combination with the "time since last drink" question for three compelling reasons: 1) the 4- and 8-month questionnaire stated the frequency question differently than did the 12-month questionnaire, 2) a comparable measure of alcohol use was needed for the three follow-up time periods in order to examine changing use over time, and 3) the time since last drink question (highly correlated with the "longest period dry" question) appeared to work well as a modifier of the quantity question: if someone had a period of nonuse prior to responding to the questionnaire, their current nonuse would classify them as improved if the nonuse was of long enough duration. Using this procedure, three alcohol use categories were selected, as illustrated in Figure 3-1, using the 12-month posttreatment format.

These three categories were intended to be pessimistic. It may be argued that an alcoholic who has not used alcohol for ten of the most recent months out of the twelve months since treatment should be classified more optimistically than *not improved*. It was reasoned, however, that usage of about as much or more alcohol during the period immediately following treatment should be judged harshly in the construction of the posttreatment alcohol use measure. Additionally, the number reporting "about as much or more" quantity in the five to ten months since last drink was small and did not have the effect of inflating the *not improved* category, nor would these few cases have increased the *improved* category appreciably.

Essentially the same classification procedure was used for the other two follow-up periods (4 and 8 months) as well as for drug use reported at the three

Figure 3-1 Quantity of Alcohol Used Since Treatment by Time Since Last Drink Alcohol Use Categorization

Quantity \ Time	0-1 mo.	2-4 mo.	5-7 mo.	8-10 mo.	11-12 mo.	13+ mo.
Not used	improved	improved	improved	improved	abstinent	abstinent
Not as much	not improved	improved	improved	improved	improved	improved
About as much	not improved	not improved	not improved	not improved	improved	improved
More	not improved	not improved	not improved	not improved	improved	improved

1. **Abstinent**
   Nonuse report, with 11 months or more since last use.

2. **Improvement**
   a. Nonuse reported, with 10 or fewer months since last use.
   b. Not as much use reported, with 2 or more months since last use.
   c. About as much use reported, with 11 or more months since last use.
   d. More use reported, with 11 months or more since last use.

3. **Not improved**
   a. Not as much use reported, with one month or less since last use.
   b. About as much use reported, with 10 months or less since last use.
   c. More use reported, with ten months or less since last use.

follow-up time periods. Approximately one-third of the patients in the study population were classified as alcohol and drug abusers. Should a composite alcohol-drug use measure be used? This question was explored and a combined chemical use indicator was developed. Comparing the combined alcohol-drug use indicator with the separate alcohol use and drug use indicators, it was found that the combined measure was less sensitive in multivariate analysis than were the separate alcohol and drug use measures. Accordingly, it was decided to use the posttreatment alcohol use measure as the principal indicator. Drug use other than alcohol and in combination with alcohol are considered, but are not the central concern of the overall analysis.

Research question one asked, "What are the alcohol and drug use outcomes of Hazelden treatment?" Using the three categories, *abstinent, improved,* and *not improved* for both posttreatment alcohol use and drug use reported at 4, 8 and 12 months after treatment discharge, it was possible to determine outcomes for each of the three follow-up intervals. Still, the composite alcohol and drug use measure, rejected as too insensitive for the multivariate analysis, was thought to be useful in considering an aspect of the posttreatment chemical use outcome question. In particular this measure reflected multiple drug use not captured by alcohol and drug use indicators singly. By considering the combinations of the three chemical use outcome categories* a sixfold classification schema resulted: *abstinent-abstinence, abstinent-improved, improved-improved, abstinent-not improved, improved-not improved,* and *not improved-not improved.*

Posttreatment chemical use outcomes were considered in three separate ways using three outcome measures. The outcomes were analyzed for: 1) all patients who returned the questionnaire, 2) all patients who had completed treatment, and 3) patients in the study population: those who had completed treatment and were having problems with alcohol only or with alcohol and drugs (excluding drugs only) at the time of treatment. Chemical use outcomes were then further analyzed for selected sociodemographic categories so as to explore the research question relative to subpopulations identified by sex, age, religious preference, marital status, and home residence of respondents.

Research question two asked, "How much change is there in posttreatment alcohol and drug use outcomes over time?" The three outcome categories were charted showing the movement of cases between the three categories over the three follow-up time periods. In this way it was possible to appreciate the dynamic properties of posttreatment alcohol and drug use as well as to establish the basic information to be subjected to further analysis relative to the fourth research question dealing with the consequences of posttreatment use.

The third research question asked, "What variables are important in predicting posttreatment abstinence?" This question was approached using posttreatment alcohol at 12 months after discharge from treatment as a dependent variable in a multiple regression analysis.** Using this statistical tech-

---

*The first mentioned outcome in the composite indicator may refer to either alcohol or drug use.

**A dependent variable is the variable you want to explain whereas independent variables are the explainers of the dependent variable. "Multiple regression is a general statistical technique through which one can analyze the relationship between a dependent variable—and a set of independent—variables."[14]

nique it became possible to isolate those sociodemographic, treatment and posttreatment variables most relevant in explaining favorable treatment outcome as judged by abstinence.

The independent variables used in the multivariate analysis should be introduced and operationalized at this point in the discussion. The principal sociodemographic variables included were sex, education and marital status. Sex and marital status were both operationalized as dichotomous variables with marital status categorized as *not married* and *married*. Education was operationalized by way of a four-fold classification: *less than high school, high school graduate, vocational school* and *some college,* and *college graduate.*

Treatment variables of importance were found in the patient's 12-month assessment of treatment activities. Ten treatment activities were listed in the 12-month follow-up questionnaire, and the respondent was asked to rate these activities according to the categories: *much help, some help, little help, no help* and *do not remember.* A factor analysis* showed these ten treatment activities to constitute two separate factors. One of these factors, individual activities in treatment, consisted of the following activities: reading, time alone, meditation, lecture and the enjoyment of the environmental setting. The other factor consisted of the collective activities in treatment and included group therapy, informal conversations with patients, the "hot seat" (which may be better described as caring confrontation), meetings with counselors, and meetings with clergy. Both "individual activities in treatment" and "collective activities in treatment" were measured for each respondent at the 12-month follow-up by way of the factor score generated by factor analysis of each treatment dimension.

Posttreatment variables were hospitalization since treatment, present AA attendance, and posttreatment prayer and meditation. Posttreatment hospitalizations were measured as the actual number of times the patient had been hospitalized since treatment as reported on the 12-month follow-up questionnaire. Present AA attendance was determined by the 12-month follow-up question, "How often do you attend AA meetings at present?" with six response categories: more than once a week, about once a week, about two or three times a month, about once a month, less than once a month, and I do not attend. Eight other AA-related questions were asked, but in examining correlations and other relationship measures, it was concluded that AA attendance was the single most important indicator of involvement in the AA program and would alone be used in the analysis. Prayer and meditation was

---

*Factor analysis is primarily a data reduction technique. Given an array of correlation coefficients for a set of variables, factor analytic techniques enable us to see whether some underlying patterns of relationship exist so that the data may be "rearranged" or "reduced" to a smaller set of factors or components that may be taken as source variables and may account for some observed interrelations in the data.[15]

measured by the 12-month follow-up question, "Since your treatment, how frequently do you maintain some kind of conscious contact with a higher power through the following means?" The means specified were prayer, meditation, church attendance, and spiritual counseling, and the respondents were asked to check one of three categories: more often, about the same, and less often. Prayer and meditation were combined into a single measure, and both church attendance and spiritual counseling were dropped because of low response frequencies.

Variables that were included among the independent variables, but did not appear as prominent explainers of outcome were age (number of years old at time of treatment), religion (Catholic and other), residence (the nine county Twin Cities metropolitan area, the rest of Minnesota, all the area outside of Minnesota), and actual frequencies for the following: primary rehabilitation days, counselor interviews, clergy interviews, family conferences, alcohol- and drug-related hospitalizations prior to treatment, and alcohol- and drug-related arrests prior to treatment. Other variables were excluded from the independent variable list because they were highly correlated with the variables retained, as in the instance of income, occupation and education. Education appeared as the more powerful of these three variables, and so it was retained as the single socioeconomic indicator. The MMPI major scales were used as independent variables, but because they had so little explanatory power in the preliminary analysis, it was decided that they be dropped as independent variables in the final study design.

The fourth research question addressed the issue of posttreatment drinking without negative consequences. "What evidence is there from the Hazelden data to refute or support the claim that treated alcoholics can resume drinking without negative consequences?" Using the movement between alcohol use categories at 4, 8 and 12 months, it was possible to calculate those cases where movement was from either *abstinence* or *improved,* to *not improved* and *no response.* The reverse movement from *not improved* and *no response* to *improved* and *abstinent* was also categorized. As mentioned earlier in the discussion of sampling bias, 25% of the nonrespondents will be considered as *abstinent-improved* and the other 75% as *not improved,* for the purpose of determining alcohol use outcome.

Crosstabulations of *quantity of use* and the respondent's reported time since last drink were used to create the posttreatment use categories of *abstinent, improved* and *not improved.* These categories were also considered in their relation to the question of whether or not treated alcoholics can resume drinking without negative consequences. The distribution of cases in the cells of this crosstabulation revealed patterns of posttreatment use that were helpful in the examination of this question. Initially the indicator and "consequences of posttreatment alcohol use" was considered relative to drinking outcomes only, but in the later analysis the outcome was examined relative to social/psychological functioning.

The fifth research question asked, "What effect does posttreatment AA participation have on alcohol use outcomes?" AA participation was examined through bivariate analysis with posttreatment alcohol use, where AA attendance was classified as *frequent attendance* (more than once a week and about once a week), *infrequent attendance* (about once a month and less than once a month), and *I do not attend*.

The sixth research question asked, "What are the characteristics of AA affiliates in contrast with non-affiliates?" Using the above three-fold classification it was possible to approach this question by way of the categories AA affiliation (frequent and infrequent attendance) and non-affiliation and then determining the sociodemographic treatment and follow-up characteristics of the two types of affiliates and the non-affiliates.

The seventh research question asked, "What variables are important in predicting posttreatment AA participation?" Multiple regression was used to consider this question, as was done in the question of predicting abstinence.

The eighth and final research question asked, "What sociodemographic, treatment and posttreatment variables explain improvement in social/psychological functioning during the year following treatment?" The improvement in social/psychological functioning was measured by responses to a list of items called growth areas. These growth areas included "relationships with friends," "general physical health," "ability to handle problems," and "ability to accept help from others." Respondents were asked to indicate one of six responses assessing the present in contrast with before treatment: *much improved, somewhat improved, same, somewhat worse, much worse,* and *does not apply.*

Factor analysis was used after some low response items were eliminated, with the result that the remaining twelve items constituted a single factor with the factor loading highest for three key items: "self-image," "general enjoyment of life" and "ability to handle problems." Factor scores were used as the measure of social/psychological improvement. Again multiple regression was the statistic used to explain the variance in the dependent variable of improvement in social/psychological functioning.

The next stage was to consider the findings from the multiple regressions where alcohol use at 12 months, AA participation at 12 months, and social/psychological functioning at 12 months after discharge were the dependent variables in a theoretical linear model with social/psychological functioning as the last variable in the linear sequence. The model was then empirically tested using the statistical technique know as path analysis.*

The linear relationships theoretically ordered in the path model were intended to represent a preliminary statement of the relationships between variables having relevance in explaining alcoholism treatment outcomes. In the path analysis, the causal ordering was assumed to be true (the ordering was not tested). Rather, a statistical method identified the co-variation and relative importance of each variable in explaining the variables that follow it in the logical sequence. Both the path model and the path analysis were seen as the summary end point in the overall study design. What resulted was that a new point of departure was established for further, more refined investigation of alcoholism treatment outcomes. That is, new research questions were raised by the path model and the relative importance and interrelationships that resulted from the path analysis. These questions were of an order that could not have been asked before the implementation of the research design described in the foregoing discussion.

Summary

Eight research questions were considered, four were concerned with the posttreatment alcohol and drug use, three with AA participation, and one with improvement in social/psychological functioning following treatment. Data for examining these research questions were from sociodemographic, treatment and follow-up sources, with the follow-up taking place at three intervals after discharge from treatment. These data were operationalized and summary measures constructed. Both bivariate and multivariate analyses were used in addressing the research questions, and the findings were reflected in a theoretical path model and path analysis as a final stage in the analysis. The findings of this study design are presented in Chapters Five through Seven; an overall discussion of implications of the findings is found in Chapter Eight.

---

*Path analysis is a statistical technique of interpreting linear relationships where it is assumed that a causal order among the variables is both known and closed. First, the causal sequence of the variables is logically formulated in a path model and second, the statistical relationships among the variables are interpreted as the direct effect each variable has on the one that follows it while controlling statistically for the other relevant variables.[16]

Reference Notes Chapter 3

[1]D. J. Anderson, S. M. L. Kammeier and H. L. Holmes, *Applied research: Impact on decision making*. Center City, MN.: Hazelden Foundation, 1978.

[2]F. Baekeland, L. Lundwall and B. Kissin, Methods for the treatment of chronic alcoholism: A critical appraisal. In R. J. Gibbins, Y. Israel, H. Kalant, R. E. Popham, W. Schmidt and R. G. Smart, *Research advances in alcohol and drug problems* (Vol. 2). New York: John Wiley & Sons, 1975, pp. 247-327.

[3]Ibid., p. 248.

[4]A. C. Ogborne, Patient characteristics as predictors of treatment outcome for alcohol and drug abusers. In Y. Israel, F. B. Glaser, H. Kalant, R. E. Popham, W. Schmidt and R. G. Smart, *Research advances in alcohol and drug problems* (Vol. 4). New York: Plenum Press, 1978, pp. 177-223.

[5]Baekeland, op. cit.

[6]Ibid., pp. 262-263, 270-271.

[7]J. C. Laundergan, J. W. Spicer and S. M. L. Kammeier, *Are court referrals effective?: Judicial commitment for chemical dependency in Washington Co., Minnesota*. Center City, MN.: Hazelden Foundation, 1979.

[8]S. M. L. Kammeier and J. C. Laundergan, *The outcome of treatment: Patients admitted to Hazelden in 1975*. Center City, MN.: Hazelden Foundation, 1978.

[9]Baekeland, op. cit., p. 51.

[10]D. J. Armor, J. M. Polich and H. B. Stambul, *Alcoholism and treatment*. Santa Monica, CA.: Rand Corporation, 1976, p. 75.

[11]Baekeland, op. cit., p. 256.

[12]W. L. Ruggels, D. J. Armor, J. M. Polich, A. Mothershead and M. Stephen, *A follow-up study of clients of selected alcoholism treatment centers funded by NIAAA*. Menlo Park, CA: Stanford Research Institute, 1975.

[13]Armor, op. cit.

[14]J. Kim, F. J. Kohout, Multiple regression analysis: Subprogram regression. In H. Nie, C. H. Hull, J. G. Jenkins, K. Steinbrenner, and D. H. Brent, *Statistical package for the social sciences* (2nd ed.). New York: McGraw-Hill, 1975, p. 321.

[15]J. Kim, Factor analysis. In H. Nie, C. H. Hull, J. G. Jenkins, K. Steinbrenner and D. H. Brent, *Statistical package for the social sciences* (2nd ed.) New York: McGraw-Hill, 1975, p. 469.

[16]Kim and Kohout, op. cit., p. 383.

Chapter Four

Alcoholism Treatment Follow-up Studies

The number of alcoholism treatment follow-up studies has been increasing in recent years, and there will probably continue to be considerable interest in evaluating the impact of treatment programs on patients. Several reviews of literature have been published summarizing the findings of treatment follow-up studies. These literature reviews differ from each other both in format and objective. Examples of these differences will be considered briefly in the following paragraphs.

Emrick reviewed 265 psychologically oriented alcoholism treatment studies and found that most studies used a drinking criteria as the principal measure of treatment outcome. About one-third of the patients studied were abstinent at follow-up and two-thirds were improved.[1] In a second review, Emrick considered outcome differences by treatment type, including no treatment, for 385 studies of psychologically oriented alcoholism treatment programs. He found that differences between treatment modalities were not significant in terms of outcome. Average abstinence rates did not differ between treated and not treated alcoholics, although treated alcoholics were significantly more "improved" than alcoholics who were not treated.[2]

One obvious shortcoming of Emrick's work was that the studies he combined for the purposes of his analysis represent considerable diversity in methodology, client characteristics, and follow-up interval. He "... attempted to review all studies published in English from 1952 through 1971 that reported specific responses of patients to some form of psychologically oriented alcoholism treatment."[3] As noted in the previous discussion of sampling bias, and as will be pointed out in this chapter, combining a collection of alcoholism treatment follow-up literature for the purpose of extracting aggregate findings produces results that are likely to be misleading.

Another example of a literature review is found in the previously mentioned work by Pattison and the Sobells. They selected 74 treatment follow-up studies which reported that some treated alcoholics ". . . successfully demonstrated an ability to resume nonproblem drinking."[4] This literature review summarized the selected studies in table form so that the reader was able to quickly identify a number of critical characteristics of each study such as investigator's name(s), year of publication, number of subjects in the original study, number of subjects followed up, number practicing controlled drinking, number abstinent, description of drinking, and description of treatment setting and modality. Forty-eight of these 74 studies reported on the outcome of abstinent-oriented treatment programs.

Of course, the critical issue in trying to draw conclusions from this selective review of literature is, "How was controlled drinking operationalized?" Some researchers used general criteria such as "moderate drinking with no adverse effects" and "drinking in a socially acceptable manner" while others used quantity measures such as "4 oz. (or 6 oz.) 86-proof liquor or equivalent in alcoholic content/day" or scores on a standardized social/psychological adjustment scale. Higher percentages of controlled drinking were reported in studies with small numbers of subjects, studies where controlled drinking was the goal of treatment and studies where the operational definition of controlled drinking was a general criteria.

In this chapter, the alcoholism treatment follow-up studies that are reviewed will not be combined into a single aggregate data base as was done by Emrick. Nor will they be selectively assembled to document a specific outcome pattern as was done by Pattison, Sobell and Sobell. Instead, the studies will be systematically identified to illustrate the diversity of alcoholism treatment programs and outcome findings. This literature review will be presented using a tabular format similar, in some respects, to that used by Pattison and the Sobells. The format to be used was developed by Kaye R. Wildasin[5] and summarizes the studies by decade of publication beginning in the 1940's. The studies are summarized by the following characteristics: author(s), date of publication, geographic location, treatment setting, mode of treatment, length of treatment, whether the patients were in treatment voluntarily or involuntarily, sex and average age of the patients, number in the study, number followed up, follow-up length, evaluative criteria, and study findings. Wildasin completed his work in 1973, reviewing 61 alcoholism treatment follow-up studies published between 1942 and 1973, and used the above format. The results of Wildasin's work will be reported here, and additional studies published during the 1970's will be added to the literature review using Wildasin's summary format.

Literature Review Selection Procedures

The 61 studies summarized by Wildasin were identified using CAAAL (Classified Abstract Archive of the Alcohol Literature), a manual peripheral punch card index maintained by the Rutgers School of Alcohol Studies. Initially 217 studies were identified sorting on "treatment of alcoholism" (main category M) and subtopics "results" (No. 57) and "follow-up" (No. 59). Of these, 107 were excluded because they were either not English publications, or did not report sufficient findings. Of the remaining 110 studies, 49 were dropped from further consideration because of apparent methodological weakness as judged either by Wildasin or identified by professional reviewers.

The studies added to Wildasin's original summary of alcoholism treatment follow-up literature were identified using the Hazelden Search Service, a computerized retrieval system that was an outgrowth of some of the work done by Wildasin. One of the topics of special concern in the Hazelden Search Service file is the evaluation of chemical dependency treatment. The Hazelden Search Service file* is presently available to researchers nationally through BRS (Bibliographic Research Service) and has filled an important need during the time the Rutgers' file has been in transition from the manual card system (CAAAL) to a computerized literature search procedure.

The Control Data Corporation and the Center on Alcohol Studies at Rutgers University are cooperating in the development of a computerized alcohol literature search procedure. Further information about the Alcohol Information Retrieval System may be obtained by contacting the Center on Alcohol Studies. Current literature is being placed into the computer file and earlier literature is being entered as time and resources permit. Unfortunately, because the Alcohol Information Retrieval System became available after this chapter was complete, it was not used to locate the treatment follow-up studies summarized and examined here.

Patterns and Diversity in Alcoholism Follow-up Studies

As was stated above, the purpose of this literature review is to illustrate or highlight the diversity of alcoholism treatment programming and the varied results of treatment outcome studies. The review does not claim to include all treatment follow-up studies done between the 1940's and 1970's. Nevertheless,

---

*Article selection and abstracting for the Hazelden Search Service file was done by Judith Howe.

although the studies included in the literature review are not exhaustive, they are representative of the treatment outcome literature for these decades. Most of the studies reviewed were done in the United States; some were done in Canada and Western Europe (Table 4-1).

To a large extent, the treatment modalities found in the studies reflect changing fads and fashions of clinical practice. Illustrative of this are the LSD therapies of the 1960's. Over the four decades psychotherapy is the most common therapeutic approach for both inpatient and outpatient treatment and for a combination of inpatient/outpatient care. Psychotherapy's popularity is difficult to assess, however, because of the broad range of different procedures that may be included under this label.

Both psychotherapy and psychiatric care vary in duration. Both therapies require more time in therapy than do aversion therapy, disulfiram and other chemotherapies. When combined with an AA adjunct, psychotherapy and psychiatric care have an even longer period of treatment. Inpatient treatment is more common than either outpatient or the combination of inpatient/outpatient. In contrast with outpatient treatment, inpatient care is usually of shorter duration because it is more intensive. Outpatient treatment most often lasted longer than three months for the studies reviewed, whereas three thresholds of treatment length are apparent in inpatient treatment: 28-34 days, 56-62 days and 84-90 days.

The range in the average age of patients was from 32 to 52 years for the studies where this information was provided. Most studies reported an average age of patients somewhere in the 40's. The patients' actual ages represent considerable disparity. To the extent that patient age is related to treatment outcome, age heterogeneity will influence the outcome findings.

Some studies report a 100% response rate for the follow-up, which appears unrealistic unless a small, select population is being studied. Most studies report response rates in the 80 to 90% range, whereas some have response rates at the 20 to 30% level. Response rates, it will be remembered, are influenced by a number of factors including the socioeconomic characteristics of the patient, follow-up interval, definition of the population being followed and the methodology of the follow-up.

Approximately one-third of the follow-up studies took place one year after treatment and slightly less than one-third were done two years or more after treatment. Most studies have an initial study population of 150 patients or less with the follow-up of more than 500 patients uncommon. For most of the follow-up studies, patient outcome was measured by improvement rather than abstinence, the opposite of Emrick's finding. The predominance of improvement as the measure of treatment outcome is found for both large and small study populations. No clear outcome pattern seems to be apparent for either improvement outcome or abstinence outcome. Expressed as percentage improved, outcomes range from a low in the 20% range to highs exceeding 80%. Abstinence outcomes show the same wide range.

What, then, can be stated from looking at alcoholism treatment outcome studies? Primarily that diversity in the treatment programs, the follow-up methodologies and the findings appear to be far more characteristic of the studies than consistent and uniform patterns. This heterogeneity severely limits the generalizability of this research literature in identifying either highly effective treatment strategies or standardized ways of determining acceptable treatment outcomes.

Some of the studies are clearly of questionable worth in furthering the understanding of treatment and recovery. *(Alcoholism and Treatment* by Armor et. al.[6], popularly known as the "Rand Report" will be examined in detail as one illustration of poor treatment outcome research.) Other studies carefully identify treatment procedures and objectives and use well-developed measurement and analysis techniques in examining the results of alcoholism treatment.

Carefully executed studies of alcoholism treatment impact need to be encouraged by funding agencies, treatment administrators, treatment staff and the patients themselves. Just as research and development has been a catalyst for greater effectiveness in industry, it is essential to the improvement of health and social services. However, the positive impact of research and development is dependent on the quality of studies. In large measure, quality studies of alcoholism treatment outcome are encouraged by the commitment to an ongoing follow-up monitoring system rather than studies of limited scope and duration. Advantages of ongoing follow-up monitoring are found both in the large number of subjects in the resulting study population and in the opportunity to refine the methodology of patient follow-up.

During the past few years the Hazelden Training Department has been offering two-day Follow-up Evaluation Workshops for treatment administrators, counselors and others interested in assessing treatment impact. These workshops have presented both the reasoning and the mechanics of installing ongoing follow-up in contrast to short, isolated, single-purpose studies.[7] Workshop participants quickly recognize the potential treatment program benefits of regular follow-up evaluation in contrast to involvement in a single-purpose study. Strong encouragement is given to seek university students and faculty to help implement ongoing program evaluation studies and assist in the analysis. It is stressed that in such an arrangement, the outside researchers should be given clear statements of what the treatment program needs to find out from the follow-up studies. Also, it must be recognized that university-based and other outside researchers have their own agendas and that any relationship between outside researchers and treatment interests need to be clearly negotiated in the early days of project planning.

Table 4-1 Alcoholism Treatment Follow-up Studies: Treatment Characteristics, Patient Characteristics and Outcomes

Author(s)	Date	Geo. Loc.	Setting	RX Mode	RX Lgth.	Pt. Status	Sex	Age	Initial Sample	Final Sample	Follow-up Length	Evaluative Criteria	Results	Findings
Miller, M.M.[13]	1942	U.S.	Outpt.	Psychotherapy	4-14 mo.	Invol.	M,F	Ave. 39	513	487	1-9 mo.	Abstinence Arrest Rec.	Abstinent - 81.4%	Treated S. - 25% rearrested Untreated S. 42%
Whitaker, C.A.[14]	1942	U.S.	Inpt.	Diagnostic	>1 mo.	Vol.	M	Ave. 37	81	26	4 yrs.	Abst. and imp.	47% improvement	
McMahan, H.G.[15]	1942	U.S.	Inpt.	Psychotherapy and A.A.	3 mo.	Vol.	?	?	146	120	1-9 mo.	Abst. and soc. adj.	A.A. contact - 84% good to fair adjustment N 50 No A.A. contact - 20% good to fair adjustment N 90	
Lemere, F. and Vogtlin, W.L.[16]	1950	U.S.	Inpt.	Aversion therapy	10 days	Vol.	?	?	4,468	4,096	13 yrs.	Abst.	51% abstinent at least 2 yrs.	
Moore, J.N.P. and Drury, M.D.[17]	1951	Ireland	Inpt.	Disulfiram	3-4 wks.	Vol.	M,F	Rge. 30-50	118	71	2½ yrs.	Abst. and imp.	50% imp. (N59) includes control	
Slater, A.D.[18]	1951	U.S.	Inpt.	Aversion	10 days	Vol.	M,F	Mean 39	63	53	3 yrs.	Abst.	23% abstinent 1 yr.	
Bell, R.G.[19]	1951	Can.	Inpt.	Psychotherapy	3 wks	Vol.	?	?	700	150	6-24 mos.	Imp. social adjustment	67% imp.	
West, L.J. and Swegan, W.H.[20]	1956	U.S.	Inpt.	Psychotherapy	?	Invol.	M	?	50	45	5-29 mos.	Imp. social adjustment	55% imp.	
Norvig, J. and Nielsen, B.[21]	1956	Denmark	Inpt.	Disulfiram	2 mo.	Vol.	M	40's	221	114	3-5 yrs.	Imp. social adjustment	77% imp.	
Pfeffer, A.Z. and Berger, S.[22]	1957	U.S.	Outpt.	Psychotherapy	22-27 mo.	Vol. & Invol.	M,F	Mean 51	160	60	1 yr.	Abst. and imp.	80% abstinent at least 1 yr.	
Selzer, M.L. and Holloway, W.H.[23]	1957	U.S.	Inpt.	Psychiat. and A.A.	Ave. 4½ mo.	Invol.	M,F	Mean 43	98	83	6 yrs.	Abst. and social adj.	41% imp.	
Thomas, R.E. et al[24]	1959	U.S.	Outpt.	Psychotherapy	Ave. 19 wks.	Vol.	M,F	Ave. 41	77	77	3 mo.	Imp. social adjustment	42% imp.	
Glatt, M.M.[25]	1959	England	Inpt.	Psychotherapy and A.A.	?	Vol.	M,F	Rge. 41-50	276	276	.5 - 3.5 yrs.	Imp. social adjustment	67% imp.	
		U.S.	Inpt.	Psycho-	90 days	Vol.	M	Ave.	100	91	Ave.	Abst. & imp.	26% imp.	

Author	Year	Country	Setting	Treatment	Duration	Vol./Invol.	Sex	Age	N	N	Follow-up	Criteria	Results
				therapy, A.A.					60 / C-group 60			imp. social adj.	S group - 30% imp. / C group - 33% imp.
Davies, D.L.[28]	1962	England	Outpt.	Disulfiram Family Counseling	2-5 mo.	Vol.	M	Rge. 26-47	7	7	7-11 yrs.	Abst. and imp.	100% imp. (7 cases ret. to normal drinking)
Gerard, D.L. et al[29]	1962	U.S.	Inpt. & Outpt.	?	?	Vol.	?	?	400	219	2, 5 & 8 yrs.	Abst. and imp.	32% imp.
Brun, K.[30]	1963	Finland	Outpt.	Psychotherapy Disulfiram	A-32 wks. M-10 wks.	Vol.	M	Rge. 26-55	A-203 M-100 C-402	A-174 M-86 C-349	2 yrs.+	Abst. and imp.	19% imp. - A clinic / 14% imp. - M clinic
Rossi, J.J., Stach, A. and Bradley, N.J.[31]	1963	U.S.	Inpt.	Psychotherapy	60 days	Vol. & Invol.	M	Ave. 44	208	149	2 yrs.	Abst. and imp.	39.6% imp.
Wolff, S. and Holland, L.[32]	1964	South Africa	Inpt. & Outpt.	Psychotherapy	3 wks.+	Vol.	M,F	Rge. 20-50	270	94	2 yrs.	Abstinence	78% respond. Abst. (N94) / 51% non. respond. Abst. (N135)
O'Reilly, P.O. and Funk, A.[33]	1964	Can.	Inpt.	LSD	7-8 days	Vol.	M,F	Mean 37	68	61	3 yrs.	Abstinence	38% abst.
Clancy, J. et al[34]	1965	U.S.	Inpt. & Outpt.	Psychotherapy	?	Vol.	?	?	90	81	1 yr.	Abst. and social adj.	45% imp.
Reinert, R.E.[35]	1965	U.S.	Inpt.	Psychotherapy & multiple modes	90 days	Vol.	M	Rge. 25-65	178	178	2 yrs.	Abst. and social adj.	Less than 30% imp.
Wedel, H.L.[36]	1965	U.S.	Outpt.	Psychotherapy	?	Vol.	?	?	C-37 Ex-33	C-35 Ex-31	14-26 mo.	Abst. and imp.	48% imp.
Vallance, M.[37]	1965	Scotland	Inpt.	Psychiat. A.A.	3 wks.	Vol.	M	Ave. 44	68	68	2 yrs.	Abst. and social adj.	25% imp.
Haberman, P.W.[38]	1966	U.S.	Outpt.	Psychiat.	Med. 20 wks.	Vol.	M,F	?	96	85	10 mo.	Abst. and imp.	Sig. imp. pt. in social class III-IV / N not indicated
Walton, H.J. et al[39]	1966	England	Inpt. & Outpt.	Psychotherapy Disulfiram	Inpt. - 3-4 wks. Outpt. - ?	Vol.	M,F	Rge. 30-50	83	83	6 mo. & 18 mo.	Abst. and imp.	54% imp. - 6 mo. / 51% imp. - 18 mo.
Edwards, G. and Guthrie, S.[40]	1966	England	Inpt. & Outpt.	Psychotherapy	2-3 mo.	Vol.	M	Mean 43	Inpt. -20 Outpt. -20	Inpt. -20 Outpt. -20	6 mo.	Abst. and social adj.	50% imp. - Inpt. / 50% imp. - Outpt.

Table 4-1 Alcoholism Treatment Follow-up Studies: Treatment Characteristics, Patient Characteristics and Outcomes (Continued)

			Treatment Characteristics				Patient Characteristics					Follow-up Characteristics			Findings
Author(s)	Date	Geo. Loc.	Setting	RX Mode	RX Lgth.	Pt. Status	Sex	Age	Initial Sample	Final Sample	Follow-up Length	Evaluative Criteria	Results		
Katz, L.[41]	1966	U.S.	Inpt.	Group therapy and A.A.	6 mo. & 1 yr.	Vol.	M	Ave. 45	287	287	2 yrs.	Abst. and imp.	48% imp.	48% imp.
Cheek, F.E. et al[42]	1966	U.S.	Inpt.	LSD & trad. Rx	1 mo.	?	Med. 46	28 LSD 34 Cont.	27 LSD 28 Cont.	3, 6 & 12 mo.	Abst. and soc. adj.	At 3 mo. LSD group imp. At 6 & 12 mo. no difference
Charnoff, S.M.[43]	1967	U.S.	Outpt.	Chemo-therapy	?	Vol.	M,F	?	229	A - 94 B - 98 C - 100	6 mo.	Abstinence	7% - A (Striatran) abst. 5% - B (Elavil) abst. 8% - C (Placebo) abst.
Blake, B.G.[44]	1967	Scotland	Inpt.	Behavior therapy (Aversion)	3-4 wks.	Vol.	M,F	Mean M-47 F-45	E - 37 C - 25	E - 33 C - 20	6 & 12 mo.	Abst. and imp.	62% imp. - E at 6 mo. 59% imp. - E at 12 mo. 60% imp. - C at 6 mo. 50% imp. - C at 12 mo.
Beaubrun, M.H.[45]	1967	Trinidad Tobago	Inpt.	Psycho-therapy Aversion A.A.	3-4 wks.	Vol.	M,F	Rge. 20-69	Grp. I -57 Grp. II -313	Grp. I -45 Grp. II -186	Grp. I -7 Yrs. Grp. II -2 yrs.	Abst. and social adj.	53% imp. - Grp. I 43% imp. - Grp. II
Pattison, E.M. et al[46]	1968	U.S.	Outpt.	Psycho-therapy	?	Vol.	M	Mean 41	46	32	Mean 20 mo.	Abst. and imp.	47% imp.
Gallant, D.M. et al[47]	1968	U.S.	Outpt.	Psycho-therapy	6 mo.	Invol.	M	Mean 33	19	C-10 V- 9	6 mo.	Abst. and social adj.	70% imp. - C (Compulsory) 1% imp. - V (Voluntary)
Burton, G. and Kaplan, H.M.[48]	1968	U.S.	Outpt.	Married couples counseling	Ave. 30 wks.	Vol.	M,F	?	47 cpls.	39 cpls.	Mean 39 mo.	Abst. and social adj.	68% imp.
Kurland, A.A.[49]	1968	U.S.	Inpt.	?	?	Vol. & Invol.	M	67% over 40	378	260	Mean 28.5 mo.	Abst. and soc. adj.	15.5% good adjustment
Bowen, W.T. and Androes, L.[50]	1968	U.S.	Inpt.	Psycho-therapy	90 days	Vol.	M	Med. 45	79	79	1 yr.	Abst. and social adj.	25% abstinent 1 yr.
Pokorny, A.D. et al[51]	1968	U.S.	Inpt.	Psycho-therapy	90 days	Vol.	M	Mean 44	113	88	1 yr.	Abst. & imp.	51% imp.
Pittman, D.J. and Tate, R.L.[52]	1969	U.S.	Inpt. & Outpt.	Psycho-therapy	E group- 3-6 wks.	Vol.	M,F	Med. 41	E group- 177	249	Med. 13 mo.	Abst. and soc. adj.	E group - 72% imp. C group - 59% imp.

74

Disulfiram

Author	Year	Country	Setting	Treatment	Duration	Vol./Invol.	Sex	Age	N	N	Follow-up	Social adj.	Outcome
Hollister, L.E. et al[54]	1969	U.S.	Inpt.	LSD & Dex.	2 days	Vol.	M	Med. 45	35 Dex. 37 LSD	19 Dex. 26 LSD	2 mo. & 6 mo.	Imp. social adjustment	At 2 mo. LSD group imp. At 6 mo. no difference
Johnson, F.G.[55]	1969	Can.	Inpt. & Outpt.	Chemotherapy LSD	?	Vol.	M,F	Rge. 20-60	95	95	1 yr.	Abst. and social adj.	Imp. significant in drinking & Empl. indices (N not indicated)
McCance, C. and McCance, P.F.[56]	1969	Scotland	Inpt.	(1)-Electro shock Aversion (2)-Group Psychotherapy LSD	6 wks	Vol.	M	?	Corn.-140 King.-54	Corn.-89 King.-54	6 mo. & 1 yr.	Abst. and social adj.	46% imp. - Cornhill 21% imp. - Kingseat (no diff. between RX 1 & RX 2 at 6 & 12 mo.)
Vincent, M.O. and Blum, D.M.[57]	1969	Can.	Inpt.	Psychotherapy	?	Vol.	M,F	Ave. M-48 F-52	128	35M 8F	5 yrs.	Abst. & imp.	88% imp. - Males 87% imp. - Females
Levinson, T. and Sereny, G.[58]	1969	Can.	Inpt.	Insight therapy	6 wks	Vol.	?	?	A-30 B-30	53	1 yr.	Imp. social adjustment	15% imp. - A (insight T.) 33% imp. - B (recreational therapy)
Kissin, B., Platz, A. and Su, W.[59]	1970	U.S.	Outpt. & Inpt.	Psychotherapy Drug Milieu	?	Vol.	M,F	?	458	225	12 mo.	Abst. & social adj.	71% imp.
Rossi, J.J.[60]	1970	U.S.	Inpt.	Synthetic	30 days	Vol.	M,F.	Ave. 45	100	73	12 mo.	Abst. and social adj.	71% imp.
Bowen, W., Soskin, R., and Chotos, J.[61]	1970	U.S.	Inpt.	Chemo/Resoc. (LSD/HRTL)	60 days	Vol.	M	LSD-43.8 HRTL-46.1	LSD-41 HRTL-40	LSD-41 HRTL-40	12 mos.	Adjustment	17% imp. LSD 22% imp. HRTL
Denson, R. and Sydiaha, D.[62]	1970	Can.	Inpt.	LSD	?	Vol.	M,F	Mean 33	Ex-25 C-26	51	12 mos.	Imp. social adj.	No significant differences between Ex. & C groups
Tomsovic, M.[63]	1970	U.S.	Inpt.	Psychotherapy A.A.	90 days	Vol.	M	43	266	161	1 yr.	Abst. and social adj.	45% imp.
Ferguson, F.N.[64]	1970	U.S.	Outpt.	Disulfiram	18 mo.	Invol.	M,F	Rge. 18-55	115	115	12, 18 & 24 mo.	Imp. social adj.	8% imp.-12 mo. 12% imp.-18 mo. 22% imp.-24 mo. 42% imp.
Gallant, D.M. et al[65]	1970	U.S.	Outpt.	Psychotherapy	?	Vol.	M,F	?	118 cpls.	24 cpls.	2-20 mo.	Abst. and social adj.	44% imp.

75

		Geo.		**Treatment Characteristics**		Pt.	**Patient Characteristics**		Initial	Final	**Follow-up Characteristics**	Evaluative		**Findings**
Author(s)	Date	Loc.	Setting	RX Mode	RX Lgth.	Status	Sex	Age	Sample	Sample	Follow-up Length	Criteria	Results	
Pahnke, W.N. et al[66]	1970	U.S.	Inpt.	Psycho-therapy LSD	?	Vol.	?	?	Ex - 64 C - 53	104	6 mo.	Imp. social adj.	44% imp. - Ex group 25% imp. - C group	
Kish, G.B. and Hermann, H.T.[67]	1971	U.S.	Inpt.	Psycho-therapy & A.A.	8 wks	Vol. & Invol.	M	Ave. 42	173	168	12 mo.	Abst. and imp.	42% imp. (1 yr.)	
Papas, A.[68]	1971	U.S.	Inpt.	Milieu	30 days	Vol.	M	33-47	80	38	12 mo.	Abst.	44.7% abst. 34.2% drinking 21.1% left military	
Fitzgerald, B.J. et al[69]	1971	U.S.	Inpt.	Psycho-therapy A.A.	16 wks	Vol. & Invol.	M,F	Mean M-42 F-42	531	217	4 yrs.	Abst. and imp.	64% imp. (M) 70% imp. (F)	
Penick, S.B. et al[70]	1971	U.S.	Inpt.	Psycho-therapy Metronidazole	Mean 22 days	Vol.	M,F	?	100	44 at 6 mo. 72 at 4 yrs.	6 mo. & 4 yrs.	Abstinence	6 mo. = 20% abst. - drug 34% abst. - Placebo 4 yrs. = 7% abst. - drug 12% abst. - Placebo	
Gordon, W.W.[71]	1971	Scotland	Inpt.	Aversive RX (differential conditioning)	12 days	Vol.	?	?	30	20	3 mo.	Abstinence and Improvement	95% imp. (19/20) None Abstinent	
Rohan, W.P.[72]	1972	U.S.	Inpt.	Psycho-therapy	60 days	Vol.	M	44	603	324	1 yr.	Abst. and social adj.	56% imp.	
Knox, W.J.[73]	1972	U.S.	Inpt.	Psycho-therapy Disulfiram	Ave. 55 days	Vol.	M	Ave 50	54	44	4 yrs.	Imp. social adj.	15% imp.	
Browne-Mayers, A.N. et al[74]	1973	U.S.	Inpt.	Psycho-therapy Family Counseling	23 wks.	Vol.	M,F	Ave. 48	74	74	1, 1½ & 2 yrs.	Abst. and imp.	59% imp. - 2 yrs.	
Obholzer, A.[75]	1974	Britain	NA	Antibuse Implant		Vol.	M-18 F-1	40-55	19	19	2½-12 mo. 5½ X	Abst.	68% Abst.	
McLauchlan, J.[76]	1974	Can.	Inpt. & Outpt.	Group therapy		Vol.	M,F	45.9	94	94	12-16 mo.	Abst.	61%; 70% pt. therapist match 50% mismatch (conceptual level)	
Shore, J. and Wilson, L.[77]	1975	U.S.	Inpt.				M	41	83	83	18 mo.	Abst.	44% abst.	

76

An examination of the report of treatment outcomes by Armor and associates is presented both as an example of poor follow-up research and of unproductive collaboration with external research expertise. This unfortunate project may have resulted either from the inability of a large bureaucracy (NIAAA) to meaningfully interact with researchers or from the opportunism of outside researchers. There were probably elements of both of these in the arrangements between NIAAA and the Stanford Research Institute and between NIAAA and the Rand Corporation. However, this example should not be interpreted as conclusive evidence of the inability of either NIAAA or individual treatment centers to develop productive external research relationships. The more recent study by Polich and associates, also done under contract with the Rand Corporation, reflects far greater programmatic insight and methodological care than did the 1976 study.

The "Rand Report": A Critique

Perhaps no other social/psychological research in alcoholism treatment and recovery has had the impact of the study published in 1976 by the Rand Corporation. This research report presented an analysis of follow-up data gathered by the NIAAA Alcoholism Treatment Center Monitoring System and a special study done for NIAAA by the Stanford Research Institute. The Rand Corporation of Santa Monica, California, was recipient of a grant from NIAAA to analyze and interpret previously gathered data. This clearly places the analysis into a retrospective design. That is, the data were gathered without an explicit plan of analysis, and the analytical strategy was later developed within the constraints of the previously gathered data.

Much of what may be criticized in the report (authored by David J. Armor, J. Michael Polich and Harriet B. Stambul) goes back to the initial data gathering and therefore is more correctly the responsibility of the NIAAA Alcoholism Treatment Monitoring System and Stanford Research Institute. There are, however, criticisms that are correctly aimed at the operationalizations and data interpretations made by the "Rand Report" author-researchers. Criticisms of both the data gathering and data analysis will be detailed in the following discussion using the topics identified by Baekeland, et. al., as methodological issues in the alcoholism treatment outcome literature as well as some other methodological points of reference.

Before proceeding with detailed criticism of the "Rand Report" it is important to raise the question, *How did methodologically substandard treatment outcome research, such as is found in the "Rand Report," gain a high level of media and general public attention and prompt so much discussion in alcoholism treatment circles?* The only ready answer is the news media's propensity to proclaim the sensational and to headline ideas contrary to the accepted attitudes and practices of the day.[8] A research report which finds the usual proportion of treated alcoholics to be abstinent or improved in their so-cial/psychological functioning would probably not be considered news-worthy. For an outcome study to state that treatment was a waste of time or that treated alcoholics could return to drinking without experiencing negative consequences is attractive as a news item because it is unusual.

Once the "Rand Report" was picked up as newsworthy by the national news services, it suddenly had national attention focused on it, not because it was a fine, or definitive example of treatment outcome research, but because it had news appeal. Without national news coverage, the "Rand Report" prob-ably would have remained as obscure as most other alcoholism treatment out-come studies. Instead, it became an item of casual conversation as well as heated debate. That some treated alcoholics took the publicized findings as empirical fact and returned to drinking is unfortunate. One would doubt that the "Rand Report" authors wanted to provide a justification for a treated al-coholic to return to drinking, especially considering these cautious and quali-fied statements made in the report:

> Therefore, we consider these results tentative but nonetheless suggestive that a sizable group of treated alcoholics, can engage in either periodic or regular moderate drinking without relapse during a 1-year interval. For these alcoholics, then, normal drinking or periodic drinking can be considered a viable form of remission (p. 126). The data from this study, and other similar studies, are simply not adequate to establish, beyond question, the long-term feasibility of normal or "controlled" drinking among alcoholics; nor do the data enable us to identify those specific in-dividuals for whom normal drinking might be appropriate (p. 140).

Even these cautious conclusions are questionable and probably unfounded given the data base and the analytical procedures used to reach these conclu-sions, as will be specified momentarily. The view that is taken here, relative to the "Rand Report," is that there was no malicious intent on the part of Armor and his associates to create a false impression. Instead, they suggested a pos-sible conclusion based on the way that they arranged the data analysis. Their conclusion was distorted by the news media in a zeal to gain readership, listenership and viewership (which may be translated into more advertising dollars and more profit). For those who personally suffered negative conse-quences or anguish from the popularized conclusion attributed to the "Rand Report" it is the serendipitous functioning of a competitive news establish-ment rather than the usually cautious and honest efforts of most alcoholism researchers that should be criticized.*

---

*The "Rand Report" authors, Armor, Polich and Stambul were not recognized alco-holism treatment outcome researchers at the time they authored the report, but they had earned reputations as researchers and evaluators.

The "Rand Report" was referred to above as methodologically substandard. What evidence is there to support that contention? The Alcoholic Treatment Center (ATC) data base was gathered from September, 1972 through April, 1974 from 44 NIAAA centers geographically situated disproportionately in the south. The clients served in the NIAAA centers were also disproportionately of lower income and minority backgrounds. Follow-up data were gathered 6 months after *intake* from 2371 male non-DWI clients representing a 21% follow-up return rate. That the data were gathered 6 months after intake rather than 6 months after discharge presents a major methodological problem as does the extremely low follow-up return.

Only 8 of the original 44 treatment centers were included in a second follow-up which used a stratified sampling procedure and obtained data from 600 male non-DWI clients (62%) 18 months after their date of intake. Because the 18-month follow-up included clients from a reduced number of ATCs and because the 6-month response rate was so low, only 219 of the 600 clients followed up at 18 months were also followed up at 6 months. The quality of the analysis over the two follow-up time periods is therefore subject to criticism because of the small number of cases represented.

In addition to using the date of intake of calculate the timing of the follow-up, an assortment of treatment *settings* were represented by the ATCs. Five identifiable treatment settings were experienced by the ATC clients, with little documentation given describing the specific treatment modalities associated with each treatment settings. Table 4-2 shows the treatment settings, the median length of treatment in months and the number of clients receiving each type of treatment. Using the date of intake to determine follow-up at 6 months and looking at the average (median) length of treatment shows that apparently half of the clients were still in treatment at the time they were interviewed for the six month follow-up.* Because clients taking part in certain treatment settings were more likely to be still receiving treatment at the time of follow-up, the treatment setting becomes a still greater confounding variable in trying to meaningfully interpret the data.

The geographic, socioeconomic and ethnic make-up of the ATC client population, the low rate of response at the 6-month follow-up, using client intake dates to determine the follow-up interval, the inclusion of clients who were still in treatment in the follow-up, the differing treatment settings (and within them "myriad forms" of therapy), and the selection of 8 out of 44 ATCs for

---

*Of the 2335 clients included in the study, 2194 were in treatment lasting an average time period greater than 6 months. If the 2194 with a longer treatment duration is divided in half, 47% of the total clients were still in treatment at 6 months after intake. However, with a median treatment duration of 7.5 months for the four longer programs, it may be reasoned that over half of the clients in the ATC 6-month follow-up were still in treatment at the time they were interviewed.

Table 4-2 Rand Report: Client Treatments Classified by
Treatment Settings[1]

Treatment Received by Client	Duration of Treatment[2]	N
Hospital care alone	1	141
Intermediate care alone	–	–
Intermediate care and hospital care	8	265
Outpatient care alone	7	820
Hospital care and outpatient care	7	661
Intermediate care and outpatient care	–	–
Intermediate, outpatient and hospital care	8	448
		2335[3]

[1]Presented on p. 103 of Armor, Polich and Stambul, *Alcoholism and Treatment,* Santa Monica, CA: The Rand Corporation, 1976.

[2]Median months between intake and last treatment.

[3]All 44 ATC, 36 cases less than 2371 total.

the 18-month follow-up constitute real and potential sampling biases. The most flagrant methodological error is the inclusion of clients still in therapy within the follow-up. The 6-month follow-up data base may be said to contain further treatment outcome distortion resulting from the overrepresentation of intermediate care (low socioeconomic status bias) and outpatient care (less severe alcoholism symptoms) among the clients followed up at 6 months after intake who were still in treatment. The 18-month follow-up was better executed, although it carries on many of the overall design problems cited for the 6-month follow-up study.

The questionnaire used in the study of ATC clients, although long, is well constructed. Designed as an interview guide, the instrument is complex and probably could not be successfully used as a mail questionnaire. It is curious, however, that valuable interviewer-respondent time was spent gathering background information such as the client's height and veteran status when this information could have been obtained more efficiently from the client treatment record. In general, the serious shortcomings of the "Rand Report" are not attributable to the data gathering instrument, but to the ways in which these data were operationalized.

The "Rand Report" speaks frequently of remission. Although remission is used in the health sciences when speaking about the course of an illness it is not commonly used in referring to treated alcoholics. It is important to be aware of how Armor, Polich and Stambul use this term in the operationalization of their data. A client was classified as being in remission if the following criteria were met:

ABSTAINED FOR 6 MONTHS: "A client falls into this category if he reports no drinking at all for 6 months or more prior to the follow-up interview."

ABSTAINED FOR 1 MONTH: "The one month abstainers are clients who reported no drinking the past 30 days but some drinking in the past 1 to 5 months prior to the follow-up."

NORMAL DRINKING: "Clients who reported drinking in the last 30 days at follow-up can fall into this category only if they meet *all* the following criteria:

1. Daily consumption of less than 3 ounces of ethanol.
2. Typical quantities on drinking days less than 5 ounces.
3. No tremors reported.
4. No serious symptoms."[9]

It is the last category, "normal drinking," that must be understood in detail in order to comprehend the remission classification. Twelve percent of the 6-month follow-up respondents and 22% of the 18-month respondents were categorized as "normal drinkers." These clients could have reported drinking either 3 to 6 cans of beer a day, 3 to 5 glasses of wine a day, or 4 to 6 shots of liquor a day for their daily drinking to equal 1 to 3 oz. "That is, a daily consumption index score of 1 oz./day for the past 30 days can be obtained by drinking one sizable (2¼ ounce) dry Martini every day, or by drinking one quart of gin on two consecutive days, but nothing on the other 28 days." The second drinking criteria that would qualify a client as a normal drinker referred to maximum quantity on a typical drinking day. The client drinking the quart of gin on two consecutive days would be disqualified as a normal drinker under this criteria. However, he could be drinking either 3 quarts of beer or 7 to 10 shots of liquor and not exceed the maximum typical daily quantity of 5 oz.

How were these "normal drinking" thresholds established? The results of surveys done for NIAAA by Louis Harris and Associates on general drinking practices were used to establish the drinking norms. Using the Harris data it was determined that the average (mean) consumption for males who drink was 3.1 oz. "Therefore, based strictly on an assessment of drinking patterns in the general population, we might set the upper limits for normal drinking at 3 oz./day for daily consumption and 5 ounces for typical quantities."[10] The obvious fault with using the average consumption from the general population survey is that the mean is seriously affected by heavy drinkers, problem drinkers and alcoholics included in the sample. Accordingly, the "normal drinking" amount is enlarged by including in the calculation of the mean the rather large intake quantities of a small number of people. Another questionable procedure is the lack of attention to individual tolerance as well as to the relatively low level of alcohol consumption that some advanced alcoholics need to sustain an ongoing "high." Certainly, the way in which the quantity and frequency of alcohol consumption was operationalized in the definition of "normal drinking" in the Rand Report raises a major limitation in accepting the remission classification.

Clients categorized as "normal drinkers" could have had no tremors reported, and "no serious symptoms." Again, "no serious symptoms" needs to be understood by way of the operational definition assigned to it by the researchers. Serious symptoms means, "Frequent episodes of at least three of the following 6 symptoms: tremors, blackouts, missing meals, morning drinking, being drunk, missing work."[11] "Frequent" was scaled on a three point scale from "did not occur" to "very often" with the "very often" end of the scale ranging from 5 or more times to 10 or more times within a 30 day period depending on the symptom. From this operationalization, it would appear that a client could have frequent blackouts and miss work often within a month, but if no other symptoms were evident and the quantity of drinking did not exceed the criteria the client would be categorized as a normal drinker and said to be in remission.

The statistical analysis of the ATC data seems appropriate and effectively used. However, the shortcomings of the data base and the operationalization of measures, principally remission, lead to some questionable interpretations and conclusions. Answers to the research questions raised in Chapter Two of the "Rand Report" are the product of the data and the ways in which the data were arranged for analysis. The computer cliche, "garbage in—garbage out" is appropriate here, except that the ATC data are probably more useful than garbage. Nevertheless, with the limitations associated with sampling biases and questionable operationalizations, the data must be seen as having minimal explanatory power.

Considerable skepticism should be exercised by the reader of research. Studies such as the "Rand Report" must be read in light of the methodological shortcomings referred to above. Concern is often expressed by practitioners of alcoholism treatment about the news media reports attributed to the "Rand Report" and the discussion the reports generated. Unfortunately, too few practitioners have either read or attempted to read the "Rand Report" itself. It is reasonable to suggest in the wake of the "Rand Report" that counselors and other alcoholism treatment practitioners improve their skills as alcoholism research consumers for the benefit of their clients and their stature in an increasingly visible profession.

As a postscript to the foregoing discussion, it needs to be mentioned that a 4-year follow-up report of the ATC population studied in 1972-74 and reported in the 1976 "Rand Report" was recently published. This new report reflects far greater caution both in the operational definitions and in the interpretation of findings. "In the 18-month study, we included people with low levels of symptoms in a 'normal drinking' category provided that they also met limits on quantity of consumption. At 4 years, we treated even a single occurrence of a symptom as a categorical indication of alcohol problems."[12] Not only did this change in criteria alter what was earlier defined as "normal drinking," it brought the researchers to a conclusion emphasizing the instability of treatment outcomes instead of viewing normal drinking as a viable form of remission. This far more cautious conclusion was apparently not considered as newsworthy as the finding of 1976. Scant news coverage has been given to the results of the 1980 report.

Conclusion

This examination of alcoholism treatment follow-up studies and the critique of a well-known, but poorly executed treatment outcome study has been intended to place the present study in perspective. Diversity of treatment programming, follow-up methodology and findings characterize the follow-up studies of the 1940's through the 1970's. Likewise, the uniqueness of the Hazelden treatment experience, the follow-up procedures used, the operationalization of variables may all be said to limit the generalizability of the findings to be reported in the following chapters. There are also characteristics of the present study that may be said to increase its generalizability. In this study, the data were gathered by a tested follow-up questionnaire over a period of years with a large study population. Furthermore, caution was exercised in the operationalization of variables so as to avoid errors of the sort identified in the "Rand Report." It is therefore hoped that the findings to be reported are generalizable not only to Hazelden, but to other treatment programs carried out within the broad framework of the Minnesota Model of treatment.

The present study is both a part of the body of alcoholism treatment outcome studies and typical of a new generation of such studies. This new generation of studies has resulted from improved computer technology and software programming. Such improvements have made multivariate analysis of data more accessible to researchers and have also permitted larger data bases to be efficiently manipulated. These improved capabilities will increase the quality of future alcoholism treatment outcome studies, especially when they are used in connection with ongoing monitoring systems. In the fifth decade of what may be defined as systematic alcoholism treatment intervention, it is important that this new generation of follow-up studies has developed, because there is every indication that such studies will be needed for the fine tuning of treatment and recovery processes that will be of increasing interest in the 1980's.

Reference Notes Chapter 4

[1]C. D. Emrick, A review of psychologically oriented treatment of alcoholism: I. The use and interrelationship of outcome criteria and drinking behavior following treatment. *Quart. J. of Studies on Alc.*, 1974, *35,* 523-549.

[2]C. D. Emrick, A review of psychologically oriented treatment of alcoholism: II. The relative effectiveness of different treatment approaches and the effectiveness of treatment versus no treatment. *Quart. J. of Studies on Alc.*, 1975, *36,* 88-108.

[3]Emrick, 1974, op. cit., pp. 523-524.

[4]E. M. Pattison, M. B. Sobell, and L. C. Sobell, *Emerging concepts of alcohol dependence.* New York: Springer, 1977, pp. 120-141.

[5]K. R. Wildasin, *An analysis of the variables in historical and contemporary literature pertaining to follow-up evaluation studies of alcoholism treatment programs.* Unpublished independent study project, University of Minnesota, 1973.

[6]D. J. Armor, J. M. Polich, and H. B. Stambul, *Alcoholism and treatment.* Santa Monica, CA: The Rand Corporation, 1976.

[7]J. W. Spicer, *Outcome evaluation: How to do it.* Center City, MN: Hazelden Foundation, 1980.

[8]W. M. Hastings, *How to think about social problems: A primer for citizens.* New York: Oxford University Press, 1979.

[9]Armor, op. cit., p. 80.

[10]Ibid., p. 77.

[11]Ibid., p. 73.

[12]J. M. Polich, D. J. Armor, and H. B. Braiker, *The course of alcoholism four years after treatment.* Santa Monica, CA.: The Rand Corporation, 1980.

[13]M. M. Miller, Ambulatory treatment of chronic alcoholism. *JAMA,* 1942, *120,* 217-275.

[14]C. A. Whitaker, Without psychosis—chronic alcoholism: A follow-up study. *Psychiat. Quart.,* 1942, *16,* 373-392.

[15]H. G. McMahan, The psychotherapeutic approach of chronic alcoholism in conjunction with the Alcoholics Anonymous program. *Ill. Psychiat. J.,* 1942, *2,* 15-20.

[16]F. Lemere and W. L. Voegtlin, An evaluation of the aversion treatment of alcoholism. *Quart. J. of Studies on Alc.,* 1950, *11,* 199-204.

[17]J. N. P. Moore and M. D. Drury, Antibuse in the management of alcoholism. *Lancet,* 1951, *2,* 1059-1061.

[18]A. D. Slater, A follow-up study of 63 alcoholics who received treatment in Utah under the Kendall Act. *Utah Alcoholism Review,* 1951, *2,* 1-8.

[19]R. G. Bell, Treatment and rehabilitation of alcohol addicts. *Ontario Med. Rev.,* 1951, *18,* 23-25, 38.

[20]L. J. West and W. H. Swegan, An approach to alcoholism in the military service. *Amer. J. Psychiat.,* 1956, *112,* 1004-1009.

[21]J. Norvig and B. Nielsen, A follow-up study of 221 alcohol addicts in Denmark. *Quart. J. of Studies on Alc.,* 1956, *17,* 633-642.

[22]A. Z. Pfeffer and S. Berger, A follow-up study of treated alcoholics. *Quart. J. of Studies on Alc.,* 1957, *18,* 624-648.

[23]M. L. Selzer and W. H. Holloway, A follow-up of alcoholics committed to a state hospital. *Quart. J. of Studies on Alc.*, 1957, *18*, 98-120.

[24]R. E. Thomas, L. H. Gliedman, S. D. Imber, A. R. Stone and J. Freund, Evaluation of the Maryland alcoholic rehabilitation clinics. *Quart. J. of Studies on Alc.*, 1959, *20*, 65-76.

[25]M. M. Glatt, An alcoholic unit in a medical hospital. *Lancet*, 1959, *2*, 397-398.

[26]R. A. Moore and F. Ramseur, Effects of psychotherapy in an openward hospital on patients with alcoholism. *Quart. J. of Studies on Alc.*, 1960, *21*, 233-252.

[27]E. H. Mitchell, Rehabilitation of the alcoholic. *Quart. J. of Studies on Alc.*, 1961, *22*, 93-100.

[28]D. L. Davies, Normal drinking in recovered alcohol addicts. *Quart. J. of Studies on Alc.*, 1962, *23*, 94-104.

[29]D. L. Gerard, G. Saenger and R. Wile, The abstinent alcoholic. *Arch. Gen. Psychiat.*, 1962, *6*, 83-95.

[30]K. Brun, Outcome of different types of treatment of alcoholics. *Quart. J. of Studies on Alc.*, 1963, *24*, 280-288.

[31]J. J. Rossi, A. Stach and N. J. Bradley, Effects of treatment of male alcoholics in a mental hospital: A follow-up study. *Quart. J. of Studies on Alc.*, 1963, *24*, 91-108.

[32]S. Wolff and L. Holland, A questionnaire follow-up of alcoholic patients. *J. of Studies on Alc.*, 1964, *25*, 108-118.

[33]P. O. O'Reilly and A. Funk, LSD in chronic alcoholism. *Canad. Psychiat. Ass'n. J.*, 1964, *9*, 258-261.

[34]J. Clancy, R. Vornbroch and E. Vanderhoof, Treatment of alcoholics: A follow-up study. *Dis. of Nerv. Sys.*, 1965, *26*, 555-561.

[35]R. E. Reinert, The alcoholism treatment program at Topeka Veterans Administration Hospital. *Quart. J. of Studies on Alc.*, 1965, *26*, 674-680.

[36]H. L. Wedel, Involving alcoholics in treatment. *Quart J. of Studies on Alc.*, 1965, *26*, 468-479.

[37]M. Vallance, Alcoholism: A two year follow-up study of patients admitted to the psychiatric ward of a general hospital. *Brit. J. Psychiat.*, 1964, *111*, 348-356.

[38]P. W. Haberman, Factors related to increased sobriety in group psychotherapy with alcoholics. *J. Clin. Psychol.*, 1966, *22*, 229-235.

[39]H. J. Walton, E. B. Ritson and R. I. Kennedy, Response of alcoholics to clinical treatment. *Brit. Med. J.*, 1966, *2*, 1171-1174.

[40]G. Edwards and S. Guthrie, A comparison of inpatient and outpatient treatment of alcohol dependence. *Lancet*, 1966, *2*, 467-468.

[41]L. Katz, The salvation army men's social service center: II. Results. *Quart. J of Studies on Alc.*, 1966, *27*, 636-647.

[42]F. E. Cheek, M. Sarett and R. S. Abbahary, Observations regarding the use of LSD-25 in the treatment of alcoholism. *J. Psychopharm.*, 1966, *1*, 56-74.

[43]S. M. Charnoff, Long-term treatment of alcoholism with amitriptyline and emylcamate: A double blind evaluation. *Quart. J. of Studies on Alc.*, 1967, *28*, 289-294.

[44]B. G. Blake, A follow-up of alcoholics treated by behavior therapy. *Behav. Res. Ther.*, 1967, *5*, 89-94.

[45]M. H. Beaubrun, Treatment of alcoholism in Trinidad and Tobago, 1956-1965. *Brit. J. Psychiat.*, 1967, *113*, 643-658.

⁴⁶E. M. Pattison, G. C. Gleser, E. B. Headley and L. A. Gottschalk, Abstinence and normal drinking: An assessment of changes in drinking patterns in alcoholics after treatment. *Quart. J. of Studies on Alc.,* 1968, *29,* 610-633.

⁴⁷D. M. Gallant, M. Faulkner, M. P. Bishop and D. Langdon, Enforced clinic treatment of paroled criminal alcoholics: A pilot evaluation. *Quart. J. of Studies on Alc.,* 1968, *29,* 77-83.

⁴⁸G. Burton and H. M. Kaplan, Marriage counseling with alcoholics and their spouses. *Brit. J. Addict.,* 1968, *63,* 161-170.

⁴⁹A. A. Kurland, Maryland alcoholics: Follow-up study I. *Psychiat. Res. Rep.,* 1968, *24,* 71-82.

⁵⁰W. T. Bowen and L. Androes, A follow-up study of 79 alcoholic patients: 1963-1965. *Bull. of the Menninger Clinic,* 1968, *32,* 26-34.

⁵¹A. Pokorny, B. Miller and S. Cleveland, Response to treatment of alcoholism: A follow-up study. *Quart. J. of Studies on Alc.,* 1968, *29,* 364-381.

⁵²D. J. Pittman and R. L. Tate, A comparison of two treatment programs for alcoholics. *Quart. J. of Studies on Alc.,* 1969, *30,* 888-889.

⁵³M. R. Goldfried, Prediction of improvement in an alcoholism outpatient clinic. *Quart. J. of Studies on Alc.,* 1969, *30,* 119-139.

⁵⁴L. E. Hollister, J. Shelton and G. Krieger, A controlled comparison of lysergic acid diethylamide (LSD) and dextroamphetamine in alcoholics. *Amer. J. Psychiat.,* 1969, *125,* 1352-1357.

⁵⁵F. G. Johnson, LSD in the treatment of alcoholism. *Am. J. of Psychiatry,* 1969, *126,* 63-69.

⁵⁶C. McCance and P. F. McCance, Alcoholism in north-east Scotland: Its treatment and outcome. *Brit. J. Psychiat.,* 1969, *115,* 189-198.

⁵⁷M. O. Vincent and D. M. Blum, A five year follow-up study of alcoholic patients. *Rep. Alc.,* 1969, *27,* 19-26.

⁵⁸T. Levinson and G. Sereny, An experimental evaluation of insight therapy for the chronic alcoholic. *Cand. Psychiat. Ass'n.,* 1969, *14,* 143-146.

⁵⁹B. Kissin, A. Platz and W. Su, Social psychological factors in the treatment of chronic alcoholism. *J. Psychiat. Res.,* 1970, *8,* 13-27.

⁶⁰J. J. Rossi, A holistic treatment program for alcoholism rehabilitation. *Med. Clin. Res.,* 1970, *3,* 6-16.

⁶¹W. Bowen, R. Soskin and J. Chotos, Lysergic acid diethylamide as a variable in the hospital treatment of alcoholism, a follow-up. *J. Nerv. Ment. Dis.,* 1970, *150 (2),* 111-118.

⁶²R. Denson and D. Sydiaha, A controlled study of LSD treatment in alcoholism and neurosis. *Brit. J. Psychiat.,* 1970, *116,* 443-445.

⁶³M. Tomsovic, A follow-up study of discharged alcoholics. *Hosp. Comm. Psychiat.,* 1970, *21,* 94-97.

⁶⁴F. N. Ferguson, A treatment program for Navajo alcoholics, results after four years. *Quart. J. of Studies on Alc.,* 1970, *31,* 898-919.

⁶⁵D. M. Gallant, A. Rich, E. Bey and L. Terranova, Group psychotherapy with married couples: A successful technique in New Orleans alcoholism clinic patients. *J. La. Med. Soc.,* 1970, *122,* 41-44.

⁶⁶W. N. Pahnke, A. A. Kurland, S. Unger, C. Savage and S. Grof, The experimental use of psychedelic (LSD) psychotherapy. *JAMA,* 1970, *212,* 1856-1863.

[67]G. B. Kish and H. T. Herman, The Fort Meade alcoholism treatment program: A follow-up study. *Quart. J. of Studies on Alc.,* 1971, *32,* 628-635.

[68]A. N. Papas, Air Force alcoholism rehabilitation program. *Milit. Med.,* 1971, *136,* 277-281.

[69]B. J. Fitzgerald, R. A. Pasewark and R. Clark, Four year follow-up of alcoholics treated at a rural state hospital. *Quart. J. of Studies on Alc.,* 1971, *32,* 636-642.

[70]S. B. Penick, J. B. Sheldon, D. I. Templer and R. N. Carrier, Four year follow-up of metronidazole treatment program for alcoholism. *Industr. Med.,* 1971, *40,* 30-32.

[71]W. W. Gordon, The treatment of alcohol (and tobacco) addiction by differential conditioning: New manual and mechanical methods. *Amer. J. Psychother.,* 1971, *25,* 394-417.

[72]W. P. Rohan, Follow-up study of problem drinkers. *Dis. Nerv. Syst.,* 1972, *33,* 196-199.

[73]W. J. Knox, Four year follow-up of veterans treated on a small alcoholism treatment ward. *Quart. J. of Studies on Alc.,* 1972, *33,* 105-110.

[74]A. N. Browne-Mayers, E. E. Seelyem and D. El Brown, Reorganized alcoholism service: Two years after. *JAMA,* 1973, *224,* 233-235.

[75]A. M. Obholzer, Follow-up study of 19 alcoholic patients treated by means of tetrethyl thiuram disulfide. *Br. J. of Addictions,* 1974, *69,* 19-23.

[76]J. F. C. McLauchlan, Therapy strategies, personality orientation and recovery from alcoholism. *Can. Psy. Assoc. J.,* 1974, *19,* 25-30.

[77]J. H. Shore and L. G. Wilson, Evaluation of a regional Indian alcohol program. *Am. J. of Psy.,* 1975, *132,* 255-258.

[78]R. Moos and F. Bliss, Difficulty of follow-up and outcome of alcoholism treatment. *J. of Stud. on Alc.,* 1978, *39,* 473-489.

Chapter Five

Posttreatment Alcohol and Drug Use and Treatment Outcomes

Alcohol and Drug Use 12 Months After Discharge

Excessive and inappropriate use of alcohol or other mood-modifying substances is central to the behavioral disabilities known as alcoholism and drug abuse. One principal goal of treatment at Hazelden is to stop such misuse. This goal is supported by the conceptualization of these chemical dependencies as chronic. The treatment prescription of total abstinence from psychoactive substances is strongly endorsed for all patients. Much of what transpires in the Hazelden rehabilitation experience is designed to convince patients of the dangers of drinking and drug use, given their histories of problems associated with abuse, and to acquaint them with the AA program and other means of realizing abstinence and sobriety. There is also a strong emphasis on freedom of choice in rehabilitation, because the patient has to take the responsibility for personal changes.

What are the alcohol and drug use outcomes of treatment at Hazelden? This question will be approached in a number of ways for it is a multifaceted question including at least four patient subgroups: 1) all patients for whom usable follow-up data are available, 2) completed treatment patients, 3) the study population, and 4) drug and alcohol users within the study population.

Questions related to the alcohol use outcomes for the first three of these subgroups are: 1) What are the posttreatment alcohol use outcomes for *all patients* discharged during the 1973-75 data gathering period for whom usable follow-up data are available? 2) What are the posttreatment alcohol use outcomes for *completed treatment patients* discharged during the 1973-75 data gathering period for whom follow-up data are available? 3) What are the posttreatment alcohol use outcomes for the *study population* (patients who completed treatment and were having problems with alcohol only or alcohol and drugs at the time of treatment)?

Usable 12-month follow-up data were obtained from 1899* of the 3638 patients discharged from treatment during the last six months of 1973 and the calendar years 1974 and 1975. As shown in Table 5-1, 50% of the 1899 respondents were *abstinent* during the year following treatment, 17.6% were *improved* and 32.4% were *not improved*. Three hundred one of the 1899 respondents were treatment dropouts leaving a completed treatment population of 1598 for which follow-up data were available. Of these 1598 patients, slightly over half (50.9%) were *abstinent* during the year following treatment, 18.3% were *improved* and 30.8% were *not improved*. By eliminating the treatment dropouts both the percentage *abstinent* and the percentage *improved* increase slightly, while the percentage *not improved* declines by about 1.5%. Sufficient 12-month follow-up data for alcohol use classification were available for 1246 of the original cases making up the study population. The percentage *abstinent* rose to 54.6% for the study population, with *not improved* declining to 27.4%. The percentage *improved* at 18% was midway between their cohort groups for all patients responding and the completed treatment patients. Although the study population had the most favorable abstinence

Table 5-1 12-Month Alcohol Use Outcomes for Three Subgroups of Patients

	Abstinent		Improved		Not Improved		Total	
	f	%	f	%	f	%	f	%
All Patients Responding	949	50.0	334	17.6	616	32.4	1899	100.0
Completed Treatment Patients	813	50.9	293	18.3	492	30.8	1598	100.0
Study Population	680	54.6	224	18.0	342	27.4	1246	100.0

*The 4-month questionnaire was used to categorize drinking so that the usable cases responded to both the 4- and 12-month questionnaire.

percentage, it will be shown that the likelihood of spurious differences has been reduced for the study population by an increased homogeneity of the patient grouping.

Before discussing some of the sociodemographic outcome differences for the three subgroups, an overall alcohol use outcome will be considered. In the discussion of sampling biases (Chapter Three) it was suggested that three-fourths of nonrespondents and patients lost to follow-up, one-half of deceased patients and all of the patients returned to Hazelden treatment should be classified as unsuccessful treatment outcomes, i.e., *not improved*. Using this procedure does not directly affect the *improved* category. It does account for another 1337 patients, however, by placing 324 more in the *abstinent* category and 1013 more placed in the *not improved* category (Table 5-2). The addition of these cases changed the percentage *abstinent* to 39.3%, reduced the percentage *improved* to 10.3% and increased the percentage *not improved* to 50.4%.

It is necessary to emphasize that the *abstinent, improved* and *not improved* percentages are relative to the population base being used. If all patients potentially in the study are accounted for, using the adjustment procedure described above, the percentage *abstinent* will drop and the percentage *not improved* will increase. Using speculative adjustments for nonrespondents, not located, returned to treatment and deceased patients thus reduces the percentage *abstinent* by slightly more than 10%. If, for the purpose of

Table 5-2 Overall Alcohol Use Treatment Outcome Adjusted Per Nonrespondent, Not Usable, Not Located, Returned to Treatment and Deceased Patients

	Usable Questionnaires Returned		Questionnaires Not Returned, Not Usable or Respondent Not Located[1]		Returned To Hazelden As Patient		Deceased[2]		Total	
	f	%	f	%	f	%	f	%	f	%
Abstinent	949	74.5	283	22.2	0	—	41	3.2	1273	39.3
Improved	334	100.0							334	10.3
Not Improved	616	37.8	850	52.2	122	7.5	41	2.5	1629	50.4
Total	1899	58.7	1133	35.0	122	3.3	82	2.5	3236*	100.0

[1]75% of patients whose questionnaires were either not returned or not usable and patients not located are considered "NOT IMPROVED."

[2]50% of deceased patients are considered "NOT IMPROVED."

*402 of the 3638 patients excluded from the study.

overall outcome, the 10.3% *improved* may be added to the *abstinent* category creating a combined *abstinent-improved* category it may be said there was an overall 50% treatment "success" rate for the patients treated at Hazelden.

Females showed slightly higher *abstinent* and *improvement* outcomes than males for the two subgroups consisting of all patients responding, and those who completed treatment. Males had a higher percentage of *not improved* in these two subgroups of patients. The differences were not statistically significant for the study population (Table 5-3). Married patients had a pattern of greater proportional *abstinence.* Unmarried patients were found to be proportionately more *not improved* for all patients responding and for those who completed treatment. These differences were not found to be statistically significant for the study population (Table 5-4). By eliminating treatment dropouts and drug only patients, the study population's posttreatment alcohol use was not found to be statistically different by sex and marital status. This finding indicates that the sex and marital status alcohol use outcome differences may be attributed to the greater heterogeneity of the subpopulations of all patients responding and of those who completed treatment.

Patients between the ages of 26 and 55 had the highest *abstinence* while patients 56 years and older were proportionately more common within the *improved* category and patients under 25 were proportionately most *not improved* (Table 5-5). These differences of posttreatment alcohol use during the year following treatment are significant for all three patient population groupings. Young people, 25 and under, are more commonly either *abstinent* or *not improved.* That is to say that if a youth began to use alcohol after treatment it appears that the use would most likely be limited neither in quantity nor duration. In contrast, even though the patients 56 years and over had the second highest percentage *not improved,* consistently around 33% more patients in the older age category appear to have either a limited period of drinking or a reduced quantity.

More education was associated with *abstinence* and less education with being *not improved* (Table 5-6). This pattern of difference was statistically significant for all three patient groupings. But in the study population, college graduates had a slightly less favorable *abstinence* percentage than was found for study population patients having some college or vocational school. For patients who completed treatment and for the study population, high school and college graduates were proportionately more *improved* than were patients who did not complete high school or college (including vocational school). This suggests that patients who had not successfully completed their educational goals may be at somewhat greater risk in limiting their drinking quantity and duration if they begin drinking than would be patients who had accomplished a recognized terminal point in their education.[1]

What does religion have to do with recovery? Although Catholics consti-

Table 5-3 Sex by Alcohol Use Categories One Year After Treatment for All Patients Responding to Follow-up, Completed Treatment Patients and the Study Population

	All Patients Responding								Completed Treatment Patients								Study Population							
	Abstinent		Improved		Not Improved		Total		Abstinent		Improved		Not Improved		Total		Abstinent		Improved		Not Improved		Total	
	f	%	f	%	f	%	f	%	f	%	f	%	f	%	f	%	f	%	f	%	f	%	f	%
Female	297	52.9	109	19.4	155	27.6	561	29.5	227	53.3	91	21.4	108	25.4	426	26.7	184	56.3	67	20.5	76	23.2	327	26.2
Male	652	48.7	225	16.8	461	34.5	1338	70.5	586	50.0	202	17.2	384	32.8	1172	73.3	496	54.0	157	17.1	266	28.9	919	73.8
Total	949	50.0	334	17.6	616	32.4	1899	100.0	813	50.9	293	18.3	492	30.8	1598	100.0	680	54.6	224	18.0	342	27.4	1246	100.0

$X^2 = 8.61$ df = 2, p < .05 $X^2 = 9.14$ df = 2, p < .05 $X^2 = 4.64$ df = 2, p > .05

Table 5-4 Marital Status by Alcohol Use Categories One Year After Treatment for All Patients Responding to Follow-up, Completed Treatment Patients and the Study Population

	All Patients Responding								Completed Treatment Patients								Study Population							
	Abstinent		Improved		Not Improved		Total		Abstinent		Improved		Not Improved		Total		Abstinent		Improved		Not Improved		Total	
	f	%	f	%	f	%	f	%	f	%	f	%	f	%	f	%	f	%	f	%	f	%	f	%
Not Married	350	45.3	134	17.3	289	37.4	773	40.7	285	45.7	119	19.1	220	35.3	624	39.1	236	51.1	86	18.6	140	30.3	462	37.1
Married	597	53.1	200	17.8	327	29.1	1124	59.3	526	54.1	174	17.9	272	28.0	972	60.9	442	56.5	138	17.6	202	25.8	782	62.9
Total	947	49.9	334	17.6	616	32.5	1897	100.0	811	50.8	293	18.4	492	30.8	1596	100.0	678	54.5	224	18.0	342	27.5	1244	100.0

$X^2 = 15.39$ df = 2, p < .01 $X^2 = 12.13$ df = 2, p < .01 $X^2 = 3.84$ df = 2, p > .05

Table 5-5 Age by Alcohol Use Categories One Year After Treatment for All Patients Responding to Follow-up, Completed Treatment Patients and the Study Population

	All Patients Responding								Completed Treatment Patients								Study Population							
	Abstinent		Improved		Not Improved		Total		Abstinent		Improved		Not Improved		Total		Abstinent		Improved		Not Improved		Total	
	f	%	f	%	f	%	f	%	f	%	f	%	f	%	f	%	f	%	f	%	f	%	f	%
25 and Under	111	42.7	27	10.4	122	46.9	260	13.7	89	42.2	25	11.8	97	46.0	211	13.2	62	47.3	12	9.2	57	43.5	131	10.5
26 - 55	717	53.3	233	17.3	394	29.3	1344	70.8	625	54.8	204	17.9	312	27.3	1411	71.4	536	58.1	164	17.8	222	24.1	922	74.0
56 and Over	121	41.0	74	25.1	100	33.9	295	15.5	99	40.2	64	26.0	83	33.7	246	15.4	82	42.5	48	24.9	63	32.6	193	15.5
Total	949	50.0	334	17.6	616	32.4	1899	100.0	813	50.9	293	18.3	492	30.8	1868	100.0	680	54.6	224	18.0	342	27.4	1246	100.0

$X^2 = 48.75$ df = 4, p < .01 $X^2 = 45.79$ df = 4, p < .01 $X^2 = 37.38$ df = 4, p < .01

Table 5-6 Education by Alcohol Use Categories One Year After Treatment for All Patients Responding to Follow-up, Completed Treatment Patients and the Study Population

	All Patients Responding								Completed Treatment Patients								Study Population							
	Abstinent		Improved		Not Improved		Total		Abstinent		Improved		Not Improved		Total		Abstinent		Improved		Not Improved		Total	
	f	%	f	%	f	%	f	%	f	%	f	%	f	%	f	%	f	%	f	%	f	%	f	%
Less than High School	126	41.7	51	16.9	125	41.4	302	15.9	108	42.5	42	16.5	104	40.9	254	15.9	84	46.7	28	15.6	68	37.8	180	14.4
High School Grad	299	49.4	107	17.7	199	32.9	605	31.9	246	48.7	95	18.8	164	32.5	505	31.6	197	51.4	74	19.3	112	29.2	383	30.7
Some College or Vocational School	167	52.2	57	17.8	96	30.0	320	16.9	143	54.4	47	17.9	73	27.8	263	16.5	123	59.4	33	15.9	51	24.6	207	16.6
College Grad	357	53.1	119	17.7	196	29.2	672	35.4	316	54.9	109	18.9	151	26.2	576	36.0	276	58.0	89	18.7	111	23.3	476	38.2
Total	949	50.0	334	17.6	616	32.4	1899	100.0	813	50.9	293	18.3	492	30.8	1598	100.0	680	54.6	224	18.0	342	27.4	1246	99.9

$X^2 = 16.21$ df = 6, p < .05 $X^2 = 20.71$ df = 6, p < .01 $X^2 = 17.24$ df = 6, p < .01

tuted only one-third of each of the three patient groupings, they accounted for a higher proportion of the *abstinent* patients and a lower proportion of the *improved* and *not improved* patients (Table 5-7). From closer inspection of these and related data it appears that familiarity with an explicitly structured set of religious beliefs, rather than a specific denomination, accounts for the more positive abstinence outcome of patients affiliated with the Roman Catholic denomination. Considering the strong spiritual component of both the AA program and the Hazelden rehabilitation experience, it is reasonable to expect that patients with an established spiritual concept may adapt that belief system to the spirituality aspect of recovery, whereas others may first have to formulate their spiritual viewpoint before being able to apply it in their own recovery.

Before proceeding further, it might be prudent to explore the three measures of alcohol use outcome: *abstinent, improved* and *not improved.* When these categories* were first introduced in Chapter Three, it was stated that the categories were intended to be pessimistic. As shown in Table 5-8, 949 of all respondents that were categorized as *abstinent* reported that they had not used alcohol and had 11 or more months of abstinence. Eighty percent of the 616 *not improved* cases were drinking not as much, about as much or more at the time they responded. The other 20% reported drinking as much or more with a recent period of abstinence of up to 10 months. Only 5 of the 334 *improved* patients who indicated drinking about as much or more had 11 to 12 months of nonuse. The largest portion of the *improved* cases, 77.5%, reported drinking less and had 2 or more months of not drinking. Seventeen cases classified as *improved* appear contradictory with *not used* combined with 0-1 month since the last drink.

There is little room for disagreement in the *abstinent* classification. By having not used alcohol for 11 or more months these patients have met the alcohol nonuse criteria (with the possible exception of a few who may have used alcohol briefly in the month following treatment).

The *improved* category is more varied and may be characterized as representing patients having used alcohol moderately as judged by quantity of use or time since last drink. What of the 62% of the *not improved* patients who report current drinking but "not as much"? These 383 cases, placed in the *not improved* category because of their current use, deserve separate attention in the later discussion of "controlled" or "normal" drinking by treated alcoholics.

---

*The categories are discussed using the subgroup of all follow-up respondents whose posttreatment alcohol use could be categorized. The construction of the alcohol use categories is the same for the completed treatment and study population subgroups with the same format also used in categorizing posttreatment drug use.

Table 5-7 Religion by Alcohol Use Categories One Year After Treatment for All Patients Responding to Follow-up, Completed Treatment Patients and the Study Population

| | All Patients Responding | | | | | | | | Completed Treatment Patients | | | | | | | | Study Population | | | | | | | |
| | Abstinent | | Improved | | Not Improved | | Total | | Abstinent | | Improved | | Not Improved | | Total | | Abstinent | | Improved | | Not Improved | | Total | |
	f	%	f	%	f	%	f	%	f	%	f	%	f	%	f	%	f	%	f	%	f	%	f	%
Catholic	339	55.4	97	15.8	176	28.8	612	32.2	302	56.4	87	16.3	146	27.3	535	33.5	250	60.5	64	15.5	99	24.0	413	33.1
Protestant and Other	610	47.4	237	18.4	440	34.2	1287	67.8	511	48.1	206	19.4	346	32.5	1063	66.5	430	51.6	160	19.2	243	29.2	833	66.9
Total	949	50.0	334	17.6	616	32.4	1899	100.0	813	50.9	293	18.3	492	30.8	1598	100.0	680	54.6	224	18.0	342	27.4	1246	100.0

$X^2 = 10.63$ df = 2, p < .01 $X^2 = 9.99$ df = 2, p < .01 $X^2 = 8.85$ df = 2, p < .05

Table 5-8 Frequencies Within Alcohol Use Categories ONE YEAR After Treatment For All Respondents

	0-1 mo.	2-4 mo.	5-7 mo.	8-10 mo.	11-12 mo.	13 mo.
Not used	17	13	21	19	746	203 [1]
Not as much	383	147	61	33	17	1 [2]
About as much	85	49	28	17 [3]	2	0
More	27	14	9	4	3	0

[1]Abstinent = 949	50.0%
[2]Improved = 334	17.6%
[3]Not Improved = 616	32.4%
Total = 1899	100.0%

At the 8-month follow-up, 56% of the cases were abstinent with one-fifth of these having used no alcohol for 11 to 12 months (Table 5-9). Those classified as *not improved* constitute 27% of the respondents with 16% in the *improved* category. Sixty-nine percent of the *not improved* cases at both the 4- and 8-month follow-ups reported current use, but not as much quantity as before treatment. A microscopic analysis of these cases will be presented later in the chapter in an examination of the "normal drinking" question. More 4-month than 8-month follow-up cases were classified as *abstinent* (65%) and there

Table 5-9 Frequencies Within Alcohol Use Categories 8 MONTHS After Treatment for All Respondents

	0-1 mo.	2-4 mo.	5-7 mo.	8-10 mo.	11-12 mo.
Not used	12	34	70	839	215 [1]
Not as much	349	135	36	10	1 [2]
About as much	90	34	12 [3]	1	2
More	13	9	1	0	0
Total	464	212	119	850	216

[1]Abstinent = 1054	56.6%
[2]Improved = 299	16.1%
[3]Not Improved = 508	27.3%
Total = 1861	100.0%

Table 5-10 Frequencies Within Alcohol Use Categories 4 MONTHS After Treatment for All Respondents

	0-1 mo.	2-4 mo.	5-7 mo.	8-10 mo.	11-12 mo.
Not used	23	268	780	100	108 [1]
Not as much	343	136	9	0	0 [2]
About as much	90	31 [3]	0	0	0
More	28	7	2	0	0
Total	484	442	791	100	108

[1]Abstinent = 1256   65.2%

[2]Improved = 170   8.8%

[3]Not Improved = 499   25.9%

    Total = 1925   99.9%

were fewer *improved* (9%) and *not improved* (26%) cases (Table 5-10). The categorization used for each of the follow-up intervals is shown in the respective tables.

The fourth subgroup is posttreatment drug users. What are the posttreatment drug user outcomes and their relationship with alcohol use outcomes for the study population? The answer requires looking both at drug use for the 12 months following treatment and at the combined alcohol and drug use for the same time period. Seventy percent of the study population reported abstinence from drugs other than alcohol. Another 25% were *improved* and 5% were *not improved*.

When the 56 patients classified as *not improved* in drug use were considered relative to their posttreatment alcohol use, 84% were found to be *not improved* in their alcohol use as well (Table 5-11). While over one-fourth of the 659 cases abstinent in alcohol use since treatment had used drugs during the posttreatment year, their drug use was classified as *improved*. Using the combined posttreatment alcohol and drug use reported at 12 months after discharge (Table 5-12), there was a reduction from 57.2% *abstinence* for "alcohol only" to 40.9% for combined alcohol and drug use.

The sixfold classification of posttreatment chemical use (Table 5-12) provides another way of looking at posttreatment alcohol and drug use. The second largest posttreatment use category was *abstinent-improved* (28.5%). It is important to note that of the 329 cases in this category, 44.4% are drug *abstinent* and alcohol *improved* while 55.6% are alcohol *abstinent* and drug *improved*. Of the 659 alcohol abstinent cases, 71.6% are also drug abstinent

Table 5-11 Study Population Alcohol Use and Drug Use ONE YEAR After Treatment

Alcohol Use	Abstinent		Improved		Not Improved		Total	
Drug Use	f	%	f	%	f	%	f	%
Abstinent	472	58.7	146	18.2	186	23.1	804	69.7
Improved	183	62.5	42	14.3	68	23.2	293	25.4
Not Improved	4	7.1	5	8.9	47	83.9	56	4.9
Total	659	57.2	193	16.7	301	26.1	1153*	100.0

with the greatest portion of the nonagreement found in the *abstinent* and *improved* categories. In contrast, alcohol *not improved* cases account for 97% of all *not improved* cases.

In looking at posttreatment drug use, the portion of the study population having problems with both alcohol and drugs at the time of treatment should be considered separately. Drug use 12 months after treatment was reported by 216 of the 442 alcohol and drug users on whom follow-up data were available (Table 5-13). Of the 63.9% (adjusted) reporting drug use, 51.8% were *improved*. For the alcohol and drug users, drug abstinence was only slightly greater than one-third (36%) while alcohol abstinence at 57% was slightly

Table 5-12 Composite Categorization of Study Population Alcohol and Drug Use ONE YEAR After Treatment

	f	%
Abstinent-Abstinent	472	40.9
Abstinent-Improved	329	28.5
Improved-Improved	42	3.6
Abstinent-Not Improved	190	16.5
Improved-Not Improved	73	6.3
Not Improved-Not Improved	47	4.1
Total	1153*	99.9

*93 missing cases are accounted for by missing drug use information.

Table 5-13 Alcohol and Drug Use Patients' 12 MONTH Alcohol and Drug Use

Alcohol Use	f	%	Adjusted %
Abstinent	188	42.5	57.1
Improved	46	10.4	14.0
Not Improved	95	21.5	28.9
No Response	113	25.6	
Total	442		
Drug Use			
Abstinent	122	27.6	36.1
Improved	175	39.6	51.8
Not Improved	41	9.3	12.1
No Response	104	23.5	
Total	442		

higher than in the study population as a whole. It is concluded that patients having problems with both alcohol and drugs at the time of treatment are more likely during the year following treatment to use drugs moderately than to use alcohol.

For the balance of the present analysis, posttreatment use of drugs other than alcohol, while it is an avenue of analysis, will not be pursued. Because the largest portion of the drug use after treatment was limited, as indicated by its classification as *improved,* it appears justified to ignore drug use for the analysis that will follow. The small number of *not improved* drug users included in the study population will not affect the upcoming analysis in an appreciable fashion.

In conclusion, Research Question One with its many facets has a multifaceted answer which is summarized below:

1. The study population had a more favorable one-year posttreatment abstinence outcome (54.6%) than either the total population for whom data were available (50%) or completed treatment patients (50.9%).

2. Overall alcohol abstinence during the year after treatment, when adjusted for nonrespondent, not usable, not located, returned to treat-

ment and deceased patients was 39.3%: or may be seen as a combined abstinent-improved percentage of 49.6.

3. There were no significant differences in alcohol use outcomes by sex or marital status for the study population although there were significantly different outcomes for those two socioeconomic variables in both the total respondent and completed treatment patient groupings.

4. Significant differences in alcohol use outcome were found for age, education and religion in all three patient groupings, with patients between 26 and 55, patients with more education and patients with Catholic religious affiliation having higher rates of abstinence.

5. Drug use during the year following treatment fell largely into the improved category and was more pronounced among patients classified as alcohol and drug users at the time of treatment than for the balance of the study population. The combination of drug-alcohol use resulted in an abstinence from mood-altering substances of 40.9%.

Predicting Abstinence

The next research question to be considered is, "What variables are important in predicting posttreatment abstinence?" This question was approached using multiple regression analysis where alcohol use at 12 months after discharge from treatment was the dependent variable. As shown in Table 5-14, 18.2%* of the variance in posttreatment alcohol use was explained by six of the independent variables.

Present AA attendance explained the greatest percent of variance (6.09%) in alcohol use after treatment. This finding translates to strong support for frequent AA meeting participation having a favorable influence on abstinence. Greater elaboration of this relationship will be found in the next chapter which deals with Alcoholics Anonymous. It is sufficient here to say that the strong treatment emphasis on AA involvement as an effective means for achieving abstinence is empirically supported.

Another important variable was posttreatment hospitalization. Patients who were not hopitalized for any reason following treatment were more likely to be abstinent than were patients who were hospitalized. Posttreatment hospitalizations explained 5.24% of the alcohol use outcome. It is reasonable to expect that for many patients, a return to drinking will result in a recurrence of health problems, especially where gastrointestinal and liver damage is evident at the time of treatment. For some, the hospitalization may signal an-

---

*Explaining this percent of the variance in the dependent variable with six independent variables in a multiple regression analysis is considered acceptable using survey data.

Table 5-14 Prediction of 12-MONTH Posttreatment Abstinence by Socio-demographic, Treatment and Follow-up Variables

	Standardized Regression Coefficient (Beta)	% Variance Explained
Present AA Attendance	.197	6.09
Times Hospitalized Since Treatment	.228	5.24
Individual Activities in Treatment	.085	2.90
Collective Activities in Treatment	.155	2.42
Education	-.069	1.14
Higher Power	.071	.42
Total		18.21

other attempt at problem recognition and treatment of alcoholism, whereas for others, the hospital environment may perform an enabling function by cushioning a crisis, thereby permitting continuation of drinking and related problems.

The next two variables in alcohol use outcome are individual activities in treatment (2.90% explained variance) and collective activities in treatment (2.42% explained variance). It will be recalled that "collective activities in treatment" is a composite measure in the form of a factor score based on patient ratings of group therapy, informal conversations with patients, the "hot seat" and meetings with counselors and clergy reported on the 12-month follow-up questionnaire. Essentially, patients who rated these activities as helpful were more *abstinent* in their outcomes and patients who rated these activities negatively were more *not improved*. The same relationship held true for the ratings of individual activities in treatment which included reading, time alone, meditation, lecture and the environmental setting although this variable explained much less of the variance in alcohol use outcome.

Education is shown with a negative standardized regression coefficient (Beta) which indicates that greater education is associated with abstinence as has already been stated. Although this variable explains only 1.14% of the outcome variance, it is worth noting education is the only previously mentioned sociodemographic characteristic included in the regression analysis as an important explainer of posttreatment alcohol use. With education the single indicator of socioeconomic status in the present analysis, the finding that higher socioeconomic status is associated with an abstinence outcome is consistent with conclusions reached by other investigators.

The last and least powerfully explained variable of posttreatment alcohol use is the "Higher Power" variable (.42%) which may be understood as increased posttreatment prayer and meditation used in maintaining some conscious contact with a Higher Power. In the next two chapters this variable will gain considerable prominence but at this point in the analysis the "Higher Power" variable appears to have only a modest influence on posttreatment alcohol use.

These findings will be used in Chapter Seven to guide the construction of an overall treatment outcome model. In considering posttreatment recovery, it becomes apparent that abstinence alone is only a part—although, relative to treatment expectations, an important part of judging the quality of alcoholism recovery. At this point in the analysis, social/psychological functioning was withheld from the regression analysis as it will be considered separately later in the discussion.

The regression analysis permits posttreatment abstainers to be characterized as frequent AA attenders who don't have posttreatment hospitalizations, but do assess group and individual activities during treatment as helpful, have greater education and have increased their use of prayer and meditation after treatment.

Posttreatment Change in Alcohol Use

How much change is there in posttreatment alcohol use outcomes over time? This research question is approached using the data gathered at the 4-, 8- and 12-month follow-up intervals. Table 5-15 shows that patterns of alcohol use during the year after treatment are consistent for some patients and fluid for others. An examination of both the consistent outcome patterns and the shifts between the outcome categories will yield an answer to the third research question.

Seventy-two percent of the patients who reported abstinence at 4 months after treatment discharge also reported abstinence at 8 months after treatment discharge. Of those classified as abstinent at 8 months after leaving treatment, 79% were also abstinent at 12 months following discharge. This represents quite a high level of stability in abstinence outcomes over the period of the year after treatment. What of those patients who moved into either of the other two use categories or became nonrespondents over the follow-up time periods?

The largest proportion lost from the *abstinent* category between the 4- and 8-month follow-up intervals (15%) were nonrespondents. Because the alcohol use of the 8-month nonrespondents is not known, these 139 cases do not help to directly answer the question of change in alcohol use. By contrast, a total

Table 5-15 Alcohol Use Stability and Change During the Year Following Treatment

4 Mo.	8 Mo.	12 Mo.
1652 patients sought	1652 patients sought	1623 patients sought
1601 usable questionnaires returned	1308 usable questionnaires returned	1246 usable questionnaires returned

12 Mo.

680 (54.6) Abstinent

224 (18.0) Improved

342 (27.4) Not Improved

377 No Response

8 Mo.

788 (60.2) Abstinent

212 (16.2) Improved

308 (23.5) Not Improved

344 No Response

4 Mo.

925 (57.7) Abstinent

339 (21.2) Improved

337 (21.1) Not Improved

51* No Response

29 dropped from study

*Did not answer question(s), questionnaire was returned.

105

of 78 cases were classified as having changed from *abstinent* to *not improved* between the 4- and 8-month follow-up intervals. Only 43 patients moved between the *abstinent* and *improved* categories between the 4- and 8-month follow-up periods.

The 8- to 12-month follow-up interval showed a slower change of *abstinent* than the 4- to 8-month interval. Only 4.6% of the 8-month *abstinent* cases reported alcohol use categorized as *not improved.* Movement from the *abstinent* category to the *improved* category between 8 and 12 months was 32 cases, proportionately lower than that reported for the previous 4 months.

Change from the 4-month *improved* category to the 8-month *abstinent* category was considerable, accounting for 116 (34.2%) of the 339 cases classified as *improved* at the 4-month follow-up interval. This shift appears to be largely due to the questionnaire categories. In formulating the alcohol use categories, 2-4 months of nonuse was classified as *improved* for the 4-month follow-up data and 8-10 months of nonuse was classified as *abstinent* for the 8-month follow-up data. If a patient's dry date was considered to have begun at the point of discharge from treatment it would be possible that the patient could be classified as *improved* at the 4-month follow-up interval and *abstinent* at the 8-month follow-up interval. Seventy-eight (23%) of the 339 cases classified as *improved* at 4 months after treatment were similarly classified at 8 months after treatment while 72 (21.2%) moved to the *not improved* category and a similar number shifted to the nonrespondent category.

Unlike the *improved* to *abstinent* shift between 4 and 8 months following treatment, which was partially explained as an artifact of questionnaire categories, the 8-month to 12-month change in cases shows more of the 212 improved patients remained improved (45.7%). Fewer cases either changed to *not improved* (52) or did not respond to the 12-month questionnaire (46) than during the previous 4 month interval.

Of the 1601 patients responding at the 4-month follow-up interval, 55.6% reported the same usage at the 8-month interval. Of the 1308 patients responding at the 8-month follow-up interval, 69.5% reported the same usage at the 12-month interval. According to these findings, stability of posttreatment alcohol use increases over time. Of the changes between the 4- and 8-month follow-up intervals (excluding shifts to the no response category) there was a similarity of movement in the direction of some drinking or more drinking (193 shifted to *improved* and *not improved*) as in the direction of less drinking or abstinence* (194 shifted to *improved* and *abstinent*). Between the 8- and 12-month follow-up, 61.8% of the 194 category changes were in the direction of some drinking or more drinking while the movement toward less drinking or abstinence represented only 38.1% of the changes. Of course, these changes

---

*Part of this shift may be accounted for as an artifact of the "time since last drink" categories referred to above.

are confounded by nonrespondents, specifically the 323 cases for which information was lost between the 4- and 8-month intervals, and the 205 cases that shifted to the no response category at the 12-month interval.

Return to Normal Drinking

The final research question to be taken up in the chapter asks, "What evidence is there from the Hazelden data to refute/support the claim that treated alcoholics can resume drinking without negative consequences?" In asking this question it is necessary to define what is meant by normal drinking. If it is agreed that alcoholism is characterized by excessive and inappropriate use of alcohol with associated negative consequences then it may be reasoned that normal drinking is nonexcessive and appropriate use of alcohol with no alcohol-associated negative occurrences in the drinker's life. The problem arises in determining drinking norms so that alcohol use may be judged either excessive or nonexcessive, appropriate or inappropriate. Even when those determinations are made it is difficult to connect negative occurrences to alcohol use with absolute certainty, although the evidence supporting these connections can, at times, be compelling.

Because the population being studied consists of persons who have been in an alcoholism rehabilitation program, it seems safe to conclude that they have histories of using alcohol excessively and/or inappropriately with associated negative consequences. Looking at the level of alcohol intake relative to what it was before treatment and making a comparative assessment of the social/psychological functioning before and after treatment should provide both a way of measuring drinking and the presence of negative consequences. Some of the preceding discussions are pertinent to this research question such as the consideration of stability or change of posttreatment alcohol use. Other data related to this question require an examination of a segment of the study population, i.e., the cases reporting not as much quantity used and 0-1 month since taking the last drink. Selected measures of social/psychological functioning will be introduced and responses contrasted between the three categories of posttreatment alcohol use with a more complete presentation of social/psychological functioning found in Chapter Seven.

With the exception of the 116 cases that shifted from *improved* to *abstinent* between the 4- and 8-month follow-ups (discussed above and shown in Table 5-15), the overall pattern of change in alcohol use for both the 4- to 8-month and the 8- to 12-month follow-up intervals is away from abstinence, with a more-or-less equal exchange of cases between the *improved* and *not improved* categories. There is no dramatic evidence from these drinking status changes to support the idea that one drink will trigger uncontrolled drinking. However, there is a clear indication that the *improved* cases are the most unstable in their use pattern over time.

How long does the slipping and sipping that characterizes the *improved,* and some of the *not improved,* cases continue? Because of the one-year limitation of the follow-up used in the present analysis, it is not possible to answer this question. In a previous 3½-year follow-up study of similar patients treated at Hazelden, 62% who drank in the first 1½ years following treatment were abstinent 3½ years after treatment. This outcome has been termed "delayed pathways to recovery" and suggests that posttreatment drinking, when considered in a time frame longer than one year after treatment, has the apparent consequence for the majority of drinkers of their eventually making a commitment to abstinence.[2]

An in-depth look at a segment of current drinkers classified as drinking less than before treatment should yield further insight into the question of drinking stability and change. At the 4-month follow-up, 248 patients reported drinking not as much in quantity with from 0-1 month since their last drink (Table 5-16). Four months later, at the 8-month follow-up, nearly one-quarter of these patients reported drinking that classified them as *improved,* one case was classified as *abstinent* and no information was available on 76 of the patients. One hundred eleven (44.8%) of the 248 cases were *not improved* at 8 months after treatment. Generally the same pattern held for the one-year interval after treatment with one more patient classified as abstinent and five more cases in the *not improved* (46.8%) category.

A more microscopic analysis of the 248 cases may be obtained by moving from the drinking categories to the specific response combinations reported at the follow-up intervals. Of the 248 cases, 39% reported at 8 months after treatment that they were drinking "not as much" with 0-1 month since the last drink and 32% were in the same response cell at the 12 month follow-up (at both time periods there was a 30% no response).

Table 5-16   Eight- and 12-Month Posttreatment Alcohol Use For 248 Patients Reporting Not as Much Quantity of Alcohol Used and 0-1 Month Since Their Last Drink at 4 MONTHS After Treatment

Drinking Categories	4 Mo.		8 Mo.		12 Mo.	
	f	%	f	%	f	%
Abstinent			1	.4	2	.8
Improved			60	24.2	56	22.6
Not Improved	248	100.0	111	44.8	116	46.8
No Information			76	30.6	74	29.9

Another way to look at currently drinking patients using not as much alcohol as before treatment is to identify those so classified at the 12-month follow-up and see what alcohol use they were reporting at the 4- and 8-month follow-up intervals. Two hundred ten patients reported not as much use of alcohol and 0-1 month since the last drink on the 12-month follow-up (Table 5-17). Eight months after treatment 55.7% of these patients were classified as *not improved* while slightly less than 10% were *abstinent,* 15 percent were *improved* and nearly 20% were nonrespondents. Dispensing with the drinking categories, half of the 210 cases classified 12 months after treatment as drinking not as much with 0-1 month since taking their last drink reported the same pattern at the 8-month follow-up and 38.1% had the same pattern of drinking at the 4-month follow-up.

Juxtaposing the reduced quantity drinkers at 4 months after treatment and the reduced quantity drinkers at 12 months after treatment gives the impression that a resumption of drinking early in the year following treatment will most likely result in continued drinking and that some drinking will lead to more drinking. By focusing on the cases drinking not as much one year following treatment, the drinking pattern becomes one of moving away from abstinence or infrequent alcohol use to greater or more frequent drinking, although less often than before treatment. Caution must be exercised in drawing these conclusions as a more detailed pattern of alcohol use should be considered. It may, however, be concluded that a pattern of either the same or greater alcohol use is not normal drinking as defined above.

The other normal drinking measure concerns comparative social/psychological functioning. For the present purpose, three indicators of social/psychological functioning will be used and their relationship with posttreatment alcohol use examined. These indicators are: 1) ability to handle problems, 2) self-image, and 3) general enjoyment of life.

Table 5-17 Four- and 8-Month Posttreatment Alcohol Use for 210 Patients Reporting Not as Much Quantity of Alcohol Used and 0-1 Month Since Their Last Drink at 12 MONTHS After Treatment

Drinking Categories	4 Mo.		8 Mo.		12 Mo.	
	f	%	f	%	f	%
Abstinent	60	28.6	20	9.5		
Improved	51	24.3	32	15.2		
Not Improved	88	41.9	117	55.7	210	100.0
No Information	11	5.2	41	19.5		

Table 5-18 Relationship Between Alcohol Use and Ability to Handle Problems ONE YEAR After Treatment

Problem Handling	Much Improved		Somewhat Improved		Same		Somewhat Worse		Much Worse		Total	
Alcohol Use	f	%	f	%	f	%	f	%	f	%	f	%
Abstinent	450	67.0	194	28.9	24	3.6	4	.6	0	—	672	54.9
Improved	120	55.0	81	37.2	16	7.3	1	.5	0	—	218	17.8
Not Improved	127	38.0	137	41.0	55	16.5	7	2.1	8	2.4	334	27.3
Total	697	56.9	412	33.7	95	7.8	12	1.0	8	.7	1224	100.0

$X^2 = 118.77$ df = 8 p < .01

As shown in Tables 5-18, 5-19, and 5-20, there are statistically significant relationships between the posttreatment improvement on the three social/psychological functioning indicators and the three posttreatment use alcohol use categories. The greatest improvement was reported for the *abstinent* patients, the least improvement for the *not improved* patients. *Improved* patients reported overall improvement similar to that of the *abstinent* patients but were more likely to report being *somewhat improved* rather than *much improved*. All three indicators of social/psychological improvements show this same pattern.

Even though these social/psychological functions differ by alcohol use, it should be noted that the overwhelming majority of all patients in the study population reported that they were improved in their ability to handle problems (90.6%), self-image (88.5%) and general enjoyment of life (87.0%). The *not improved* patients showed less social/psychological functioning improvement by these three measures than either the *abstinent* or *improved* patients,

Table 5-19 Relationship Between Alcohol Use and Self Image Functioning ONE YEAR After Treatment

Self Image Functioning	Much Improved		Somewhat Improved		Same		Somewhat Worse		Much Worse		Total	
Alcohol Use	f	%	f	%	f	%	f	%	f	%	f	%
Abstinent	473	70.4	163	24.3	28	4.2	6	.9	2	.3	672	55.0
Improved	117	53.4	82	37.4	10	4.6	7	3.2	3	1.4	219	17.9
Not Improved	119	36.0	128	38.7	53	16.0	21	6.3	10	3.0	331	27.1
Total	709	58.0	373	30.5	91	7.4	34	2.8	15	1.2	1222	100.0

$X^2 = 147.63$ df = 8 p < .01

Table 5-20 Relationship Between Alcohol Use and General Enjoyment of Life ONE YEAR After Treatment

Enjoyment of Life	Much Improved		Somewhat Improved		Same		Somewhat Worse		Much Worse		Total	
Alcohol Use	f	%	f	%	f	%	f	%	f	%	f	%
Abstinent	466	69.2	164	24.4	27	4.0	13	1.9	3	.4	673	54.9
Improved	128	58.4	62	28.3	20	9.1	4	1.8	5	2.3	219	17.9
Not Improved	121	36.3	124	37.2	57	17.1	18	5.4	13	3.9	333	27.2
Total	715	58.4	350	28.6	104	8.5	35	2.9	21	1.7	1225	100.0

$X^2 = 125.88$ $df = 8$ $p < .01$

but the report at one year after discharge is still high: 79% improvement in ability to handle problems, 75% improvement in self image and 73% improvement in general enjoyment of life. More *not improved* patients were only *somewhat improved* in their social/psychological functioning than patients either in the *abstinent* or *improved* alcohol use categories.

Using the aggregate social/psychological functioning and alcohol use outcome data and isolating one portion of drinkers—those currently using less alcohol than before treatment—provides evidence that: a) drinkers have less social/psychological functioning improvement than do abstainers, b) drinkers classified as *improved* in alcohol use are more *somewhat improved* in social/psychological functioning improvement than are abstainers, and c) drinkers who have moderated their quantity or frequency of alcohol use have unstable alcohol use patterns over time.

What does this say about "normal drinking" or, more specifically, what evidence is there from these data to either refute or support the claim that treated alcoholics can resume drinking without negative consequences? The findings presented here do not support the contention that treated alcoholics can resume drinking in moderation without negative consequences, although reduced drinking is associated with greater social/psychological functioning improvement than is the same or more drinking. The problem seems to be that it is difficult for the treated alcoholics in the study population to maintain reduced drinking over time, i.e., both the *improved* alcohol use and the reduced quantity cell of the *not improved* category are unstable over the follow-up intervals. There is, however, a problem in trying to state anything conclusive from the present data about "normal drinking" for treated alcoholics because the period of follow-up is too short to gain an appreciation of the full dynamic of either drinking with negative consequences or drinking followed by abstinence.

The 3½-year follow-up study referred to earlier is in agreement with the present data. It also suggests that over a longer period of time following treatment some alcoholics who drank during the year after treatment will move toward abstinence with a reduction of life problems and others will become more immersed in a pattern of regular drinking with an increase in associated life problems. Certainly, more studies of treated alcoholics over a time period of three or more years since treatment discharge will be needed if a more definitive answer to the question is to be found. Given the data available here it is safe to say that abstinence is highly related to a low incidence of negative consequences in the lives of treated alcoholics and that although the negative consequences are only slightly less frequent for patients who have reduced their drinking, maintaining a pattern of reduced drinking over time seems unlikely.

Conclusion

Most often when inquiries are made about chemical dependency treatment outcomes the inquirer expects to be told that the program has a certain "success rate"; that of the patients receiving treatment for chemical dependency a portion had favorable rehabilitation results. What this chapter has intended to communicate is that reporting treatment outcomes depends on numerous factors: a) What is the treatment population being studied? b) What adjustments are made for nonrespondents? c) What sociodemographic variables influence treatment outcome? d) What posttreatment behaviors and attitudes are associated with abstinence? e) How are the posttreatment dynamics of alcohol use handled? f) What about the possibility of "normal drinking" for some treated alcoholics?

Abstinence ranged between 50-55% for the year following treatment with the higher abstinence found for the study population consisting of patients who had completed treatment and excluding those abusing only drugs other than alcohol. This abstinence rate dropped when adjustments were made for nonrespondents and for combined alcohol and drug use.

For patients with both alcohol and drug problems who used drugs following treatment the pattern was moderate or infrequent drug use, which was classified as *improved*. A return to drinking was more uncommon than for patients who abused alcohol only, and resulted in the same or more alcohol use. Abstinence was more likely for patients between the ages 26-55 having more formal education and a Catholic religious preference.

Rather than trying to reach a single outcome percentage that represents the entire patient population it seems far more productive to appreciate the diversity of outcome found among the categories of patients being treated. Some patients come into treatment with high risk profiles and others with low risk profiles relative to the probability of abstinence. These differences need to be acknowledged in the treatment process. Perhaps more importantly, they become critical in aftercare planning and the posttreatment recovery process. Individual treatment plans can be helpful in maximizing the effectiveness of the treatment experience, but somehow the high risk outcome patients must be encouraged more strongly to use recovery resources, including AA and other means of gaining support and insight.

A return to drinking following treatment will not, in all probability, result in the establishment of a "normal drinking" pattern. Instead, drinking the same or more is related to low improvement in social/psychological functioning. Whereas moderate drinking is associated with greater social/psychological functioning improvement, it is still improbable that moderate drinking can be maintained for a long duration. What seems to occur is that some treated alcoholics return to drinking and clearly demonstrate for themselves that they cannot maintain their lives without negative consequences if they continue to drink. They then negotiate abstinence by way of this delayed pathway of proving to themselves that drinking won't work for them. Others return to the drinking and problems that they were experiencing before entering treatment. For them there will be continued difficulty with health, social relationships and psychological well-being as drinking continues (as will be shown in the following chapters). Some will eventually return to treatment, or in some way be forced into abstinence. Others will play out the tragic scenario of the long-term practicing alcoholic.

Reference Notes Chapter 5

[1] A. Campbell, P. E. Converse and W. L. Rodgers, *The quality of American life: Perceptions, evaluations and satisfactions.* New York: Russel Sage Foundation, 1976, pp. 231-238.

[2] D. Brissett, J. C. Laundergan, S. M. L. Kammeier and M. Biele, Drinkers and nondrinkers at three and a half years after treatment: Attitudes and growth. *J. of Studies on Alc.,* 1980, *41,* 945-952.

Chapter Six

Posttreatment Alcoholics Anonymous Attendance and Treatment Outcome

Alcoholics Anonymous (AA) is recognized by professional alcoholism practitioners and recovering alcoholics alike as probably the most valuable treatment method available for alcoholics. Many practitioners are themselves recovering alcoholics and have their personal experience and the experiences of their clients as testimony to the effectiveness of AA.

Recovering alcoholics find that AA outlines a set of principles which prescribe a life-style and value orientation effective in guiding recovery from alcoholism. AA members who are seriously working their programs make it clear that AA has succeeded in keeping them from active alcoholism while promoting personal growth. However, such individual case histories raise important research questions that need to be considered by examining treatment outcomes for a larger number of recovering alcoholics.

Two of the research questions are: 1) What effect does posttreatment AA participation have on alcohol use outcomes? and 2) What are the sociodemographic, treatment and follow-up characteristics of alcoholics who affiliate with AA in contrast with nonaffiliates?

The first question has received considerable research attention which generally shows favorable recovery results with AA involvement. However, according to Leach and Norris, "No valid claim to a success rate can be established for AA,—because no records are kept either on how many alcoholics are exposed to AA only to go away and die unremitted, or how many alcoholics who, after minimal exposure to AA, go away and recover."[1] The same authors have been working on an analysis of the AA General Service Board "sobriety census" for 1968 and 1971 which represents an internal effort to determine AA effectiveness by surveying some AA members. Slightly over 60% of the AA members studied in these two time periods (60.3% out of 6,861 in 1968 and 60.6% out of 3,636 in 1971) were found to have been sober one or more years.[2] This consistent finding obtained in two separate surveys is impressive but, as Leach and Norris caution, it does not give a clear indication of the "success rate" for AA. To satisfactorily determine the "success rate" of AA it would be necessary to maintain detailed records of all who either are or have been affiliated with AA and to make contact with this population in order to determine the impact that AA has had on their recovery process.

Lacking such complete information, much of what is known about the success of AA as a means of recovery from alcoholism comes from follow-up studies of alcoholics who have received treatment for their condition in either a residential or outpatient program. Kish and Herman found a significant relationship between AA attendance and degree of improvement, although a relatively small portion of their follow-up population attended AA frequently.[3] Robson, et. al., identified motivation (measured by attitude toward treatment) and posttreatment AA attendance as the most important variables in predicting successful rehabilitation.[4] Repeatedly, the variable of posttreatment AA attendance has been identified as positively related to abstinence.[5, 6] Abstinence, in turn, has been found to be associated with favorable social, occupational and physical functioning.[7]

The second research question concerning the characteristics of AA affiliates has been examined descriptively by Trice[8] as a social process and again by Trice and Roman[9] using multivariate analysis of treatment follow-up to identify sociophysiological characteristics of AA affiliates. Affiliative and group dependency needs, physical stability, guilt proneness and intensive external labeling were found to be the attributes most associated with successful AA affiliation (measured as attendance at least twice a week for one year). Other researchers have found AA affiliates to be more often unmarried[10] and middle class.[11]

This chapter will further explore the two research questions using follow-up data gathered from the Hazelden study population (1,652). Recovery from alcoholism may be viewed both as abstinence from alcohol and maintenance of a "quality" sobriety. Both aspects of recovery need to be considered in examining the effectiveness of AA in promoting recovery from active alcoholism.

AA Participation: Effect on Recovery

The measure of AA participation used in the analysis was developed from patient responses at 12 months after treatment. There was some attrition in frequent AA attendance over the three follow-up intervals as shown in Tables 6-1 and 6-2. Nonetheless, there was a remarkable stability in the overall pattern with more than 90% of the frequent AA participators at both 4 and 8 months after discharge also frequent participators 12 months after leaving treatment.

Frequent AA participation was found to be associated with alcohol abstinence at 4, 8 and 12 months after discharge from treatment (Tables 6-3, 6-4 and 6-5). The actual number of *abstinent,* frequent AA participators declined slightly between the time periods but, in general, relationship between the *abstinent* and frequent AA attendance categories remains similar for all three intervals. The overall *abstinent* category was reduced by 6.1% from the 4-month to the 12-month follow-up periods, in spite of a small increase over the 4-month percentage shown at 8-months. Within the *not improved* category, there was an increase of 9.1%, with the largest part of this increase taking place between the 8- and 12-months intervals. Most of the growth in the *not improved* category appeared to come from the "do not attend" AA category while the proportion in the *improved* category showed an irregular decline.

At 4 months after treatment 110 *not improved* patients reported frequent AA attendance. Similarly, 107 *not improved* patients reported frequent AA

Table 6-1 AA Attendance at 4 Months by AA Attendance at 12 Months

12 Mo. 4 Mo.	Frequent		Infrequent		Do Not Attend		Total	
	f	%	f	%	f	%	f	%
> Once a week	465	35.3	48	3.6	32	2.4	545	41.4 ⟩72.8
Once a week	255	19.4	83	6.3	75	5.7	413	31.4
2-3 times a mo.	27	2.1	38	2.9	30	2.3	95	7.2
> Once a month	11	1.4	27	2.1	16	1.2	54	4.1 ⟩15.8
Once a month	6	.5	19	1.4	34	2.6	59	4.5
Do not attend	15	1.1	11	.8	124	9.4	150	11.3 ⟩11.3
Total	779	59.8	226	17.1	311	23.6	1316	

$$\chi^2 = 612.12, \text{df} = 10, \text{p} < .001$$

Table 6-2 AA Attendance at 8 Months by AA Attendance at 12 Months

8 Mo. \ 12 Mo.	Frequent		Infrequent		Do Not Attend		Total		
	f	%	f	%	f	%	f	%	
> Once a week	415	34.5	21	1.7	10	.8	446	37.1	63.9
Once a week	245	20.4	55	4.6	23	1.9	323	26.8	
2-3 times a mo.	28	2.3	40	3.3	12	1.0	80	6.7	
> Once a month	12	1.0	33	2.7	12	1.0	57	4.7	18.5
Once a month	10	11.6	34	2.8	42	3.5	86	7.1	
Do not attend	12	1.0	23	1.9	176	14.6	211	17.5	17.5
Total	722	70.8	206	17.0	275	22.8	1203		

$$\chi^2 = 914.64, df = 10, p < .001$$

attendance at the 8-month follow-up interval. At 12 months after treatment 130 were *not improved* and attending AA frequently. Although AA attendance is highly related to abstinence, between 15 and 18% of the frequent AA attenders were *not improved*. It is not part of the present purpose to consider *not improved* frequent AA attenders in detail, although the recovery pattern of this grouping certainly warrants further examination. It is important to make clear that not all frequent AA attenders are *abstinent,* and that a portion of those drinking have used alcohol in what has been categorized as a *not improved* fashion.

Table 6-3 Alcohol Use at 4 Months by AA Attendance at 12 Months

4 Mo. \ 12 Mo.	Frequent		Infrequent		Do Not Attend		Total	
	f	%	f	%	f	%	f	%
Abstinent	509	39.2	126	9.7	150	11.6	785	60.6
Improved	152	11.7	52	4.0	68	5.3	272	21.0
Not improved	110	8.5	40	3.1	88	6.8	338	18.4
Total	771	59.4	218	16.8	306	23.7	1395	100.0

$$\chi^2 = 37.48, df = 4, p < .001$$

Table 6-4 Alcohol Use at 8 Months by AA Attendance at 12 Months

8 Mo. \ 12 Mo.	Frequent		Infrequent		Do Not Attend		Total	
	f	%	f	%	f	%	f	%
Abstinent	488	41.6	118	10.1	132	11.3	738	63.0
Improved	108	9.2	33	2.8	40	3.4	181	15.4
Not improved	107	9.1	49	4.2	97	8.3	253	21.6
Total	703	59.9	200	17.1	269	23.0	1172	100.0

$$\chi^2 = 53.68, df = 4, p < .001$$

The effectiveness of frequent AA participation in promoting abstinence has been supported, but how is frequent AA participation related to improved social/psychological functioning? Examining this question using bivariate analysis yields the findings below.*

- Frequent AA participation was positively related with improvement in job performance and participation in community affairs.
- Frequent AA participation was positively related to increased Higher Power contact as well as to an improved relationship with a Higher Power.

Table 6-5 Alcohol Use at 12 Months by AA Attendance at 12 Months

12 Mo. \ 12 Mo.	Frequent		Infrequent		Do Not Attend		Total	
	f	%	f	%	f	%	f	%
Abstinent	457	36.8	108	8.7	112	9.0	677	54.5
Improved	141	11.4	45	3.6	38	3.1	224	18.0
Not improved	130	10.5	61	4.9	150	12.1	341	27.5
Total	728	58.7	214	17.2	300	24.2	1242	100.0

$$\chi^2 = 112.62, df = 4, p < .001$$

---

*The interaction between improved social/psychological functioning and both posttreatment alcohol use and AA participation is, however, more complex than suggested by the bivariate analysis.

- Frequent AA participation was not positively related in an improved relationship with a spouse but was positively related to improved relationships with children, other relatives and friends.

Analysis of the follow-up data supports the previous findings that AA participation is effective in promoting recovery from alcoholism. Not only was frequent AA participation related to abstinence but it was also associated with indicators for improved social/psychological functioning including job performance, community involvement and spiritual and social relationships. These findings, and the consensus of previous research findings on this question, suggest the second research question: "What are the characteristics of alcoholics who affiliate with AA?"

Characteristics of AA Participators

Fifty-nine percent of the patients in the study population were classified as frequent AA participators, 17% as infrequent participators and 24% as non-participators. A number of patient sociodemographic, treatment and follow-up variables were considered relative to frequent AA participation with the following results.

- Frequent AA participation was not related to length of stay ($\overline{X}=34$ days), number of counselor interviews ($\overline{X}=9$), number of clergy interviews ($\overline{X}=3$) or prior chemical dependency-related hospitalizations ($\overline{X}=1$).
- Frequent AA participation was not related to the type of drinking (daily, binge, etc.) prior to treatment or to abstinence prior to treatment.
- Frequent AA participation was proportionately greater for female patients than for male patients (67% female, 56% male).
- Frequent AA participation was proportionately less for patients under 21 and over 60 years of age than for patients between 21 and 60 years of age (38% under 21, 44% over 60, 62% between 21 and 60).
- Frequent AA participation was proportionately greater for married patients than for currently unmarried patients (63% married and 53% unmarried).
- Frequent AA participation was proportionately greater for patients having attended or graduated from college than for patients with high school educations or less (65% college, 52% high school or less).
- Frequent AA participation was proportionately greater for patients living outside the metropolitan Twin Cities area than for residents of the nine-county Twin Cities metropolitan area (61% outside Twin Cities, 55% Twin Cities metro).
- Frequent AA participation was slightly greater proportionately for patients abusing both alcohol and drugs prior to treatment than for

patients abusing only alcohol prior to treatment (62% alcohol and drugs, 58% alcohol only).

- Frequent AA participation was not proportionately different between Catholics and noncatholics (60% Catholics, 59% noncatholics).

Some of the relationships between frequent AA participation and patient sociodemographic characteristics were interrelated. For example, the difference in frequent AA attendance between residents of the metropolitan Twin Cities area and the geographic area outside of the Twin Cities area was found to be related both to patient age and sex. A larger proportion of the nonmetropolitan Twin Cities population was female and a smaller proportion was aged 21 and under when contrasted with the metropolitan Twin Cities patients. The higher participation of females and lower participation of youth in AA have the effect in the bivariate analysis of showing lower AA participation for the metro Twin Cities area. Because of these and other interrelationships between the variables, multivariate analysis was used which controlled for variable interaction. The sociodemographic, treatment and follow-up variables were analyzed using a stepwise multiple regression to determine the characteristics that were most salient in explaining AA participation. The results of this analysis are shown in Table 6-6.

Two of the treatment and follow-up variables were identified as explaining 11.1% of the variance in AA participation. The variable referred to as Higher Power contact, which represented increased prayer and meditation since treatment, explained 8.5% of the variance and was, therefore, the strongest

Table 6-6 Prediction of AA Attendance by Sociodemographic, Treatment and Follow-up Variables

	Standardized Coefficient (Beta)	% Variance Explained
Higher power	.214	8.48
Treatment group	.176	2.90
Education	−.127	1.52
Marital status	−.119	1.26
Sex	.103	.86
Total		15.02

single predictor of AA participation. Of course, it is not known for certain if patients who had increased their prayer and meditation were more likely to attend AA frequently or whether frequent AA attenders were more likely to have increased their prayer and meditation. But, interpretation of sequence that will be discussed further in the next chapter places increased prayer and meditation sequentially prior to frequent AA participation.

The second strongest predictor of frequent AA attendance was the patient's posttreatment assessment of group activities in treatment which explained 2.9% of the variance in AA attendance. Patients who favorably rated the helpfulness of group therapy, supportive confrontation, counselor and clergy meetings and informal conversation with other patients while in treatment were AA attenders. Although group activities in treatment is a retrospective measure it may be seen as a motivational indicator similar to that used by Robson and his associates who found posttreatment AA attendance positively related to abstinence.

The three sociodemographic variables, education, marital status and sex were identified in combination to explain 3.6% of the variance in AA attendance. As pointed out above, being better educated, currently married and female are all related to frequent AA attendance. (The negative regression coefficients for education and marital status represent an inverse relationship that resulted from the coding arrangement of these two variables.)

Both the "Higher Power" and "treatment-group" variables suggested differences in recovering alcoholics' capacity for and willingness to relate outside themselves. Patients who learned to relate to a Higher Power and to benefit from the group dimension of treatment were most likely to be frequent AA attenders following treatment. In contrast, frequent AA attendance was less probable for patients who had not learned to use resources outside themselves.

The analysis of posttreatment AA participation has contributed additional empirical support to the claim of AA effectiveness in promoting recovery from alcoholism. Not only were frequent AA attenders more likely to be abstinent, but they were more likely to have shown improvements in personal and social functioning.

In answer to the question, "What are the characteristics of AA affiliates?", five patient attributes were identified as the best predictors of patients who would become frequent AA attenders. Patients who developed the ability to relate outside of themselves as indicated by increased Higher Power contact and a favorable rating of group related treatment activities were probable frequent AA participators. This probability of frequent AA attendance was greater for patients who were better educated, married and female.

What are the implications of these findings for treatment practitioners? The findings may be summarized as: *unmarried patients with low education who have trouble relating in group settings and developing comfortable means of maintaining contact with a Higher Power are least likely to attend AA regularly following treatment and therefore have a higher risk of using alcohol and not realizing improved social/psychological functioning.* Treatment personnel need to view patient relational development as equivalent in importance to treatment objectives such as breaking the denial system and developing a personal inventory. In practice, this means that patients need to be tutored in meaningful relational skill development, both spiritual and interpersonal. Developing an improved capability in relational skills should result in frequent AA attendance which will, in turn, both enhance these skills and contribute to abstinence and personal growth.

Reference Notes Chapter 6

[1]G. B. Leach and J. L. Norris, Factors in the development of Alcoholics Anonymous (A.A.). In B. Kissin and H. Begleiter (eds.) *The biology of alcoholism: Treatment and rehabilitation of the chronic alcoholic* (Vol. 5) New York: Plenum Press, 1977, p. 459.

[2]Ibid., p. 498.

[3]G. B. Kish and H. T. Herman, The Fort Meade alcoholism treatment programs: A follow-up study. *Quart. J. of Studies on Alc.*, 1971, *32,* 628-635.

[4]R. A. Robson, H. I. Paulus and G. G. Clarke, An evaluation of the effect of a clinic treatment program on the rehabilitation of alcoholic patients. *Quart. J. of Studies on Alc.*, 1965, *26,* 264-278.

[5]F. Baekeland, L. Lundwall and B. Kissin, Methods for the treatment of chronic alcoholism: A critical appraisal. In R. J. Gibbins, Y. Israel, H. Kalant, R. E. Popham, W. Schmidt and R. G. Smart, *Research advances in alcohol and drug problems* (Vol. 2) New York: John Wiley & Sons., 1975.

[6]Leach, op. cit., p. 464.

[7]D. L. Gerard, G. Saenger and R. Wile, The abstinent alcoholic. *Arch. of Gen. Psychiat.*, 1962, *6,* 83-95.

[8]H. M. Trice, A study of the process of affiliation with Alcoholics Anonymous. *Quart. J. of Studies on Alc.*, 1970, *31,* 932-949.

[9]H. M. Trice and P. M. Roman, Sociopsychological predictors of affiliation with Alcoholics Anonymous: A longitudinal study of treatment success. *Social Psychiatry,* 1970, *5,* 51-59.

[10]M. D. Gynther and P. I. Brilliant, Marital status, remission to hospital, and intrapersonal and interpersonal perceptions of alcoholics. *Quart. J. of Studies on Alc.* 1971, *32,* 628-635.

[11]R. K. Jones, Sectarian characteristics of Alcoholics Anonymous. *Sociology,* 1970, *4,* 181-195.

Chapter Seven

Social/Psychological Functioning and Development of an Empirically Based Model of Treatment Outcome

Mention has been made in the preceding chapters of social/psychological functioning improvement during the year after treatment for alcoholism. In the present chapter, posttreatment social/psychological functioning improvement will be the principal focus or dependent variable. Detailed attention to social/psychological functioning has been reserved for elaboration because it is seen as the primary measure of treatment outcome.

Since the alcoholic's reduced life quality or level of social/psychological functioning is considered to be a problem brought about by inappropriate, repetitive use of alcohol (the social/psychological maladaption discussed in Chapter Two), abstinence from alcohol is considered a requisite to improved social/psychological functioning. The objective of treatment is to create patient awareness of the effect that alcohol has had on social/psychological functioning, to demonstrate that abstinence from alcohol will be a necessary first step in bringing about an improvement in social/psychological functioning and to show that through the fellowship and program of AA it will be possible to work toward a quality sobriety consisting of abstinence and personally satisfying social/psychological functioning. Accordingly, improved social/psychological functioning is the principal goal of treatment which is achievable through the combined means of AA participation and abstinence from alcohol and other mood-altering substances. The present purpose is to empirically examine this principal treatment goal in relation to other socio-demographic, treatment and posttreatment variables.

E. Mansell Pattison has been a most persistent advocate of considering social/psychological functioning as a principal treatment outcome variable. In a recent discussion of this position he states, "If we consider rehabilitation in terms of total 'life health,' then we may consider subsets of rehabilitation outcome in terms of the following: (1) Drinking Health, (2) Emotional Health, (3) Vocational Health, (4) Interpersonal Health, and (5) Physical Health."[1] Pattison contends that impairment need not occur in all five life health subsets. In fact, improvement may take place in subsets two through five without abstinence, according to Pattison, who further contends that abstinence from alcohol is not necessarily related to improvement in subsets two through five.

The measures of social/psychological functioning used in the present analysis are related to Pattison's life health subsets and will be used to examine (a) the empirical reality of the subsets, (b) the contention that social/psychological improvement can take place without abstinence, and (c) that abstinence and social/psychological functioning improvement are not related. Examination of these contentions is within the purview of the final research question to be considered: What sociodemographic, treatment and posttreatment variables explain social/psychological functioning improvement during the year following treatment? Later in the chapter a path model of the relationships between selected variables will be presented and explored.

Social/Psychological Functioning Improvement

Twelve items were used to measure social/psychological functioning improvement. For each of the items the respondent was to check the most appropriate of five categories ranging from "much improved" to "much worse" with a "does not apply" response category also available. The respondents were instructed to compare the way in which they dealt with each of the items before treatment and the way in which they dealt with the items at the time of response to the questionnaire. Three items that relate to Pattison's subset Emotional Health were self-image, enjoyment of life and ability to handle problems. Five items were designed to measure Interpersonal Health: relationship with relatives, relationship with friends, relationship with Higher Power, ability to accept help, and ability to give help. The Higher Power relationship item may not be considered interpersonal but it is certainly in the area of relational skill. Two items correspond to Vocational Health: job performance and ability to manage finances. Physical Health has a single item measured: physical health. Drinking Health a single measure, ability to accept need for abstinence.

Are the life health subsets as related to the social/psychological functioning improvement items empirically distinct from each other? The statistical tool of factor analysis was used to address this question. Factor analysis indicates whether a number of measures constitute one or more measurement dimensions. The factor scores for the twelve social/psychological functioning improvement measures shown in Table 7-1 were found to constitute a single factor rather than to support the five subsets of life health suggested by Pattison. Interpretation of the factor analysis indicates that social/psychological functioning improvement should be seen as constituting a single dimension rather than subsets. Therefore, in most of the following analysis a single dimension of social/psychological functioning improvement will be measured by an overall factor score.

In looking at Table 7-1, it will be noted that the three items associated with Emotional Health have the highest individual factor score coefficients. This factor loading suggests that within the single factor of social/psychological improvement, enjoyment of life, ability to handle problems and self-image capture much of the essence of the overall measure. This finding shows that improvements in interpersonal relationships, physical health and job per-

Table 7-1 Social/Psychological Functioning Improvement One Year After Treatment Discharge

	Factor Score Coefficients
1. Relationships with Relatives	.074
2. Relationships with Friends	.115
3. Relationships with Higher Power	.071
4. Job Performance	.111
5. Physical Health	.093
6. Self Image	.137
7. Enjoyment of Life	.160
8. Ability to Handle Problems	.156
9. Ability to Accept Help	.101
10. Ability to Give Help	.116
11. Ability to Manage Finances	.087
12. Ability to Accept Need for Abstinence	.082

formance are directly reflected in improved emotional health. Put another way, an enhanced enjoyment of life, self-image and ability to handle problems may be said to result as a corollary to improvement in the other indicators of social/psychological functioning.

How are these individual measures of social/psychological functioning related to alcohol use/nonuse following treatment? Abstinence at 4, 8 and 12 months after treatment is significantly related to greater social/psychological functioning improvement for each of the twelve measures at 4, 8 and 12 months as shown in Table 7-2. These data support the idea that, while patients with a pattern of posttreatment drinking show social/psychological functioning improvement, they do not show it to the same extent as abstainers. The relationship between functioning improvement and alcohol use is consistent, as graphically shown by the three emotional health measures (Figure 7-1). This pattern has been repeatedly confirmed in separate analyses of the Hazelden follow-up data. The interpretation of this finding is that overall quality of life

Table 7-2 Relationship* Between Social/Psychological Functioning Measures and Alcohol Use at 4-, 8-, and 12-Month Follow-ups

	4 mo.		8 mo.		12 mo.	
	χ^2	p	χ^2	p	χ^2	p
Relationship with Relatives	49.55	< .01	41.33	< .01	53.02	< .01
Relationship with Friends	73.85	< .01	68.15	< .01	100.78	< .01
Relationship with Higher Power	132.52	< .01	115.19	< .01	110.07	< .01
Job Performance	83.13	< .01	33.98	< .01	77.04	< .01
General Physical Health	73.14	< .01	55.54	< .01	85.30	< .01
Self Image	176.52	< .01	98.36	< .01	147.63	< .01
General Enjoyment of Life	154.82	< .01	102.76	< .01	125.88	< .01
Ability to Handle Problems	131.85	< .01	104.75	< .01	118.77	< .01
Ability to Accept Help	85.28	< .01	83.97	< .01	110.77	< .01
Ability to Give Help	83.16	< .01	87.62	< .01	95.93	< .01
Ability to Manage Finances	79.19	< .01	50.93	< .01	72.86	< .01
Acceptance of Need for Abstinence	241.57	< .01	209.35	< .01	304.72	< .01

*df = 8

Figure 7-1 Relationship Between Posttreatment Alcohol Use and Emotional Health Improvement

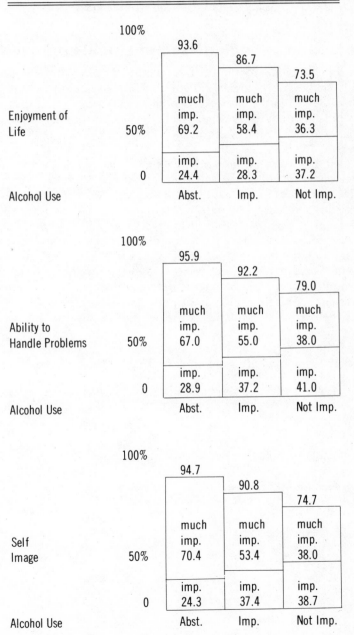

for those using alcohol is lower than for abstainers although treatment is beneficial to the social/psychological functioning improvement of patients in all three alcohol use categories.

Prediction of Social/Psychological Improvement

What other sociodemographic, treatment and posttreatment variables are related to social/psychological functioning improvement? This question will be approached as in the previous two chapters by using multiple regression analysis but this time with social/psychological functioning improvement as the dependent variable. Results of the multiple regression analysis are shown in Table 7-3.

The most important variable in explaining social/psychological functioning improvement was "collective activities in treatment." Positive evaluation of collective activities in treatment (group therapy, informal conversations with patients, the "hot seat," meetings with counselors and meetings with clergy) may be seen, in part, as a kind of motivational indicator and, in part, as a treatment process indicator. In the prediction of posttreatment social/psychological functioning improvement, "collective activities" accounted for 16% of the variance. The second most important predictor of improved social/psychological functioning, posttreatment abstinence, accounted for 7% of the variance. This finding could be anticipated from the strong relationship between the social/psychological variables and abstinence that was just discussed.

Unlike the multiple regression analysis findings for either alcohol abstinence at 12 months after treatment where 18% of the variance was ex-

Table 7-3 Prediction of Posttreatment Social/Psychological Functioning

Variable	Standardized Coefficient (Beta)	% Variance Explained
Collective Activities in Treatment	.236	15.91
Alcohol Use	.247	6.99
Private Activities in Treatment	.163	6.16
Higher Power	.266	6.13
Marital Status	.064	.01
Total		35.20

plained, or posttreatment AA attendance where 15% of the variance was explained, a total of 35% of the variance was explained in the prediction of social/psychological functioning improvement. This large percent of explained variance is accounted for by the predictive strength of two variables, "private activities in treatment" and "Higher Power," each of which was nearly as powerful a predictor of social/psychological functioning improvement as was abstinence at one year after treatment. Private activities in treatment (positive evaluation of reading, time alone, meditation, lecture and the environmental setting) accounted for 6.16% of the variance and "Higher Power" (increased prayer and/or meditation after treatment) accounted for 6.13% of the variance. Abstinence at 12 months after treatment, combined with favorable rating of private activities in treatment and increased prayer and meditation explained nearly 20% of the variance in social/psychological functioning. Following these variables, the amount of variance explained declines abruptly. Marital status, by contrast, explained only .01% of the variance in posttreatment functioning improvement.

What do the four strong predictors of posttreatment functioning improvement say about treatment outcome and how are they related back to rehabilitation goals? One primary long-range rehabilitation goal is abstinence and the other is improved life-style. The analysis of follow-up data clearly supports abstinence as being positively related to improved social/psychological functioning which is another way of saying improved life-style. Favorable ratings of collective and private activities in treatment are more difficult to interpret.

As previously mentioned, there is a motivational aspect to favorable treatment ratings. If the treatment experience served as a catalyst to taking actions seen as necessary for recovery, the extent to which the patient may be said to be motivated in that recovery is likely to be reflected in the ratings of treatment activities one year after discharge. The motivational component in the ratings of both collective and private activities in treatment is more suggestive than definitive. Because of the strong predictive performance of the treatment rating measures, it may be concluded that more rigorous measurement of patient recovery motivation be a recommended part of future research on alcoholism treatment outcomes.

The other part of the treatment rating measures of collective and private activities in treatment has to do with the way in which a patient tracks through the treatment experience. Findings presented thus far do not show sociodemographic variables to be especially useful as predictors of treatment outcome. Similarly, the psychological variable as measured by the Minnesota Multiphasic Inventory (MMPI) were so low in their predictive power that they were eliminated from the variable pool in the preliminary analysis. In contrast, the multivariate analysis places the ratings of collective and private activities in treatment as important predictors of treatment outcome. It is recognized in treatment that different patients move through the phases of treatment at different rates. One patient may need to spend more time and effort working on breaking the denial system while another patient may remain stalled at the formulation of a meaningful Higher Power understanding. The importance of the varying patterns of patients' movement through the treatment experience has been largely ignored in alcoholism treatment outcome studies although it has been recognized as important in other treatment outcome research.[2] The predictive importance of the collective and private activity ratings suggests that it may be very productive to try to explain treatment outcome by way of more detailed measurement of patients' progress through the treatment process.

Increased prayer and meditation following treatment (Higher Power variable) also appears as an important predictor of social/psychological functioning improvement. This variable explained only .42% of the variance in the prediction of abstinence but was the major explainer of variance in the AA participation accounting for 8.48% of the variance. In the explanation of variance in the social/psychological functioning improvement, the Higher Power variable explains 6.13% of the variance. The consistent appearance of the Higher Power variable in the prediction of the three dependent variables (posttreatment alcohol use/nonuse, posttreatment AA participation, and posttreatment social/psychological functioning improvement) is consistent with the spiritual emphasis of the Hazelden treatment approach and in a larger context, the Minnesota Model of treatment. Patients who increase their prayer and/or meditation as a way of maintaining a spiritual relationship are more likely to have favorable treatment outcomes than are patients who do not increase prayer and/or meditation following treatment. This finding strongly reinforces the centrality of the spiritual aspect of the alcoholism recovery process and thereby supports the inclusion of the spiritual emphasis within the treatment rehabilitation process.

A Path Model of Posttreatment Recovery

Thus far, ten variables have been identified through multiple regression analysis as predictors of the three dependent variables (posttreatment alcohol use/nonuse, posttreatment AA attendance, and posttreatment social/psychological functioning improvement). After their identification, these ten variables were used in the construction of a path model of alcoholism recovery process where improved social/psychological functioning was positioned as the recovery goal or end point in the chain of variables. It will be remembered that in the construction of the path model a causal sequence of variables is logically formulated and in doing so it is assumed that an order among the variables is both known and causally closed. After the path model has been determined, a path analysis is performed where linear relationships among the variables are calculated. The calculation shows the direct effect of each variable in the path model on the variables that follow in sequence while statistically controlling for other relevant variables.

The ten variables that comprise the path model are: 1) sex, 2) education, 3) marital status, 4) rating of private activities in treatment, 5) ratings of collective activities in treatment, 6) number of posttreatment hospitalizations, 7) Higher Power (increased prayer and/or meditation), 8) posttreatment AA participation, 9) posttreatment alcohol use, and 10) posttreatment social/psychological functioning improvement. These ten variables were ordered first by selecting the set of biodemographic variables. The three biodemographic variables were, in turn, ordered by whether the characteristic was ascribed or achieved. Sex is an ascribed or given characteristic so it was designated as the first variable in the path model sequence. Education and marital status are both achieved or earned characteristics with education logically preceding marital status although there may be some chronological overlap during the years of higher education. Education was therefore placed as the second variable in the path model and marital status third.

Both private and collective ratings of treatment activities, comprising the treatment variable set, were placed next in the path model. Private activities were placed prior to collective activities with the somewhat tenuous rationale that private activities, because they were more personal and psychological, should be placed prior to collective activities with their interactional involvement.

The posttreatment set of variables began with the "number of posttreatment hospitalizations" variable which was seen as a weak but necessary variable in the linear sequencing. Next, the Higher Power variable was selected to follow the "posttreatment hospitalizations" variable and precede the AA participation variable. This placement is empirically supportable. According to the multiple regression, the Higher Power variable, because of its predictive power in explaining AA attendance, should come before the AA participation variable. Frequent AA attendance can, and probably does, lead to greater frequency of prayer and meditation. But, for the purposes of the path model, the strong predictive power of the Higher Power variable in explaining frequent AA attendance was used to determine the linear sequencing.

The three outcome variables were arranged differently in the path model than in the order of chapters. In the path model, AA attendance was placed as the first of the three outcome variables in that it was seen as a means to the goal of abstinence. Abstinence in turn, was viewed as a strong predictor of social/psychological functioning improvement. This ordering was done with the recognition that there are some frequent AA attenders who are concurrently drinking.[3, 4] Also, the relatively high level of social/psychological functioning improvement for drinkers needs to be acknowledged in positing the causal ordering leading up to the end point in the model which stands as the principal goal of alcoholism recovery—social/psychological functioning improvement. The resulting path model is shown in Figure 7-2.

The path analysis following the path model is shown in Figure 7-3. At first glance the number of arrows and the path coefficients shown in the path analysis seem confusing, but if it is kept in mind that this represents a linear diagram where the relationships are calculated following their sequential order the meaning of the analysis becomes more discernable. The relationships between the variables will be highlighted according to their sequential order in the following summary statements.

1. Sex

Sex—Private Activities (path coefficient .058) represents a weak relationship where females are more positive in their ratings of private activities in treatment than are males.

Sex—Higher Power (path coefficients .078) represents a weak to moderate relationship where females show greater increases in prayer and meditation than do males.

Sex—Marital Status (path coefficient .100) represents a moderate relationship of more females being single than males.

Figure 7-2 Alcoholism Recovery Path Model

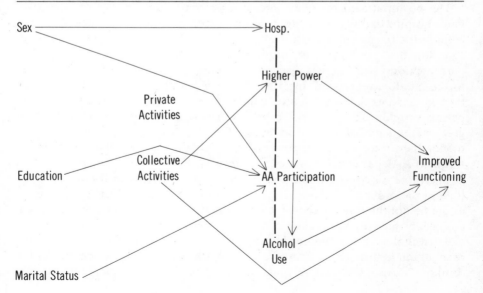

Figure 7-3 Alcoholism Recovery Path Diagram

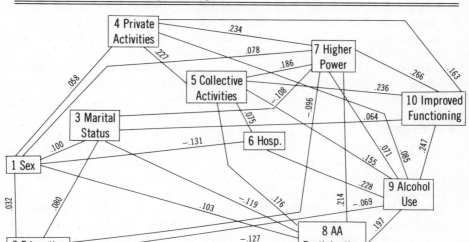

Sex—Number of Hospitalizations (path coefficient –.131) represents a moderate relationship of more females having more posttreatment hospitalizations than males.

Sex—AA Attendance (path coefficient .103) represents a moderate relationship where females attend AA more frequently than do males.

Sex—Education (this is a noncausal relationship and should be ignored for the present purpose).

2. *Education*

Education—Marital Status (path coefficient .080) represents a weak to moderate relationship where those with lower education are less often married than are those with higher education.

Education—Higher Power (path coefficient –.096) represents a weak to moderate relationship where those with more education show greater prayer and meditation increases than do those with less education.

Education—Alcohol Use (path coefficient –.069) represents a weak relationship where those with more education are more often abstinent than are those with less education.

Education—AA Attendance (path coefficient –.127) represents a moderate relationship where those with more education have greater AA attendance than those with less education.

3. *Marital Status*

Marital Status—Higher Power (path coefficient –.108) represents a moderate relationship where married persons have more increase in prayer and meditation than do unmarried persons.

Marital Status—Functioning Improvement (path coefficient .064) represents a weak relationship where married persons have greater social/psychological functioning improvement than nonmarried persons.

Marital Status—AA Attendance (path coefficient –.119) represents a moderate relationship where married persons have more frequent AA attendance than unmarried persons.

4. Private Activities

Private Activities—Functioning Improvement (path coefficient .163) represents a moderately strong relationship where those who rate private activities in treatment favorably are more improved in their social/psychological functioning than are those who rate these activities unfavorably.

Private Activities—Higher Power (path coefficient .234) represents a strong relationship where those who rate private activities in treatment favorably show a greater increase in their posttreatment prayer and meditation than do those who rate these activities unfavorably.

Private Activities—Alcohol Use (path coefficient .085) represents a weak to moderate relationship where those who rate private activities in treatment favorably are more abstinent than those who rate these activities unfavorably.

5. Collective Activities

Collective Activities—Higher Power (path coefficient .186) represents a moderately strong relationship where those who rate collective activities in treatment favorably show a greater increase in their posttreatment prayer and meditation than those who rate these activities unfavorably.

Collective Activities—Functioning Improvement (path coefficient .236) represents a strong relationship where those who rate collective activities in treatment favorably show greater posttreatment functioning improvement than do those who rate these activities unfavorably.

Collective Activities—Alcohol Use (path coefficient .155) represents a moderately strong relationship where those who rate collective activities in treatment favorably show greater abstinence than do those who rate these activities unfavorably.

Collective Activities—Number of Hospitalizations (path coefficient .075) represents a weak to moderate relationship where those who rate collective activities in treatment favorably have more posttreatment hospitalizations than do those who rate these activities unfavorably.

Collective Activities—AA Attendance (path coefficient .176) represents a moderately strong relationship where those who rate collective activities in treatment favorably have greater posttreatment AA attendance than do those who rate these activities unfavorably.

6. Number of Hospitalizations

Number of Hospitalizations—Alcohol Use (path coefficient .228) represents a strong relationship where those with posttreatment hospitalizations are more likely to use alcohol after treatment than are those without posttreatment hospitalizations.

7. Higher Power

Higher Power—Functioning Improvement (path coefficient .266) represents a strong relationship where those with increased posttreatment prayer and meditation are more improved in social/psychological functioning than are those without increased prayer and meditation after treatment.

Higher Power—Alcohol Use (path coefficient .071) represents a weak to moderate relationship where those with increased posttreatment prayer and meditation are more abstinent than are those without increased prayer and meditation.

Higher Power—AA Attendance (path coefficient .214) represents a strong relationship where those with increased posttreatment prayer and meditation are more frequent AA attenders than are those without increased prayer and meditation.

8. AA Attendance

AA Attendance—Alcohol Use (path coefficient .197) represents a moderately strong relationship where those who attend AA frequently are more abstinent than are those who attend AA infrequently.

9. Alcohol Use

Alcohol Use—Functioning Improvement (path coefficient .247) represents a strong relationship where those who are abstinent are more likely to show greater posttreatment social/psychological functioning improvement than are those who drink.

Six of the ten variables have moderately strong or strong relationships with other variables as shown in Figure 7-1. Both private and collective treatment activity ratings are related to the Higher Power variable and to functioning improvement. Private activities are more strongly related to functioning improvement. The number of posttreatment hospitalizations is negatively related to abstinence as a strong but separate relationship within the paths.

The Higher Power variable is the most important variable in relation to functioning improvement. What appears to happen in the path analysis is that part of the predictive power of the collective activity variable noted in the previous regression analysis becomes modified when sequenced through the Higher Power variable so that the Higher Power variable becomes dominant in its relationship to functioning improvement. The strong relationship identified is between Higher Power and AA attendance. This relationship is important because it is part of a path from the Higher Power variable to frequent AA attendance to abstinence to improvement in social/psychological functioning. In other words, *the Higher Power variable emerges in the path analysis as the principal variable, both directly and indirectly, in explaining functioning improvement.*

Summary

Several different statistical techniques support the finding that social/psychological functioning improvement is positively related to abstinence from alcohol during the year following discharge from treatment. Abstinence is, in turn, positively related to frequent AA attendance which is related to increased prayer and meditation, and increased prayer and meditation is also directly related to improved posttreatment social/psychological functioning. The other two variables that fit into the path arrangement are ratings of private and collective activities in treatment which may be seen in both a motivational and treatment process context. Because of the importance of the private and collective activity ratings, it is recommended that future research should move toward separating out the motivational and treatment process aspects of these variables. The variable areas have the potential of greater explanatory power than either the sociodemographic or psychological variables that have been used in research on treatment outcome and the recovery process. The importance of increased prayer and meditation in the posttreatment recovery process strongly reinforces the spiritual emphasis of the Minnesota Model treatment approach and the way that the spiritual part of recovery complements frequent AA attendance with its direct recovery benefits.

More will be said in the next chapter about how we might build on the understanding of the recovery process identified in the path analysis. This analysis must be seen as early empirical exploration of alcoholism recovery processes. More refinement of the path model is needed, but what it is possible to say with confidence at this time is that the analysis of the follow-up data validates the efficacy of the treatment approach identified earlier as the Minnesota Model of which treatment at Hazelden is a part.

Reference Notes Chapter 7

[1]E. M. Pattison, A conceptual approach to alcoholism treatment goals. *Addictive Behavior,* 1976, *1,* 177-192.

[2]R. Almond, *The healing community: Dynamics of the therapeutic milieu.* New York: Jason Aronson, 1974.

[3]M. Q. Patton, *The outcome of treatment: Patients admitted to Hazelden 1977.* Center City, MN: Hazelden Foundation, 1979.

[4]J. C. Laundergan, *The outcome of treatment: The relationship between previous treatment and client outcome.* Center City, MN: Hazelden Foundation, 1981.

Chapter Eight

Conclusions

Minnesota has evolved an extensive alcoholism treatment capability. It is based on common definitions and a common heritage. The Minnesota Model of treatment, discussed in Chapter 1, has three underlying assumptions: 1) alcoholism can be described and identified, 2) alcoholism is an involuntary disablement, and 3) alcoholism is responsive to treatment. These assumptions are elaborated in Chapter 2. The conceptualization of alcoholism at Hazelden is also presented in Chapter 2, along with a description of the goals and processes of treatment at Hazelden. This conceptualization of alcoholism goals and processes, while specific to Hazelden, is assumed to be widely accepted and practiced by alcoholism treatment programs utilizing the Minnesota Model (both within Minnesota and in other locations where this treatment model has been adopted). This assumption has not been tested, however, and it is recognized that there are both similarities and differences among specific treatment programs identified with the Minnesota Model.

Many practitioners and former patients seem confident that the Minnesota Model represents an effective approach in the treatment of alcoholism and other chemical dependencies. This presumed effectiveness of the Minnesota Model needs to be empirically tested. Even though data gathered from patients of a single treatment center, Hazelden, may not be entirely adequate to test the effectiveness of the Minnesota Model of treatment, it is intended that findings from the Hazelden follow-up be generalized to alcoholism treatment carried out according to the precepts of the Minnesota Model.

Specifically, the Hazelden follow-up data were gathered from Hazelden patients discharged during the last six months of 1973 and the calendar years

1974 and 1975. Follow-up questionnaires were sent to these patients 4, 8, and 12 months after their discharge from treatment. Both the methodology used in the follow-up research and the research questions examined are presented in Chapter 3.

The term "operationalization" is also introduced in Chapter 3. This term continues to represent a prominent idea in Chapter 4, the review of literature dealing with treatment follow-up studies, and in the data analysis chapters that follow. Operationalization refers to a set of procedures used to measure an abstract concept. Researchers must decide how to categorize and label the information they seek to systematically gather. It is important to be aware that research findings can be artifacts of the ways a researcher has chosen to measure, categorize, and define the objective properties of the topic being researched. In order to show how the central variables used in the present treatment outcome research are being used, the operationalization of these variables is introduced in Chapter 3.

A diversity of treatment programs and follow-up procedures is characteristic of alcoholism treatment as shown in Chapter 4. Some follow-up research has been carefully done and some is of marginal quality. *Alcoholism and Treatment,* published by the Rand Corporation and popularly known as the "Rand Report," is critiqued as an example of poor alcoholism treatment outcome research. When the operationalizations used in the Rand study are understood, the worth of the controversial findings it reports becomes questionable.

Abstinence from alcohol and other mood-altering chemicals is one of the Hazelden treatment goals. At first glance, posttreatment chemical use appears to be a straightforward "yes" or "no" determination. The discussion and presentation of findings found in Chapter 5 shows chemical use outcome to be a complex issue. Extent of use, duration of use, moving into and out of use, and social/psychological functioning while using and not using all combine with other contingencies to caution against simplistic reporting of posttreatment chemical use outcome. What is perhaps more relevant than focusing only on a percentage of favorable outcome is the identification of variables associated with abstinence. Current AA attendance was found to be the most important variable in predicting abstinence. The obvious question, then, is "What variables explain AA affiliation and participation?"

The AA questions are discussed in Chapter 6 where "Higher Power," operationalized as increased prayer and meditation following treatment, emerges as the strongest predictor of AA attendance. It is not claimed that the direction of the relationship between AA participation and increased prayer and meditation is completely understood, i.e., do people attend AA meetings because they have increased their prayer and meditation or vice versa? What is important is that behaviors encouraged as a part of the treatment process (prayer and meditation, AA attendance) have greater predictive power relative to abstinence that do the sociodemographic characteristics of patients. This is an important finding because a behavior change is more likely to be accomplished or begun as part of a treatment experience than are changes in sociodemographic characteristics (sex, marital status, education, etc.).

"The mission of the primary rehabilitation program is to help the chemically dependent person achieve two long-term goals: 1) abstinence from mood-altering chemicals, and 2) an improved life-style." This statement of purpose presented in Chapter 2 identifies two goals that are empirically demonstrated to be interrelated in the presentation of findings found in Chapter 7. Abstainers show more social/psychological functioning improvement than do the *improved* patients, who in turn, do better than those who are *not improved*. However, even the patients classified as *not improved* in terms of posttreatment alcohol use show some social/psychological functioning improvement, although their improvement is significantly less than that of the *abstinent* patients.

What variables other than abstinence predict improved social/psychological functioning? Favorable assessment of the collective and the private activities in treatment are both important variables in explaining improved social/psychological functioning. Increased prayer and meditation, the "Higher Power" variable, is also an important predictor of social/psychological functioning improvement.

These and other predictors of outcome were assembled first into a path model presented in Chapter 7. This path model moves sequentially from the sociodemographic variables to the treatment variables and then to the posttreatment variables. This path model is empirically tested with the result that the "Higher Power" variable is identified as the most important variable in contributing to the dual treatment goals of abstinence and improved life-style.

As in many research activities, new findings pose new questions. The path model identifies the interrelationships between the variables that contribute to successful attainment of treatment purposes. Furthermore, the treatment process, with its emphasis on spirituality and AA participation, is empirically reinforced by the analysis. It becomes clear, however, that more sensitive measures of the treatment process need to be developed if treatment outcome is to be better understood. Both the collective activities in treatment and the private activities in treatment are prominent predictors of desired outcome, but both of these variables are too multifaceted in their present form. Also, because these measures are retrospective and have a motivational component, there is a need to create different treatment measures in the future refinement of the model.

Another limitation that was keenly felt, especially in the discussion of "return to normal drinking," was the relatively brief follow-up period. One year is probably adequate for treatment evaluation purposes but it does not permit a sufficient unfolding of posttreatment experiences to adequately chart the recovery process. A multi-year follow-up would supply additional insight into the process of recovery and thereby help to further refine the path model.

In Chapter 4, emphasis was placed on the benefits of having an ongoing follow-up monitoring system instead of carrying out isolated follow-up studies. It is the ongoing follow-up of patients that provides the cornerstone of the Hazelden evaluation and research efforts. Using this continuous data base as a point of departure, several new directions will be explored by Hazelden Evaluation and Research staff and consultants during the decade of the 1980's. New treatment process indicators will be developed, studies of specific populations of patients will be undertaken and a five-year follow-up will be conducted. These projects are all intended to improve the understanding of what constitutes effective treatment and successful recovery. Results of these efforts will be applied to the further refinement of the Hazelden rehabilitation program and disseminated to others interested in the Minnesota Model. This dissemination will continue to be carried out through counselor training, continuing education workshops, presentations at alcoholism conferences, and publications.

The analysis presented in Chapters 5 through 7 indicates that the Minnesota Model of treatment and corresponding conceptualization of alcoholism, as exemplified by Hazelden, yield positive rehabilitation results. Not all patients complete treatment, and not all who complete treatment show major improvements. However, of those who respond to the follow-up questionnaires, most give evidence that they have been positively affected by the treatment experience. As impressive as these findings are, it is important to note that the impact of alcoholism treatment is greater than the aggregate personal impacts reported by the patients.

Alcoholism is recognized as a family illness and the impact of treatment is felt by individual family members and the family as a system. Furthermore, alcoholism is seen as a community problem and a problem of the workplace. Here, too, the effect of treatment has positive implications. In order to adequately judge the outcome of treatment it would be necessary to take measurements among patients, their significant others and the social systems in which patients and significant others participate. Such a large-scale evaluation and research undertaking would be a major effort. Although such a comprehensive study is not a project being contemplated by this researcher, it is important that the full impact of alcoholism treatment not be overlooked in assessing treatment outcomes. The emphasis on behavior changes among the patients that have been reported here should be seen as only the first level indication of treatment outcome.

Another related matter concerns the recent strong and growing interest in prevention of chemical dependency problems. Because there is no way of knowing who prealcoholics are, although some people are at a higher risk than others, most prevention efforts are necessarily "broad brush" affairs designed to have wide impact. Frequently, prevention programs are pitted against treatment programs for funding in the present era of fiscal scarcity.

It is important to recognize that effective treatment is quickly translated into effective prevention. Former alcoholism rehabilitation patients frequently serve as inspired "good will ambassadors," informing others of the pitfalls of alcoholism and other chemical dependencies and making friends and acquaintances aware of some of the danger signs of early chemical abuse. Rather than viewing treatment and prevention as separate, the latent prevention outcomes of effective treatment need to be nurtured and developed. In this way, the considerable benefits of successful alcoholism treatment can be further multiplied.

The Minnesota Model of chemical dependency has attracted national and international attention. Patient follow-up, as reported here and elsewhere, shows that this treatment model is making a significant contribution to the rehabilitation of alcoholics and other chemically dependent people. When the positive benefits to the family, community, and workplace of successful outcome are considered, and further indirect benefits such a prevention are accounted for, it is possible to gain a more complete appreciation of the impact of treatment.

There are major contributions that research can make as the Minnesota Model continues to evolve. The development of improved and refined procedures for chemical dependency diagnosis must be a high priority because this activity both defines the "gatekeeper" criteria for treatment and helps in the formulation of treatment plans. Better understanding and measurement of patient treatment paths is another necessary activity, according to the findings of this study. Continued improvement of treatment follow-up measures and analysis should emerge from the experience of working with large data bases like the one resulting from Hazelden's ongoing evaluation monitoring system. In these and other ways, behavior sciences can continue to interact with the spiritual emphasis and dedicated clinical practice found in the Minnesota Model. Such a combination of purpose and effort will contribute new insight and awareness that will further improve primary rehabilitation as an effective way of moving chemically dependent people toward recovery. From the experience of being a part of the Minnesota Model for three decades, Hazelden has placed a high priority on refining and improving the effectiveness of this treatment approach. Hopefully, the findings reported here, and the new research directions suggested by the findings, will contribute to this purpose and to a better understanding of chemical dependency treatment and outcome.

Appendix A

Validity and Reliability of Hazelden Treatment Follow-up Data*

Alcoholism Treatment Evaluation

What happens to people who participate in chemical dependency programs after they leave treatment? Are treatment programs effective? Does chemical dependency treatment have any lasting effects? In order to answer these questions, it is necessary to study the program participants *after* they leave treatment.

But can we believe reports from treated alcoholics about their own drinking? After all, they know they're not supposed to be drinking. Why should they send back a questionnaire to Hazelden—of all places—admitting that they've returned to their old ways? Are these questionnaire results valid? Are they reliable? These are the questions this chapter will address.

Representativeness

The first issue in considering the credibility of the questionnaire is to establish the extent to which the results really represent the total population of people treated for chemical dependency at Hazelden. How many people sent

---

*This chapter is written by Michael Q. Patton, past director of the Minnesota Center for Social Research at the University of Minnesota.

back the questionnaire? From July, 1973 through December, 1975, the response rate for the 4-month questionnaire was 71%;* the return rate for the 8-month follow-up was 67% and the percentage responding 12 months after treatment was 72%. A special effort was made to increase the response rate for the 12-month follow-up questionnaires by telephoning people who did not mail back their questionnaires. Twenty percent of the 2040 12-month follow-up responses were obtained by telephone. By comparison, 5% of the 2943 8-month responses came from telephone interviews and less than 1 percent of the 2220 4-month responses were obtained by telephone.

Clearly a 100% return rate would be ideal, but no survey research ever obtains a perfect response rate. The rule of thumb among survey researchers is that one can expect about a 60% return rate in the typical mail questionnaire study. The two-thirds level of return for the 8-month questionnaire can be considered at least typical and basically adequate. *The 72% response rates after 4 and 12 months are satisfactory and constitute an acceptable data set in terms of probable representativeness.*

An additional factor in judging representativeness is the degree to which the background characteristics of questionnaire respondents are representative of the entire population of people who enter treatment at Hazelden. From July, 1973 through December, 1975, Hazelden admitted 3638 persons to treatment. We have 12-month follow-up questionnaires for 2040 of these people. How similar are these questionnaire respondents to the 1598 people for whom we do not have questionnaires?**

Table A-1 shows the background comparison between respondents and nonrespondents. People who sent back the questionnaire tended to be somewhat older, more educated, and wealthier than those who are not included in the follow-up study. Proportionately more out-of-state clients returned questionnaires, thus, Minnesota residents are somewhat underrepresented in the questionnaire sample. These are the kinds of differences that would be expected since younger, poorer, and less educated persons are less likely to be responsive to a mail questionnaire. The most important difference is in percentage of persons who completed treatment. To complete treatment at Ha-

---

*This is based on 2220 responses, including 20 by telephone, out of 3085 questionnaires excluding persons who were deceased (48), who asked not to be included in the evaluation when they were in treatment (173), people who had returned to treatment (69), those who could not be located (124), and those omitted through clerical errors (139); thus, the total number of people treated from July, 1973 through December, 1975 was 3638.

**This total of 1598 persons includes people who did not return a questionnaire (809), people who asked not to be included in the evaluation (268), those who were deceased 12 months after treatment (82), people who had returned to treatment (122), those who could not be located (183), and those excluded due to clerical error (134).

Table A-1 REPRESENTATIVENESS DATA: Comparison of 12-Month Follow-up Questionnaire Respondents to Nonrespondents on Available Background Characteristics

Background Characteristics	Questionnaire Respondents (N = 2040)	Non-Respondents (N = 1598)	Total July 1973-1975 Hazelden Population (N = 3638)
1. Percentage male	70%	73%	71%
2. Age: Under 26	14%	20%	17%
26-55	70%	65%	67%
Over 55	16%	15%	16%
3. Percentage completing treatment	84%	60%	73%
4. Percentage Minnesota residents	39%	47%	42%
5. Percentage who completed high school or above	82%	70%	81%
6. Percentage with income below $10,000 per year	28%	40%	30%

zelden a person must leave with staff approval. Among respondents, 84% left with staff approval; an additional 4% were transferred to extended care; and 12% either left without staff approval or were dismissed involuntarily at the request of staff. Among nonrespondents the program completion rate was 60%; an additional 3% were transferred or left for medical reasons; and 37% either left without staff approval or were dismissed. Thus, a large percentage of nonrespondents failed to complete treatment. This places special limitations on the generalizability of results from the follow-up data. *The questionnaires can be considered basically representative of that portion of the total Hazelden population which completed treatment (73%).* However, the results cannot be considered representative of the total population of patients who entered Hazelden from July, 1973 through December, 1975 since 27% did not formally complete treatment.

Our final comparison may help clarify the degree to which the questionnaire results can be considered representative. Since 20% of the 2040 12-month follow-up responses had to be obtained by telephone, it is possible to consider clients interviewed by telephone as nonrespondents to the mail questionnaire. Comparing the posttreatment drinking behavior of mail question-naire respondents to telephone interview respondents will give some indica-tion of any systematic differences that exist. The results shown in Table A-2 are quite significant. Data obtained by telephone shows a substantially lower abstinence rate than data obtained on the mail questionnaire; 60% of the mail respondents were abstinent while only 34% of the telephone interviewees were abstinent. Thus, it is likely that the drinking behavior of nonrespondents does indeed differ significantly from the alcohol consumption patterns of re-spondents. While the return rate (72%) obtained by combining mail re-sponses with telephone interviews is reasonable, the combined study sample should not be considered representative of the total Hazelden population. There is a high probability that the success rate for the total population, which includes those who did not complete treatment, is consistently lower than that for the sample contained in the 1975 follow-up study, most of whom (84%) did complete treatment.

Reliability

The question of representativeness is aimed at determining how much error is involved in generalizing to a larger group, findings that are based only on a sample of people in that larger group. The question of reliability, on the other

Table A-2 REPRESENTATIVENESS DATA: Comparison of Reported Drinking Behavior for Mail Questionnaire Respondents and Telephone Interviewees 12 Months After Treatment, July 1973 - December 1975

Reported Drinking Behavior Twelve Months After Treatment	Mail Ques-tionnaire Respondents (N = 1582)	Telephone Inter-viewees (N = 393)	Total Sample (N = 1975)*
1. Abstinent	60%	34%	55%
2. Drinking Reduced Since Treatment	29%	50%	33%
3. Drinking the Same as Before Treatment	9%	11%	9%
4. Drinking More	2%	5%	3%
	100%	100%	100%

*Sixty-five clients out of 2040 responses did not answer this question, thus the reduced total sample size. Most of this missing data is probably due to clients who were treated only for drug abuse and thus skipped alcohol questions.

hand, is aimed at determining how much error is contained in the actual results obtained from the sample. All social science measurement involves some error. Henry Dyer, in his keynote address at the 1973 Invitational Conference on Measurement and Evaluation, told of trying to explain to a government official that even the best education tests have enough measurement error that they must be used with caution. The government official responded that test makers should "get on the ball" and start producing tests that "are 100 percent reliable under all conditions."

Dyer's comments on this conversation are particularly relevant to an understanding of error in evaluation measurement. He asks:

> How does one get across the shocking truth that 100 percent reliability in a test is a fiction that, in the nature of the case, is unrealizable? How does one convey the notion that the test reliability problem is not one of reducing measurement error to absolute zero, but of minimizing it as far as practicable and doing one's best to estimate whatever amount of error remains, so that one may act cautiously and wisely in a world where all knowledge is approximate and not even death and taxes are any longer certain?

Sources of error are many. Simple mechanical errors such as accidentally marking the wrong box on the questionnaire, skipping a question, or missing a word while reading are common problems for all of us. People who have trouble reading will have difficulty with questionnaires. The health of a person on the day the questionnaire is completed can affect reliability. The mental state of the respondent—depression, elation, boredom, anxiety, self-esteem—can introduce error. Poor concentration, trying to complete questions in a hurry, and interruptions can lead to mistakes.

There are two kinds of error that are considered in estimating the degree to which any particular questionnaire is reliable. One issue in reliability is the *internal consistency* of responses. Do the answers on the questionnaire result in contradictions? The second issue is *response stability*. This issue only arises when, as in the case of the Hazelden evaluation, the same questionnaire has been administered on several occasions over some period of time. Are responses on identical items stable from one time to the next? Both types of reliability will be examined here.

Tables A-3 and A-4 present findings on the internal consistency of responses concerning alcoholic consumption after treatment. Table A-3 shows the degree of correspondence between reported *frequency* of drinking and reported quantity of drinking 4 months after treatment. The consistency is very nearly perfect. Since the response categories for quantity and frequency are somewhat different one would not expect perfect symmetry in responses. Table A-4 presents the same data from the 8-month follow-up questionnaires. Again the consistency is nearly perfect.

Table A-3 RELIABILITY DATA: Correspondence Between Reported Frequency of Drinking and Quantity of Drinking at 4 Months After Treatment

Frequency \ Quantity	Not Used	Less Used After Treatment	Same Used After Treatment	More Used After Treatment	TOTAL
Not used	66%	0	0	0	66%
Used once	3%	7%	2%	0	12%
Less often after treatment	0	16%	2%	0	18%
Same frequency after treatment	0	1%	2%	0	3%
More often after treatment	0	0	0	1%	1%
TOTAL	69%	24%	6%	1%	100% (N = 2146)

Pearson Correlation, $r = .85$ ($p < .001$)

A different type of consistency measure is obtained by examining the abstinence rates suggested by different questions. On the 8-month follow-up the following results were obtained: 60% reported they had not used alcohol since treatment on the frequency of use question; 63% said they had not had a drink on the quantity of use question; 64% responded that they had not had a drink in 8 months; and 66% said that their longest dry period was at least 8 months. Some of the variation in percentages is due to missing data and varying response rates for the four questions. Overall these data present a pattern of high consistency. At 12 months the results are again consistent: 55% reported no use of alcohol since treatment on the quantity question; 52% said that they had never consumed alcohol since treatment on the frequency question; 50% responded that their longest period dry was 12 months or longer; and 52% reported abstinence as their current drinking status 12 months after treatment. Again, the data show a high degree of internal consistency. *On the issue of internal consistency, then, the Hazelden data are highly reliable.*

The second reliability issue concerns response stability over time. To accurately assess response stability it is necessary to compare answers on identical questions for the same person at two different points in time, e.g., at 4 months and 8 months after treatment. Moreover, the question on which this

Table A-4 RELIABILITY DATA: Correspondence Between Reported Frequency of Drinking and Quantity of Drinking at 8 Months After Treatment

Frequency \ Quantity	Not Used	Less Used After Treatment	Same Used After Treatment	More Used After Treatment	TOTAL
Not used	60%	0	0	0	60%
Used once	3%	7%	1%	0	11%
Less often after treatment	0	21%	3%	0	24%
Same frequency after treatment	0	1%	3%	0	4%
More often after treatment	0	0	0	1%	0
TOTAL	63%	29%	7%	1%	100% (N = 1895)

Pearson Correlation, r = .87 (p < .001)

comparison is made over time, must *not* be subject to change. Thus, current drinking status cannot be used for such a comparison because the response after 4 months could well be different from the true response 8 months after treatment.

There are two questions that permit an assessment of response stability between 4 months and 8 months. The first question on the questionnaire asks: "At the time of your treatment would you say you were having problems with . . . (1) alcohol, (2) drugs, or (3) both?" Ninety-six percent of those who identified alcohol as their primary problem on the 4-month questionnaire did so again on the 8-month questionnaire ($N=1104$); there was 85% response stability after 8 months for those who reported drugs as their primary problem on the 4-month questionnaire ($N=113$); and there was 87% consistency over the two time periods for those who initially reported having both problems when they entered treatment ($N=424$). There appears to be some error over time in reporting whether the initial treatment problem was *both* alcohol and drugs thus reducing reliability for persons who were having at least some problem with drugs. Respondents for whom alcohol was the primary problem have highly stable responses on this reliability measure.

The greater the number of categories on the question, the greater the opportunity for making an error and/or forgetting relatively minor distinctions.

153

The second item on which a response reliability test can be made illustrates this point. At both four months and eight months respondents were asked the following question:

Which one of the following best categorizes your drinking before your treatment?

_____ Abstinent

_____ Light or moderate social drinking

_____ Inappropriate drinking restricted mainly to social events or week-ends

_____ Inappropriate drinking on more than one occasion most weeks, but not restricted to social events or weekends

_____ Inappropriate drinking occurring almost every day or evening

_____ Periodic binge drinking

Of 1687 respondents for whom both 4-month and 8-month questionnaires were returned, 76% chose the same category both times; another 16% moved up or down an adjacent category and the remaining 8% moved up or down two or more categories. Errors were not more likely to occur upward than downward; 12% reported less drinking *before treatment* on the 8-month questionnaire compared to their response at 4 months. After 8 months, 12% reported more drinking before treatment compared to their 4-month report. The reliability coefficient for this question measuring stability from 4 months to 8 months is .66 ($p < .001$). Given the content of this question and the similarity among response categories, *the stability rate for this item is within an acceptable range.* The greatest error, i.e., the main reason for reduced reliability on this question, was movement among the three categories that begin "inappropriate drinking . . ." It is not difficult to understand how a respondent might mark two different responses on two separate occasions.

Validity

So far we have found that the response rate is relatively high for a study of this kind and the findings can be considered fairly representative of treated alcoholics who formally completed the Hazelden program. Internal consistency is high and response stability is at an acceptable level. But how much confidence can we have that the respondents told the truth about their drinking behavior? Do the questionnaire results reflect actual drinking patterns? Does the follow-up questionnaire really measure posttreatment patterns of alcohol consumption? These are issues of validity. Such questions go to the very heart of the research process. If the results are false or misleading then it doesn't matter if they are representative or reliable. Consistent and reliable responses are useless if the data are inaccurate. And there is no reason to even consider representativeness if findings are not valid. Generalizations based on misleading results merely compound the error. *There is, then, no issue more important than that of validity.*

The Hazelden evaluation project is an exception in that an assessment of data validity was systematically built into the research design. In order to establish the degree to which treated alcoholics responded truthfully to the questionnaire, follow-up questionnaires were also sent to a relative or close friend of the former patient 8 months after treatment. During treatment at Hazelden each patient was asked to identify a "significant other" who could be contacted about posttreatment chemical dependency behavior. A "significant other" is someone who is close to the patient, close enough to be knowledgeable about the patient's drinking patterns or drug use after treatment. Data from "significant others" constitute a validity check on the responses of treated patients.

From July, 1973 through December, 1975, validity questionnaires were returned by 1166 significant other respondents. Forty-two percent of the significant other respondents were spouses of treated patients; an additional 21% were family members other than spouses, particularly parents of younger patients; and the remaining 38% consisted of friends, clergymen, or employers.

Table A-5 shows the degree of agreement between patients and significant others on 13 chemical dependency questions 8 months after treatment. The sample size is different for each question because not everyone answered all the questions. Table A-5 shows the percentage of cases where the response of the significant other was identical to the response of the treated patient. The highest percentage of agreement is 87% for the question on type of patient problem (alcohol, drug, or both). The average agreement rate for the five questions on patient drinking behavior 8 months after treatment is 81% (items 3, 4, 5, 6 and 7). The question requiring significant others to recall patient's drinking habits *before* treatment (item 2) has a lower validity quotient (64%) as one would expect.

One might expect that where there are inconsistencies the significant other would report more drinking behavior than that reported by patients. Such a hypothesis would be derived from the assumption that some patients tend to systematically report slightly less drinking than they actually do in order to look good in the follow-up study. Such is, indeed, the pattern. Where there are inconsistencies between patients and significant others, the differences are more likely to be in the direction of more drinking reported by the significant other instead of in the direction of less drinking. For example, the question on drinking habits 8 months after treatment asks both significant others and patients to mark one of the following categories to describe the posttreatment alcohol use patterns of the patients:

_____ Abstinent

_____ Light or moderate social drinking

(Continued on page 157)

Table A-5 VALIDITY DATA BY TYPE OF CHEMICAL DEPENDENCY PROBLEM: Degree of Agreement Between Clients and Significant Others 8 Months After Treatment

	Alcohol Abusers Only	Total Sample (Treated for Alcohol Abuse, Drug Abuse, or Both)	Total Sample Validity Coefficient (Pearson Correlation)
1. Type of problem at treatment (alcohol, drug, both)	89% (N = 629)	87% (N = 878)	not applicable
2. Client's drinking habits before treatment	64% (N = 645)	64% (N = 884)	r = .43 (p < .001)
3. Client's drinking eight months after treatment	84% (N = 601)	85% (N = 840)	r = .58 (p < .001)
4. Frequency of drinking eight months after treatment compared to drinking at time of treatment	87% (N = 656)	81% (N = 904)	r = .80 (p < .001)
5. Quantity of drinking eight months after treatment compared to drinking at time of treatment	84% (N = 613)	83% (N = 844)	r = .76 (p < .001)
6. Length of time since last drink	82% (N = 609)	81% (N = 849)	r = .81 (p < .001)
7. Longest dry period since treatment	77% (N = 597)	76% (N = 842)	r = .74 (p < .001)
8. Frequency of attendance at AA meetings	66% (N = 610)	65% (N = 857)	r = .82 (p < .001)
9. Attendance at AA meetings eight months after treatment compared to attendance before treatment	76% (N = 322)	75% (N = 454)	r = .50 (p < .001)

(Continued from page 155)

_____ Inappropriate drinking mostly restricted to social events or weekends
_____ Inappropriate drinking on more than one occasion most weeks, but not restricted to social events or weekends
_____ Inappropriate drinking occurring almost every day or evening
_____ Periodic binge drinking

Table A-6 VALIDITY DATA BY AGE OF PARTICIPANTS: Degree of Agreement Between Clients and Significant Others on Quantity of Drinking 8 Months After Treatment Compared to Before Treatment

Question: Which one statement most nearly represents this person's use of alcohol today, in **terms of quantity,** compared to what it was before treatment?

_____ This person **has not used** alcohol since treatment.
_____ When this person uses alcohol, he (or she) **doesn't take as much** as before treatment.
_____ When this person uses alcohol, he (or she) **takes about as much** as before treatment.
_____ When this person uses alcohol, he (or she) **takes more** than before treatment.

Degree of Agreement	Client Age			
	25 or Under (N = 79)	26-55 (N = 636)	Over 55 (N = 129)	Total (N = 844)
1. S.O. reports lower amount of drinking than reported by client	14%	5%	6%	6%
2. S.O. and client report same quantity of drinking	77%	85%	78%	83%
3. S.O. reports higher quantity of drinking than reported by client	9%	10%	16%	11%
TOTAL	100%	100%	100%	100%

Pearson Correlation Between Client and Significant Other Responses
25 or under, $r = .69 \ (p < .001)$
26-55, $r = .78 \ (p < .001)$
Over 55, $r = .71 \ (p < .001)$
Total sample, $r = .76 \ (p < .001)$

In 85% of the cases, significant other and the patient reported exactly the same pattern of drinking. In 5% of the cases, the significant other reported *less* serious drinking than that reported by the patient; and in 10% of the cases the significant other reported *more* serious drinking than that reported by the former patient. The validity coefficient (Pearson correlation) was .58 (p < .001).

On the question concerning frequency of drinking 8 months after treatment, there was 80% agreement between significant others and patients. Seven percent of the significant others reported less frequent drinking than

Table A-7 VALIDITY DATA BY AGE OF PARTICIPANTS: Degree of Agreement Between Clients and Significant Others On Frequency of Client Drinking Before Treatment Compared to Drinking 8 Months After Treatment

Question: What is the extent of this person's drinking today, **in terms of frequency,** compared to what it was before treatment?

_____ This person **has not used** alcohol since treatment.

_____ This person has used alcohol **on only one occasion** (non-continuous) since treatment.

_____ This person uses alcohol **about as often** as before treatment.

_____ This person uses alcohol **more often** than before treatment.

Degree of Agreement	Client Age			
	25 or Under (N = 86)	26-55 (N = 676)	Over 55 (N = 142)	Total (N = 904)
1. S.O. reports less serious drinking than reported by client	13%	5%	9%	7%
2. S.O. and client report same degree of drinking	78%	83%	73%	80%
3. S.O. reports more serious drinking than reported by client	9%	12%	18%	13%
TOTAL	100%	100%	100%	100%

Pearson Correlation Between Client and Significant Other Responses

25 or under,	r = .79 (p < .001)
26-55,	r = .82 (p < .001)
Over 55,	r = .73 (p < .001)
Total sample,	r = .80 (p < .001)

reported by the patients while 13% of the significant others reported more frequent drinking by the patient than that reported by the patient.

To further investigate validity patterns the data were analyzed by age of treated patient. On alcohol consumption questions, data for younger and older patients show a pattern of somewhat lower validity compared to middle-aged patients. For older patients there is a marked tendency for significant others to report both higher quantity and frequency of alcohol use. The converse is true for younger patients with significant others consistently less aware of patient drinking. Tables A-6 and A-7 illustrate this point. These age-related patterns were consistent for all of the outcome questions in this study.

Overall, the validity findings establish a strong case for believing the self-reports of patients concerning their posttreatment drinking behavior. Just as no social science measurement can attain 100% reliability, validity coefficients will always be less than perfect. The degree of agreement between significant other responses and patient responses is consistently high. While the data for younger and older patients show somewhat lower levels of validity, all of the results are within an acceptable range—and most of the findings show an unusually high degree of validity.

Conclusion

This analysis has examined the Hazelden evaluation data on three dimensions: representativeness, reliability and validity. With regard to representativeness, we found that the response rate is reasonable for a study of this kind. Further analysis established that the findings can be considered basically representative for treated alcoholics who have formally *completed* the Hazelden program.

Reliability was examined in two ways. First, internal consistency among similar questions was found to be relatively high. Second, response stability over time was analyzed and found to be at an acceptable level. Thus, the Hazelden evaluation data can be considered essentially reliable.

Finally, and most importantly, we examined the evidence on validity. Overall, the validity findings establish a strong case for believing the data. While the data for younger and older patients showed somewhat lower levels of validity, all of the results are within an acceptable range—and most of the findings show a high degree of validity.

Appendix B

Questionnaires used in the 1973-75 Patient Follow-up

Two questionnaire forms were used in the 1973-75 patient follow-up. The form identified as Exhibit One was used at both four and eight months after treatment. This follow-up questionnaire form has the longest period of use of any of the Hazelden follow-up questionnaires being used through 1979. Apart from the advantage of using a single questionnaire form as a standard instrument over a number of years so as to accumulate a comparable data base, this questionnaire has the advantage of being read by an opti-scan reader thereby eliminating keypunching. This form is no longer used in the ongoing Hazelden follow-up although many of the items it contains have been retained in the questionnaires used presently.

Exhibit Two is the follow-up questionnaire form used at the 12-month follow-up interval. In many ways it is similar to the form used at the 4- and 8-month follow-ups, making comparisons over the three time periods possible. However, the phrasing and categorization of some of the items is different from the questionnaire shown in Exhibit One and some of the items are unique to this questionnaire. The 12-month questionnaire was not used again after 1975.

Hazelden's Evaluation-Research Department has used follow-up questionnaires similar to those shown in this appendix in chemical dependency treatment evaluation consulting with other treatment centers. The questionnaires have also been shared in the Follow-up Evaluation Workshops that are held several times each year through the Hazelden Training Department. Further information on Hazelden's follow-up instruments and procedures may be obtained by contacting the Evaluation-Research Department at Hazelden.

Patient form sent
at 4 and 8 months

CONTINUATION PROGRAM

EXHIBIT ONE

© The Hazelden Foundation, 1975.

DIRECTIONS: Read the enclosure letter first.
1. Mark the circles that correspond with your answer.
2. Use lead pencil only (No. 2 or softer).
3. Do NOT use ink or ball point pens.
4. Make heavy black marks that completely fill the circle.

5. Erase thoroughly any marks you wish to change.
6. Make no stray marks on the sheet.

GOOD MARKS ●○ ●○ ●○

POOR MARKS ⊘○ ⊗○ ○◐

ALCOHOL AND DRUG USAGE

1. At the time of your treatment would you say you were having problems with .
   ○ Alcohol   ○ Drugs   ○ Both

2. Which one of the following best categorizes your drinking before your treatment?
   ○ Abstinent
   ○ Light or moderate social drinking
   ○ Inappropriate drinking restricted mainly to social events or weekends
   ○ Inappropriate drinking on more than one occasion most weeks, but not restricted to social events or weekends
   ○ Inappropriate drinking occurring almost every day or evening
   ○ Periodic binge drinking

3. Which one of the following best categorizes your drinking at present?
   ○ Abstinent
   ○ Light or moderate social drinking
   ○ Inappropriate drinking restricted mainly to social events or weekends
   ○ Inappropriate drinking on more than one occasion most weeks, but not restricted to social events or weekends
   ○ Inappropriate drinking occurring almost every day or evening
   ○ Periodic binge drinking

4. What is the extent of your drinking today, in terms of frequency, compared to what it was before your treatment? (Mark one.)
   ○ I have not used alcohol since leaving treatment
   ○ I have used alcohol on only one occasion (non–continuous) since leaving treatment
   ○ I have used alcohol but not as often as before treatment
   ○ I use alcohol about as often as before treatment
   ○ I use alcohol more often than before treatment

5. Which one statement most nearly represents your use of alcohol today, in terms of quantity, compared to what it was before your treatment?
   ○ I have not used alcohol since leaving treatment
   ○ When I use alcohol, I don't take as much as before treatment
   ○ When I use alcohol, I take about as much as before treatment
   ○ When I use alcohol, I take more than before treatment

6. How long ago did you last take a drink?
   ○ 0 – 1 month
   ○ 2 – 4 months
   ○ 5 – 7 months
   ○ 8 – 10 months
   ○ 11 – 12 months (or longer)
      (BE SURE TO ANSWER QUESTION 7)

7. Which one best categorizes the longest dry period since your treatment?
   ○ 0 – 1 month
   ○ 2 – 4 months
   ○ 5 – 7 months
   ○ 8 – 10 months
   ○ 11 – 12 months (or longer)

8. Which one statement below best categorizes your use of drugs, other than alcohol, just before treatment?
   ○ No use of drugs
   ○ Appropriate prescribed use for medical reasons
   ○ Inappropriate use of prescribed drugs above recommended dosage
   ○ Inappropriate use of non-prescription drugs on more than one occasion most weeks
   ○ Inappropriate use of non-prescription drugs occurring almost every day or evening

9. Which one statement below best categorizes your use of drugs, <u>other than</u> alcohol, at present?
   - O No use of drugs
   - O Appropriate prescribed use for medical reasons
   - O Inappropriate use of prescribed drugs above recommended dosage
   - O Inappropriate use of non-prescription drugs on more than one occasion most weeks
   - O Inappropriate use of non-prescription drugs occurring almost every day or evening

10. Which one statement below best categorizes your use of drugs today, <u>other than</u> alcohol, <u>in terms of frequency</u>, compared with what it was before treatment?
    - O I have not used drugs since leaving treatment
    - O I have used drugs since leaving treatment but only those prescribed <u>for medical reasons</u>
    - O I have used drugs inappropriately on only one occasion (non-continuous) since leaving treatment
    - O I use drugs inappropriately but <u>not as often</u> as before treatment
    - O I use drugs inappropriately <u>about as often</u> as before treatment
    - O I use drugs inappropriately <u>more often</u> than before treatment

11. Which one statement most nearly represents your use of drugs, <u>other than</u> alcohol, <u>in terms of quantity</u>, compared with what it was before treatment?
    - O I have <u>not used</u> drugs since leaving treatment
    - O I have used drugs since leaving treatment but only <u>for medical reasons</u>
    - O When I use drugs, I <u>don't take as much</u> as before treatment
    - O When I use drugs, I <u>take about as much</u> as before treatment
    - O When I use drugs, I <u>take more</u> than before treatment

12. How long ago did you last use drugs inappropriately (other than alcohol)?
    - O 0 - 1 month
    - O 2 - 4 months
    - O 5 - 7 months
    - O 8 or more months (BE SURE TO ANSWER QUESTION 13)
    - O Did not use

13. What is the longest period since treatment during which you did not use drugs inappropriately?
    - O 0 - 1 month
    - O 2 - 4 months
    - O 5 - 7 months
    - O 8 or more months
    - O Did not use

MATURATION AND GROWTH

The following is a list of possible growth areas. Think about how you dealt with each of these areas before your treatment and how you presently deal with each of them. Choose the response which best describes your development in each of these areas.

	MUCH IMPROVED	SOMEWHAT IMPROVED	SAME	SOMEWHAT WORSE	MUCH WORSE	DOES NOT APPLY
14. Relationship with spouse	O	O	O	O	O	O
15. Relationship with children	O	O	O	O	O	O
16. Relationship with parents	O	O	O	O	O	O
17. Relationship with other relatives	O	O	O	O	O	O
18. Relationship with friends	O	O	O	O	O	O
19. Relationship at work	O	O	O	O	O	O
20. Relationship with Higher Power	O	O	O	O	O	O
21. Your own job performance	O	O	O	O	O	O
22. Participation in community affairs	O	O	O	O	O	O
23. General physical health	O	O	O	O	O	O
24. Self image (How you feel about yourself)	O	O	O	O	O	O
25. General enjoyment of life	O	O	O	O	O	O
26. Ability to handle problems	O	O	O	O	O	O
27. Ability to accept help and advice from others	O	O	O	O	O	O
28. Ability to give help and advice to others	O	O	O	O	O	O
29. Ability to assume responsibility	O	O	O	O	O	O
30. Ability to manage financial affairs	O	O	O	O	O	O
31. Acceptance of sexual role	O	O	O	O	O	O
32. Acceptance of need for abstinence	O	O	O	O	O	O

33 - 36. Since your treatment do you maintain some kind of conscious contact with a Higher Power through

	MORE OFTEN	ABOUT THE SAME	LESS OFTEN	NEVER DID & STILL DON'T
33. Prayer	O	O	O	O
34. Meditation	O	O	O	O
35. Church attendance	O	O	O	O
36. Spiritual counseling	O	O	O	O

ALCOHOLICS ANONYMOUS

37. How often do you attend A.A. meetings at present?
- O More than once a week
- O About once a week
- O About two or three times a month
- O About once a month
- O Less than once a month
- O I do not attend

38 - 41. Have you participated in the following A.A. activities since leaving treatment?

38. Led a meeting	O YES	O NO
39. Told my story	O YES	O NO
40. Did 12th step work	O YES	O NO
41. Sponsored an A.A. member	O YES	O NO

42. How does your present A.A. participation differ from what it was before treatment?
O More   O Same   O Less   O Did not attend

43. Would you like to take or retake the Fourth or Fifth Step?
O Yes
O No

44. Have you consciously continued working Steps Six through Twelve of the A.A. Program after leaving treatment?
O Yes
O No

BE SURE YOU ARE USING A NO. 2 PENCIL
MAKE DARK MARKS COMPLETELY FILLING
THE CIRCLE
GO ON TO QUESTION 45 IN THE NEXT
COLUMN OF THIS SIDE ———→

FRIENDS

45. Is there anyone with whom you talk over personal problems?
O Yes
O No

46. With whom do you most often talk about personal problems?
- O Spouse
- O Parent(s)
- O Children
- O Friend
- O AA sponsor or contact
- O Clergyman
- O Other
- O No One

47. Did your treatment have anything to do with acquiring or developing this relationship?
O Yes
O No
O Does not apply

48. How often do you communicate with this person on an average?
- O Daily
- O 2-3 times a week
- O Weekly
- O 2-3 times a month
- O Monthly
- O 2-3 times a year
- O Less frequently
- O Does not apply

49. Do you find it easy to talk about your personal problems with this person?
O Yes
O No
O Does not apply

50. How many times during the past month have you talked with this person about personal problems?
- O None
- O Once
- O 2-3 times
- O 4 or more times
- O Does not apply

HEALTH AND MORALE

51 - 56. Which best describes how often you have had the following complaints since your treatment?

	OFTEN	SOMETIMES	RARELY	NEVER
51. Upset stomach	O	O	O	O
52. Headaches	O	O	O	O
53. Felt tense, nervous, or worried	O	O	O	O
54. Colds or allergies	O	O	O	O
55. Felt depressed or "blue"	O	O	O	O
56. Difficulty sleeping	O	O	O	O

HEALTH AND MORALE (Continued)

57 - 62. Since your treatment how often have you used <u>non-prescription,</u> <u>over-the-counter,</u> medication for relief from the following complaints?

	NEVER	ONCE OR TWICE	3 OR MORE TIMES
57. Upset stomach	O	O	O
58. Headaches	O	O	O
59. Felt tense, nervous, or worried	O	O	O
60. Colds or allergies	O	O	O
61. Felt depressed or "blue"	O	O	O
62. Difficulty sleeping	O	O	O

63 - 68. Since your treatment how often have you used <u>prescription</u> medication (<u>on</u> <u>your</u> <u>doctor's</u> <u>orders</u>) for relief from the following complaints?

	NEVER	ONCE OR TWICE	3 OR MORE TIMES
63. Upset stomach	O	O	O
64. Headaches	O	O	O
65. Felt tense, nervous, or worried	O	O	O
66. Colds or allergies	O	O	O
67. Felt depressed or "blue"	O	O	O
68. Difficulty sleeping	O	O	O

BEHAVIOR PATTERNS

69. When you do get angry which of the following best describes what you usually do?
    O Keep it to yourself
    O Show it but do not lose your temper
    O Lose temper

70. Since your treatment do you find yourself becoming angry or resentful
    O More often than before
    O About as often as before
    O Less often than before

71. Since your treatment do you find yourself becoming anxious or nervous
    O More often than before
    O About as often as before
    O Less often than before

72. When you become anxious or nervous which of the following best describes what you usually do? (Mark as many as apply)
    O Smoke
    O Eat
    O Drink liquor
    O Take a drug
    O Work or play harder than usual
    O Go to church or pray
    O Talk it over with a friend or relative
    O Just try to forget about it
    O None of the above

73. As a result of your treatment, to what extent do you feel you learned new ways to deal with your anxieties or nervousness?
    O I learned several alternatives
    O I learned a new way
    O Nothing new was learned
    O I have no new ways and don't use the old ones. (Please explain on separate sheet)

74. Since your treatment do you find yourself becoming depressed or "blue"
    O More often than before
    O About as often as before
    O Less often than before

75. When you become depressed which of the following best describes what you usually do first?
    O Smoke
    O Eat
    O Drink liquor
    O Take a drug
    O Work harder than usual
    O Go to church or pray
    O Talk it over with a friend or relative
    O Just try to forget about it
    O Other (Please explain on separate sheet)

76. If you resumed the use of alcohol or other chemicals after your discharge from treatment, please answer the following item: (Check as many as apply)

    To the best of my knowledge, I used chemicals
    O impulsively-spur of the moment without thinking.
    O because I weighed the consequences and decided the risks were minimal.
    O because I decided I was not chemically dependent.
    O because I really don't care what happens to me.
    O because I found myself in a <u>tense</u> or <u>difficult</u> situation.
    O because I found myself in a <u>happy</u> or <u>exciting</u> situation.

NCS Trans-Optic F2557-5

EASY DOES IT

CONTINUATION PROGRAM
© The Hazelden Foundation, 1974

Staff researchers are trying to learn what happens to people after their treatment. We are asking you to cooperate in this study by checking the appropriate answers to the questions below. Your replies will be confidential, you will never be identified by name and results will be reported in statistical tables.

NOTE: Please answer all items. (Don't forget the back page!) If none of the answers provided seem to fit, please explain in the space provided on page 2. The phrase "Mood-altering drugs" refers to mood-altering chemicals other than alcohol. Many of the questions will ask you to compare now with what you were doing before treatment. These questions always refer to your treatment at _____
which ended _____

ALCOHOL & DRUG USAGE

1. Which one of the following best categorizes your drinking at present?
    _____ Abstinent
    _____ Light or moderate social drinking
    _____ Inappropriate drinking restricted mainly to social events or weekends
    _____ Inappropriate drinking on more than one occasion most weeks, but not restricted to social events or weekends
    _____ Inappropriate drinking occurring almost every day or weekend
    _____ Periodic binge drinking

2. In the year since you left treatment, how many times have you used alcohol?
    _____ Not at all   _____ About 4–6 times
    _____ Only on one occasion   _____ More than 6 times
    _____ Probably 2 or 3 times

3. Which one statement most clearly represents your use of alcohol today, in terms of quantity, compared to what it was before your treatment?
    _____ I have not used alcohol since leaving treatment.
    _____ When I use alcohol, I don't drink as much as I did before treatment.
    _____ When I use alcohol, I drink about as much as I did before treatment.
    _____ When I use alcohol, I drink more than I drank before treatment.

4. How long ago did you last take a drink?
    _____ 0–1 month   _____ 8–10 months
    _____ 2–4 months   _____ 11–12 months
    _____ 5–7 months

5. Which one best categorizes the longest dry period since your treatment?
    _____ 0–1 month
    _____ 2–4 months
    _____ 5–7 months
    _____ 8–10 months
    _____ 11–12 months

6. Which one statement below best categorizes your use of mood-altering drugs (other than alcohol) at present?
    _____ No use of mood-altering drugs
    _____ Appropriate prescribed use for medical reasons
    _____ Inappropriate use of mood-altering drugs restricted mainly to social events or weekends
    _____ Inappropriate use of mood-altering drugs on more than one occasion most weeks, but not restricted to social events or weekends
    _____ Inappropriate use of mood-altering drugs almost every day or evening

166

7. What is your mood-altering drug use today, in terms of frequency, compared to what it was before treatment?

_____ I have not used mood-altering drugs since leaving treatment.

_____ I have used mood-altering drugs since leaving treatment but only those prescribed for medical reasons.

_____ I have used mood-altering drugs on only one occasion (non-continuous) since leaving treatment.

_____ I use mood-altering drugs inappropriately but not as often as before treatment.

_____ I use mood-altering drugs inappropriately about as often as before treatment.

_____ I use mood-altering drugs inappropriately more often than before treatment.

8. Which one statement most nearly represents your use of mood-altering drugs, in terms of quantity, compared to what it was before treatment?

_____ I have not used mood-altering drugs since leaving treatment.

_____ I have used mood-altering drugs since leaving treatment but only for prescribed medical reasons.

_____ When I use mood-altering drugs, I don't take as much as before treatment.

_____ When I use mood-altering drugs, I take about as much as before treatment.

_____ When I use mood-altering drugs, I take more than before treatment.

9. How long ago did you last use mood-altering drugs inappropriately?

_____ 0–1 month   _____ 8 or more months

_____ 2–4 months   _____ Did not use

_____ 5–7 months

10. What is the longest period since treatment during which you did not use mood-altering drugs inappropriately?

_____ 0–1 month   _____ 8 or more months

_____ 2–4 months   _____ Did not use

_____ 5–7 months

EXPLANATIONS:

Are you willing to be an AA contact for a person in your area?

_____ Yes _____ No   Later (Date)_____

MATURATION AND GROWTH

The following is a list of possible growth areas. Think about how you dealt with each of these areas before your treatment, and how you presently deal with each of them. Select the response that best describes your development in each of these areas.

		Much Improved	Somewhat Improved	Same	Somewhat Worse	Much Worse	Does not Apply
11.	Relationship with spouse	_____	_____	_____	_____	_____	_____
12.	Relationship with children	_____	_____	_____	_____	_____	_____
13.	Relationship with parents	_____	_____	_____	_____	_____	_____
14.	Relationship with other relatives	_____	_____	_____	_____	_____	_____
15.	Relationship with friends	_____	_____	_____	_____	_____	_____
16.	Relationship with Higher Power	_____	_____	_____	_____	_____	_____
17.	Your own job performance	_____	_____	_____	_____	_____	_____
18.	General physical health	_____	_____	_____	_____	_____	_____
19.	Self-image (how you feel about yourself)	_____	_____	_____	_____	_____	_____
20.	General enjoyment of life	_____	_____	_____	_____	_____	_____
21.	Ability to handle problems	_____	_____	_____	_____	_____	_____
22.	Ability to accept help from others	_____	_____	_____	_____	_____	_____
23.	Ability to give help and advice to others	_____	_____	_____	_____	_____	_____
24.	Ability to manage financial affairs	_____	_____	_____	_____	_____	_____
25.	Acceptance of sexual role	_____	_____	_____	_____	_____	_____
26.	Acceptance of need for abstinence	_____	_____	_____	_____	_____	_____

27.–30. Since your treatment, how frequently do you maintain some kind of conscious contact with a Higher Power through the following means?

		More Often	About the Same	Less Often
27.	Prayer	_____	_____	_____
28.	Meditation	_____	_____	_____
29.	Church Attendance	_____	_____	_____
30.	Spiritual Counseling	_____	_____	_____

31. What seems to be the best way for you to keep in touch with a Higher Power? (Select only one item)

_____ Sharing in a formal worship   _____ Sharing with friends in AA

_____ Private prayer or meditation   _____ Reading spiritual material

_____ Sharing with like minded friends other than in AA   _____ Attending retreats

                                                        _____ Other ways (please specify)

ALCOHOLICS ANONYMOUS

32. How often do you attend AA meetings at present?

_____ More than once a week   _____ About once a month

_____ About once a week   _____ Less than once a month

_____ About two or three times a month   _____ I do not attend

33.–36. Have you participated in the following AA activities since leaving treatment?

33. Led a meeting   _____ Yes   _____ No

34. Told your story   _____ Yes   _____ No

35. Did 12th step work   _____ Yes   _____ No

36. Sponsored an AA member   _____ Yes   _____ No

37. How active is your present AA participation compared with what it was before treatment?

_____ More   _____ Less

_____ Same   _____ Did not attend

38. Since leaving treatment, have you frequently made use of the 10th step inventory?

_____ Yes   _____ No

39. Have you consciously continued working on steps six through twelve of the AA program after leaving treatment?

_____ Yes   _____ No

40. To what extent do you feel that AA is continuing to help you improve life?

_____ It is essential   _____ It is not at all essential

_____ It helps very much   _____ I do not attend

_____ Sometimes it helps, and sometimes it doesn't help

41. With whom do you most often talk about personal problems? (Select one.)

_____ Spouse   _____ Clergyman

_____ Other relative(s)   _____ Other (please specify)

_____ Friend other than AA   _____

_____ AA member   _____ No one

42. Since your treatment, do you find yourself becoming angry or resentful?

_____ More often than before treatment

_____ About as often as before treatment

_____ Less often than before treatment

43. Since your treatment, do you find yourself becoming anxious or nervous?

_____ More often than before

_____ About as often as before

_____ Less often than before

44. Which one of the following seems to be the most common source of anxiety for you?

_____ Job or occupation   _____ My own health

_____ Money problems   _____ Health of family member or friend

_____ Problems with family   _____ Loneliness or boredom

_____ World situations and politics

45. When you become anxious or nervous which one of the following best describes what you **usually** do? (Select one.)

_____ Smoke
_____ Eat
_____ Take a drink
_____ Take medication
_____ Lie down, go to sleep
_____ Attend an AA meeting

_____ Work or play harder than usual
_____ Go to church or pray
_____ Talk it over with someone
_____ Engage in hobbies or sports activities
_____ Just try to forget it
_____ None of the above

46. Since your treatment, do you find yourself becoming depressed or "blue"?

_____ More often than before
_____ About as often as before
_____ Less often than before

47. When you become depressed, which one of the following best describes what you usually do first? (Select one.)

_____ Smoke
_____ Eat
_____ Take a drink
_____ Take medication
_____ Lie down, go to sleep
_____ Attend an AA meeting

_____ Work or play harder than usual
_____ Go to church or pray
_____ Talk it over with someone
_____ Engage in hobbies or sports activities
_____ Just try to forget it
_____ None of the above

48. Since leaving treatment, how many times have you been picked up or arrested by the police? _____

49. Since leaving treatment, how many times have you been hospitalized for any reason? _____

RESOURCES

50.–54. Since your treatment, have you turned to any of the following resources for help when you resumed using alcohol or drugs?

	Yes	No	Does Not Apply
50. AA	_____	_____	_____
51. Physician	_____	_____	_____
52. Hospital	_____	_____	_____
53. Referral centers	_____	_____	_____
54. Detoxification or out-patient facilities	_____	_____	_____

PRESENT JOB STATUS

55. What is your present job?

_____ Self employed

_____ Housewife and/or homemaker
_____ Permanent job
_____ Part-time job
_____ Unemployed

_____ Unemployed and receiving unemployment compensation
_____ Retired
_____ Military service

56. How long have you worked at your present job?

_____ 0–5 months   _____ More than 3 years

_____ 6–11 months   _____ Does not apply

_____ 1–3 years

57. Since leaving treatment, have you experienced any of the following changes in your job status?

_____ No change   _____ I am now unemployed

_____ I have received a promotion   _____ I am now retired

_____ I have a new job with same company   _____ Other

_____ I have changed jobs and company

58. Since leaving treatment, how do you feel you are able to get along with the other people you work with at your job?

_____ Better than before treatment

_____ About the same as before treatment

_____ Worse than before treatment

_____ Does not apply

59. Since leaving treatment, how do you feel about your relationship with your immediate supervisor?

_____ Better than before treatment

_____ About the same as before treatment

_____ Worse than before treatment

_____ Does not apply

60. During the last year, how many weeks have you worked?

_____ Less than 27 weeks (please explain)

_____ 27–49 weeks

_____ 50–52 weeks

_____ Does not apply

61. At any time during the year prior to your treatment, had you received unemployment compensation?

_____ Yes   _____ No

TREATMENT

62.–71. As you recall your treatment activities, after one year, how do you rate the activities in this list that were most helpful to you? (Mark them according to their effectiveness, not how well you liked them.)

		Much Help	Some Help	Little Help	No Help	Do not Remember
62.	Individual meetings with counselors					
63.	Individual meetings with clergymen					
64.	Group therapy					
65.	Informal conversations with patients					
66.	Lectures					
67.	Environmental setting					
68.	Reading					
69.	Time alone for thought					
70.	Group or personal meditation					
71.	"Hot seat"					

Reference List

Alcoholics Anonymous: The story of how thousands of men and women have recovered from alcoholism. (rev. ed.). New York: Alcoholics Anonymous World Services, Inc. 1955.

Almond, R., *The healing community: Dynamics of the therapeutic milieu.* New York: Jason Aronson, 1974.

Anderson, D. J. and Burns, J. P., Hazelden Foundation: Part of the caring community. In V. Groupe (ed.), *Alcoholism rehabilitation: Methods and experiences of private rehabilitation centers.* New Brunswick, N.J.: Rutgers Center of Alcohol Studies, 1978.

Anderson, D. J., Kammeier, S. M. L., and Holmes, H., *Applied research: Impact on decision making.* Center City, MN. Hazelden Foundation, 1978.

Armor, D. J., Polich, J. M., and Stambul, H. B., *Alcoholism and treatment.* Santa Monica, CA: The Rand Corporation, 1976.

Bacon, S. D., The process of addiction to alcohol: Social aspects. *Quart. J. of Studies on Alc.,* 1973, *34,* 1-27.

Baekeland, F., Lundwall, L. and Kissin, B., Methods for the treatment of chronic alcoholism: A critical appraisal. In R. J. Gibbins, Y. Israel, H. Kalant, R. E. Popham, W. Schmidt, and R. G. Smart (eds.), *Research advances in alcohol and drug problems* (Vol. 2). New York: John Wiley & Sons, 1975.

Beaubrun, M. H., Treatment of alcoholism in Trinidad and Tobago. 1956-65. *Brit. J. Psychiat.,* 1967, *113,* 643-658.

Bell, R. G., Treatment and rehabilitation of alcohol addicts. *Ontario Med. Rev.,* 1951, *18,* 23-25, 38.

Blake, B. G., A follow-up of alcoholics treated by behavior therapy. *Behav. Res. Ther.,* 1967, *5,* 89-94.

Bowen, W. T., and Androes, L., A follow-up study of 79 alcoholic patients: 1963-1965. *Bull. of the Menninger Clinic,* 1968, *32,* 26-34.

Bowen, W. T., Soskin, R., and Chotos, J., Lysergic acid diethylamide as a variable in the hospital treatment of alcoholism, a follow-up. *J. Nerv. Ment. Dis.,* 1970, *150(2),* 111-118.

Brissett, D., Laundergan, J. C., Kammeier, S. M. L., and Biele, M., Drinkers and nondrinkers at three and a half years after treatment: Attitudes and growth. *J. of Studies on Alc.* 1980, *41,* 945-952.

Browne-Mayers, A. N., Seelyem, E. E. and Brown, D. E., Reorganized alcoholism service: Two years after *JAMA,* 1973, *224,* 233-235.

Brun, K., Outcome of different types of treatment of alcoholics. *Quart. J. of Studies on Alc.,* 1963, *24,* 280-288.

Burton, G. and Kaplan, H. M., Marriage counseling with alcoholics and their spouses. *Brit. J. addict.,* 1968, *63,* 161-170.

Cadort, R. J., Genetic determinants of alcoholism. In R. E. Tarter and A. A. Sugarman (eds.) *Alcoholism: Interdisciplinary approaches to an enduring problem.* Reading, MA: Addison-Wesley, 1976.

Campbell, A., Converse, P. E. and Rodgers, W. L., The quality of American life: Perceptions, evaluations and satisfactions. New York: Russell Sage Foundation, 1976.

Charnoff, S. M., Long-term treatment of alcoholism with amitriptyline and emylcamate: A double blind evaluation. *Quart. J. of Studies on Alc.,* 1976, *28,* 289-294.

Cheek, F. E., Osmond, H., Sarett, M., and Abbahary, R. S., Observations regarding the use of LSD-25 in the treatment of alcoholism. *J. Psychopharm.,* 1966, *1,* 56-74.

Clancy, J., Vornbrock, R., and Vanderhoof, E., Treatment of alcoholics: A follow-up study. *Dis. of Nerv. Sys.,* 1965, *26,* 555-561.

Crewe, C., A short history of Hazelden. In V. Groupe (ed.), *Alcoholism rehabilitation: Methods and experiences of private rehabilitation centers.* New Brunswick, N.J.: Rutgers Center of Alcohol Studies, 1978.

Curlee, J., *Alcoholism and the empty nest.* Center City, MN: Hazelden Foundation, 1969.

Davies, D. L., Normal drinking in recovered alcohol addicts. *Quart. J. of Studies on Alc.,* 1962, *23,* 94-104.

Denson, R. and Sydiaha, D., A controlled study of LSD treatment in alcoholism and neurosis. *Brit. J. Psychiat.,* 1970, *116,* 443-445.

Edwards, G. and Guthrie, S., A comparison of inpatient and outpatient treatment of alcohol dependence. *Lancet,* 1966, *2,* 467-468.

Emrick, C. D., A review of psychologically oriented treatment of alcoholism. I. The use and interrelationship of outcome criteria and drinking behavior following treatment. *Quart. J. of Studies on Alc.,* 1974, *35,* 523-549.

Emrick, C. D., A review of psychologically oriented treatment of alcoholism: II. The relative effectiveness of different treatment approaches and the effectiveness of treatment versus no treatment. *Quart. J. of Studies on Alc.,* 1975, *36,* 88-108.

Ferguson, F. N., A treatment program for Navajo alcoholics, results after four years. *Quart. J. of Studies on Alc.,* 1970, *31,* 898-919.

Fitzgerald, B. J., Pasewark, R. A., and Clark, R., Four year follow-up of alcoholics treated at a rural state hospital. *Quart. J. of Studies on Alc.,* 1971, *32,* 636-642.

Gallant, D. M., Faulkner, M., Bishop, M. P. and Langdon, D., Enforced clinic treatment of paroled criminal alcoholics: A pilot evaluation. *Quart. J. of Studies on Alc.,* 1968, *29,* 77-83.

Gallant, D. M., Rich, A., Bey, E., and Terranova, L., Group psychotherapy with married couples: A successful technique in New Orleans alcoholism clinic patients. *J. La. Med. Soc.,* 1970, *122,* 41-44.

Gerard, D. L., Saenger, G. and Wile, R., The abstinent alcoholic. *Arch. Gen. Psychiat.,* 1962, *6,* 83-95.

Glatt, M. M., An alcoholic unit in a medical hospital. *Lancet,* 1959, *2,* 397-398.

Goldfried, M. R., Prediction of improvement in an alcoholism outpatient clinic. *Quart. J. of Studies on Alc.,* 1969, *30,* 119-139.

Goodwin, D., *Is alcoholism hereditary?* New York: Oxford University Press, 1976.

Gordon, W. W., The treatment of alcohol (and tobacco) addiction by differential conditioning: New manual and mechanical methods. *Amer. J. Psychother.,* 1971, *25,* 394-417.

Gross, M. M. and Hastey, J. M., Sleep disturbances in alcoholism. In R. E. Tarter and A. A. Sugarman (eds.), *Alcoholism: Interdisciplinary approaches to an enduring problem.* Reading, MA: Addison-Wesley, 1976.

Gynther, M. D. and Brilliant, P. I., Marital status, remission to hospital, and intrapersonal and interpersonal perceptions of alcoholics. *Quart. J. of Studies on Alc.,* 1971, *32,* 628-635.

Haberman, P. W. Factors related to increased sobriety in group psychotherapy with alcoholics. *J. Clin. Psychol.,* 1966, *22,* 229-235.

Hastings, W. M., *How to think about social problems: A primer for citizens.* New York: Oxford University Press, 1979.

Hazelden caring community guidebooks: Identification, Implementation, the Crisis, the New awareness, Emergency care, Dealing with denial, the New understanding, Winning by losing/the decision, Personal inventory and planned re-entry, Challenges to the new way of life. Center City, MN: Hazelden Foundation, 1975.

Heilman, R. O., *Early recognition of alcoholism and other drug dependence.* Center City, MN: Hazelden Foundation, 1980.

Hoffman, H., Loper, R. and Kammeier, S. M. L., Identifying future alcoholics with MMPI alcoholism scales. *Quart. J. of Studies on Alc.,* 1974, *35,* 490-498.

Hollister, L. E., Shelton, J. and Krieger, G., A controlled comparison of lysergic acid diethylamide (LSD) and dextroamphetamine in alcoholics. *Amer. J. Psychiat.,* 1969, *125,* 1352-1357.

Howe, R. L., *Survival plus.* New York: The Seabury Press, 1971.

Jellinek, E. M., *The disease concept of alcoholism.* New Haven, CT: College and University Press, 1960.

Johnson, F. G., LSD in treatment of alcoholism. *Am. J. Psychiat.,* 1969, *126,* 63-69.

Jones, R. K., Sectarian characteristics of Alcoholics Anonymous, *Sociology,* 1970, *4,* 181-195.

Kammeier, S. M. L., Hoffman, H. and Loper, R. G., Personality characteristics of alcoholics as college freshmen and at the time of treatment. *Quart. J. of Studies on Alc.,* 1973, *34,* 390-399.

Kammeier, S. M. L., and Laundergan, J. C., *The outcome of treatment: Patients admitted to Hazelden in 1975.* Center City, MN: Hazelden Foundation, 1977.

Katz, L., The Salvation Army men's social service center. II. Results. *Quart. J. of Studies on Alc.,* 1966, *27,* 636-647.

Keller, M., The disease concept of alcoholism revisited. *J. of Studies on Alc.,* 1976, *37,* 1964-1777.

Keller, M and McCormick, M. *A dictionary of words about alcohol.* New Brunswick, N.J.: Rutgers Center of Alcohol Studies, 1968.

Kim, J., Factor analysis. In H. Nie, C. H. Hull, J. G. Jenkins, K. Steinbrenner and D. H. Brent, *Statistical package for the social sciences* (2nd ed.). New York: McGraw-Hill, 1975.

Kim, J., Kohout, F. J., Multiple regression analysis: subprogram regression. In H. Nie, C. H. Hull, J. G. Jenkins, K. Steinbrenner, and D. H. Brent, *Statistical package for the social sciences* (2nd ed.). New York: Mcgraw-Hill, 1975.

Kish, G. B. and Herman, H. T., The Fort Meade alcoholism treatment program: A follow-up study. *Quart. J. of Studies on Alc.,* 1971, *32,* 628-635.

Kissin, B., Theory and practice in the treatment of alcoholism. In B. Kissin and H. Begleiter (eds.), *The biology of alcoholism: Treatment and rehabilitation of the chronic alcoholic* (Vol. 5). New York: Plenum Press, 1977.

175

Kissin, B., Platz, A. and Su, W., Social and psychological factors in the treatment of alcoholism. *J. Psychiat. Res.,* 1970, *8,* 13-27.

Knox, W. J., Four year follow-up of veterans treated on a small alcoholism treatment ward. *Quart. J. of Studies on Alc.,* 1972, *33,* 105-110.

Kurland, A. A., Maryland alcoholics: Follow-up study I. *Psychiat. Res. Rep.,* 1968, *24,* 71-82.

Laundergan, J. C., *The outcome of treatment: The relationship between previous treatment and client outcome.* Center City, MN: Hazelden Foundation, 1981.

Laundergan, J. C. and Johnson, K., Hazelden's research data terminals can get it for you quickly. *Hazelden Research Notes,* Hazelden Foundation, 1977. (No. 1)

Laundergan, J. C., Spicer, J. W. and Kammeier, S. M. L., *Are court referrals effective? Judicial commitment for chemical dependency in Washington Co., Minnesota.* Center City, MN: Hazelden Foundation, 1979.

Leach, G. B. and Norris, J. L., Factors in the development of Alcoholics Anonymous (A.A.). In B. Kissin and H. Begleiter (eds.), *The biology of alcoholism: Treatment and rehabilitation of the chronic alcoholic* (Vol. 5). New York: Plenum Press, 1977.

Lemere, F., and Voegtlin, W. L., An evaluation of the aversion treatment of alcoholism, *Quart. J. of Studies on Alc.,* 1950, *11,* 199-204.

Levinson, T., and Sereny, G., An experimental evaluation of insight therapy for the chronic alcoholic. *Canad. Psychiat. Ass'n.,* 1969, *14,* 143-146.

Loper, R. G., Kammeier, S. M. L. and Hoffman, H., MMPI characteristics of college freshmen males who later became alcoholics. *J. of Abnor. Psy.,* 1973, *82,* 159-162.

Lucero, R. J., Jensen, K. F., Alcoholism and teetotalism in blood relatives of abstaining alcoholics. *Quart. J. of Studies on Alc.,* 1971, *32,* 183-185.

Ludwig, A. M., Winkler, A. and Stark, L. H., The first drink: Psychobiological aspects of craving. In E. M. Pattison, M. B. Sobell and L. C. Sobell, *Emerging concepts of alcohol dependence.* New York: Springer, 1977.

McCance, C., and McCance, P. F., Alcoholism in north-east Scotland: Its treatment and outcome. *Brit. J. Psychiat.,* 1969, *115,* 189-198.

McLauchlan, J. F. C., Therapy strategies, personality orientation and recovery from alcoholism. *Can. Psy. Asso. J.,* 1974, *19,* 25-30.

McMahan, H. G., The psychotherapeutic approach of chronic alcoholism in conjunction with the Alcoholics Anonymous program. *Ill. Psychiat. J.,* 1942, *2,* 15-20.

Mendelson, J. H., Biochemical mechanisms of alcohol addiction. In B. Kissin and H. Begleiter, (eds.), The biology of alcoholism: Biochemistry (Vol. 1). New York: Plenum Press, 1971.

Miller, M. M., Ambulatory treatment of chronic alcoholism. *JAMA,* 1942, *120,* 217-275.

Miller, P. M. and Mastria, M. A., *Alternatives to alcohol abuse: A social learning model,* Champaign, IL: Research Press, 1977.

Mitchell, E. H., Rehabilitation of the alcoholic. *Quart. J. of Studies on Alc.,* 1961, *22,* 93-100.

Moore, J. N. P., and Drury, M. D., Antibuse in the management of alcoholism. *Lancet,* 1951, *2,* 1059-1061.

Moore, R. A., Ramseur, F., Effects of psychotherapy in an open-ward hospital on patients with alcoholism. *Quart. J. of Studies on Alc.,* 1960, *21,* 233-252.

Moos, R. and Bliss, F., Difficulty of follow-up and outcome of alcoholism treatment. *J. of Stud. on Alc.,* 1978, *39,* 473-489.

National council on alcoholism committee. Criteria for the diagnosis of alcoholism. *Amer. J. Psychiat.* 1972, *129,* 127-135.

Norvig, J., and Nielsen, B., A follow-up study of 221 alcohol addicts in Denmark. *Quart. J. of Studies on Alc.,* 1956, *17,* 633-642.

Obholzer, A. M., Follow-up study of 19 alcoholic patients treated by means of tetraethyl thiuram disulfide. *Br. J. of Addiction,* 1974, *69,* 19-23.

Ogborne, A. C., Patient characteristics as predictors of treatment outcome for alcohol and drug abusers. In Y. Israel, F. B. Glaser, H. Kalant, R. E. Popham, W. Schmidt and R. G. Smart, *Research advances in alcohol and drug problems* (Vol. 4). New York: Plenum Press, 1978.

O'Reilly, P. O., and Funk, A., LSD in chronic alcoholism. *Canad. Psychiat. Ass'n. J.,* 1964, *9,* 258-261.

Pahnke, W. N., Kurland, A. A., Unger, S., Savage, C., and Groff, S., The experimental use of psychedelic (LSD) psychotherapy. *JAMA,* 1970, 212, 1856-1863.

Papas, A. N., Airforce alcoholic rehabilitation program. *Milit. Med.,* 1971, *136,* 277-281.

Paredes, A., The history of the concept of alcoholism. In R. E. Tarter and A. A. Sugarman (eds.), *Alcoholism: Interdisciplinary approaches to an enduring problem.* Reading, MA: Addison-Wesley Publishing Co., 1976.

Pattison, E. M., A conceptual approach to alcoholism treatment goals. *Addic. Beh.,* 1976, *1,* 177-192.

Pattison, E. M., Gleser, G. C., Headley, E. B., Gottschalk, L. A., Abstinence and normal drinking: An assessment of changes in drinking patterns in alcoholics after treatment. *Quart. J. of Studies on Alc.,* 1968, *29,* 610-633.

Pattison, E. M., Sobell, M. B. and Sobell, L. C. *Emerging concepts of alcoholism.* New York: Springer, 1977.

Patton, M. Q., *The outcomes of treatment: A study of patients admitted to Hazelden in 1977.* Center City, MN: Hazelden Foundation, 1979.

Penick, S. B., Sheldon, J. B., Templer, D. I., and Carrier, R. N., Four year follow-up of metronidazole treatment program for alcoholism. *Industr. Med.,* 1971, *40,* 30-32.

Pfeffer, A. Z., and Berger, S., A follow-up study of treated alcoholics. *Quart. J. of Studies on Alc.,* 957, *18,* 624-648.

Pokorny, A., Miller, B., and Cleveland, S., Response to treatment of alcoholism: A follow-up study. *Quart. J. of Studies on Alc.,* 1968, *29,* 364-381.

Polich, J. M., Armor, D. J., and Braiker, H. B., *The course of alcoholism four years after treatment.* Santa Monica, CA: The Rand Corporation, 1980.

Pittman, D. J. and Tate, R. L., A comparison of two treatment programs for alcoholics. *Quart. J. of Studies on Alc.,* 1969, *30,* 888-889.

Reinert, R. E., The alcoholism treatment program at Topeka Veterans Administration Hospital, *Quart. J. of Studies on Alc.,* 1965, *26,* 674-680.

Richeson, F., *Courage to change: Beginnings and influence of Alcoholics Anonymous in Minnesota.* Minneapolis, MN: M&M Printing, 1978.

Ringer, C., Kufner, H., Antons, K., and Feuerlein, The NCA criteria for the diagnosis of alcoholism. *J. of Studies on Alc.*, 1977, *38*, 1259-1273.

Robson, R. A., Paulus, H. I. and Clarke, G. G., An evaluation of the effect of a clinic treatment program on the rehabilitation of alcoholic patients. *Quart. J. of Studies on Alc.*, 1965, *26*, 264-278.

Rohan, W. P., Follow-up study of problem drinkers. *Dis. Nerv. Syst.*, 1972, *33*, 196-199.

Rossi, J. J., A holistic treatment program for alcoholism rehabilitation. *Med. Ecol. Clin. Res.*, 1970, *3*, 6-16.

Rossi, J. J., Stach, A. and Bradley, N. J., Effects of treatment of male alcoholics in a mental hospital: A follow-up study. *Quart. J. of Studies on Alc.*, 1963, *24*, 91-108.

Ruggels, W. L., Armor, D. J., Polich, J. M., Mothershead, A., and Stephen, M., *A follow-up study of clients at selected alcoholism treatment centers funded by NIAAA*. Menlo Park, CA: Stanford Research Institute, 1975.

Selzer, M. L., and Holloway, W. H., A follow-up of alcoholics committed to a state hospital, *Quart. J. of Studies on Alc.*, 1957, *18*, 98-120.

Shellum, B., Sobriety, Minnesota's newest industry. *Minneapolis Tribune* (summary supplement) May 20-28, 1979.

Shepard, E. A. (ed), Reports on government sponsored programs. *Quart. J. of Studies on Alc.*, 1950, *11*, 351-359.

Shore, J. H. and Wilson, L. G., Evaluation of a regional Indian alcohol program. *Am. J. of Psy.*, 1975, *132*, 255-258.

Slater, A. D., A follow-up study of 63 alcoholics who received treatment in Utah under the Kendall Act. *Utah Alcoholism Review*, 1951, *2*, 1-8.

Sontag, S., *Illness as metaphor*. New York: Farrar, Straus and Giroux, 1978.

Spicer, J. W., *Outcome evaluation: How to do it*. Center City, MN: Hazelden Foundation, 1980.

State of Minnesota directory chemical dependency programs. St. Paul, MN: Chemical Dependency Programs Division, Department of Public Welfare, 1977.

Stokes, P. E., Alcohol-endocrine interrelationships. In B. Kissin and H. Begleiter, *The biology of alcoholism: Biochemistry* (Vol. 1). New York: Plenum Press, 1971.

Tarter, R. E. and Schneider, D. V., Models and theories of alcoholism. In R. E. Tarter and A. A. Sugarman (eds.), *Alcoholism: Interdisciplinary approaches to an enduring problem*. Reading, MA: Addison-Wesley, 1976.

Thomas, R. E., Gliedman, L. H., Imber, S. D., Stone, A. R. and Freund, J., Evaluation of the Maryland alcoholic rehabilitation clinics. *Quart. J. of Studies on Alc.*, 1959, *20*, 65-76.

Tomsovic, M., A follow-up study of discharged alcoholics. *Hosp. Comm. Psychiat.*, 1970, *21*, 94-97.

Trice, H. M., A study of the process of affiliation with Alcoholics Anonymous. *Quart. J. of Studies on Alc.*, 1970, *31*, 932-949.

Trice, H. M. and Roman, P. M., Sociopsychological predictors of affiliation with Alcoholics Anonymous: A longitudinal study of treatment success. *Soc. Psychiat.*, 1970, *5*, 51-59.

Twenty-four hours a day. Center City, MN: Hazelden Foundation, 1955.

Vallance, M., Alcoholism: A two year follow-up study of patients admitted to the psychiatric ward of a general hospital. *Brit. J. Psychiat.,* 1965, 111, 348-356.

Vincent, M. O., and Blum, D. M., A five year follow-up study of alcoholic patients. *Rep. Alc.,* 1969, *27,* 19-26.

Walton, H. J., Ritson, E. B., and Kennedy, R. I., Response of alcoholics to clinic treatment. *Brit. Med. J.,* 1966, *2,* 1171-1174.

Websters third new international dictionary of the English language (unabridged). Springfield, MA: G. and C. Merriam Co. 1967.

Wedel, H. L., Involving alcoholics in treatment. *Quart. J. of Studies on Alc.,* 1965, *26,* 468-479.

West, L. J., and Swegan, W. H., An approach to alcoholism in the military service. *Amer. J. Psychiat.,* 1956, 112, 1004-1009.

Whitaker, C. A., Without psychosis—chronic alcoholism: A follow-up study. *Psychiat. Quart.,* 1942, *16,* 373-392.

Wildasin; K. R., *An analysis of the variables in historical and contemporary literature pertaining to follow-up evaluation studies of alcoholism treatment programs.* Unpublished independent study project, University of Minnesota, 1973.

Williams, A. F., The alcoholic personality. In B Kissin and H. Begleiter (eds.), *The biology of alcoholism: Social aspects of alcoholism* (Vol. 4). New York: Plenum Press, 1976.

Williams, H. L. and Salamy, A., Alcohol and sleep. In B. Kissin and H. Begleiter (eds.), *The biology of alcoholism: Physiology and behavior* (Vol. 2). New York: Plenum Press, 1972.

Wolff, S. and Holland, L., A questionnaire follow-up of alcoholic patients. *Quart. J. of Studies on Alc.,* 1964, *25,* 108-118.